Lexicography

This book is an accessible introduction to lexicography – the study of dictionaries.

We rely on dictionaries to provide us with definitions of words, and to tell us how to spell them. They are used at home and at school, cited in law courts, sermons and parliament, and referred to by crossword addicts and scrabble players alike. But why are dictionaries structured as they are? What types of dictionary exist, and what purposes do they serve? Who uses a dictionary, and for what?

Lexicography: An Introduction provides a detailed overview of the history, types and content of these essential reference works. Howard Jackson analyses a wide range of dictionaries, from those for native speakers to thematic dictionaries and learners' dictionaries, including those on CD-ROM, to reveal the ways in which dictionaries fulfil their dual function of describing the vocabulary of English and providing a useful and accessible reference resource.

Beginning with an introduction to the terms used in lexicology to describe words and vocabulary, and offering summaries and suggestions for further reading, *Lexicography: An Introduction* is concise and student-friendly. It is ideal for anyone with an interest in the development and use of dictionaries.

Howard Jackson is Professor of English Language and Linguistics at the University of Central England. His publications include *Grammar and Vocabulary* (Routledge, 2002), *Words and their Meaning* (Longman, 1988), and *Words, Meaning and Vocabulary* (Cassell, 2000).

Lexicography

An introduction

Howard Jackson

London and New York

First published 2002
by Routledge
11 New Fetter Lane, London EC4P 4EE

Simultaneously published in the USA and Canada by Routledge
29 West 35th Street, New York, NY 10001

Routledge is an imprint of the Taylor & Francis Group

© 2002 Howard Jackson

Typeset in Bembo by
The Running Head Limited, Cambridge
Printed and bound in Great Britain by
TJ International Ltd, Padstow, Cornwall

British Library Cataloguing in Publication Data
A catalogue record for this book is available
from the British Library

Library of Congress Cataloging in Publication Data
A catalog record has been requested

ISBN 0–415–23172–8 (hbk)
ISBN 0–415–23173–6 (pbk)

Contents

Preface   vii
Dictionaries cited   ix

1 Words   1

2 Facts about words   10

3 The dictionary   21

4 The beginnings   31

5 *The New English Dictionary*   47

6 Up to the present   61

7 Users and uses   74

8 Meaning in dictionaries   86

9 Beyond definition   101

10 Etymology   117

11 Dictionaries for learners   129

12 Abandoning the alphabet   145

13 Compiling dictionaries   161

14 Criticising dictionaries   173

References   184
Index   189

Preface

Much has happened, both in respect of the making of dictionaries and in respect of their academic study, in the twelve or so years since my previous book on dictionaries (*Words and Their Meaning*, Longman, 1988). Then, the 'corpus revolution' (Rundell and Stock 1992) had only just begun – *Words and Their Meaning* just managed to catch the first (1987) edition of the *Collins COBUILD English Dictionary*. Now virtually all dictionaries published in the UK make some claim to have used a computer corpus in their compilation. Not only have learners' dictionaries developed by leaps and bounds – the *Oxford Advanced Learner's Dictionary* was in its third edition then, now in its sixth, and the *Cambridge International Dictionary of English* was still a long way off – but native speaker dictionaries have also seen significant developments – the publication of the *New Oxford Dictionary of English* in 1998, as well as three editions of the *Concise Oxford*, not to mention the second edition of the great OED in 1989 and the beginning of the massive revision that will result in the third edition, planned for 2010.

Dictionaries have also appeared during the period in electronic format, notably as CD-ROMs, opening up new possibilities, not only in how dictionaries can be used and exploited, but also in how dictionary material can be organised and presented. Dictionaries are also accessible online, through the internet, including the OED, enabling subscribers to view the revisions that will constitute the third edition, as they are posted quarterly.

The study of lexicography has also developed and flourished during the last dozen years. They saw the launch of the highly successful *International Journal of Lexicography* in 1988, for the first ten years under the editorship of Robert Ilson, and latterly that of Tony Cowie. The mighty three-volume *Encyclopedia of Lexicography* (Hausmann *et al.* 1989–91) delineated the state of the art, and the *Dictionary of Lexicography* (Hartmann and James 1998) mapped the territory. More recently, Reinhard Hartmann's *Teaching and Researching Lexicography* (2001) has set the agenda for the business of academic lexicography. And Sidney Landau has updated his readable *Dictionaries: The Art and Craft of Lexicography* (second edition, 2001) with its transatlantic perspective.

It is time for a new treatment of the subject in the UK. I am grateful to Louisa Semlyen and to Routledge for taking this on. The book is dedicated to all the final-year students who have enabled me to develop the material by taking my 'Lexicography' module on the English degree at the University of Central England in Birmingham over more years than I care to recall.

Howard Jackson
Birmingham
August 2001

Dictionaries cited

The following dictionaries are mentioned in the course of this book. (Note: a superscript number, e.g. 1988^2, refers to the edition; in this case, the second edition published in 1988.)

Native speaker dictionaries

Chambers English Dictionary, (1988^7) edited by Catherine Schwarz, George Davidson, Anne Seaton and Virginia Tebbit.

Chambers 21st Century Dictionary (1996) edited by Mairi Robinson.

Collins Concise Dictionary (1982; 1988^2; 1992^3; 1999^4, edited by Diana Treffry).

Collins English Dictionary (1979 edited by Patrick Hanks, 1986^2 edited by Patrick Hanks, $1991/94^3$ edited by Marian Makins, 1998^4 edited by Diana Treffry).

Concise Oxford Dictionary (1911 edited by H.G. and F.W. Fowler, 1929^2, 1934^3, 1951^4, 1964^5, 1976^6, 1982^7, 1990^8, 1995^9, 1999^{10} edited by Judy Pearsall).

Encarta Concise English Dictionary (2001) edited by Kathy Rooney, Bloomsbury.

Longman Dictionary of the English Language (1984, 1991^2 edited by Brian O'Kill).

A New English Dictionary on Historical Principles (1888–1928) edited by James Murray, Henry Bradley, W.A. Craigie and C.T. Onions.

New Oxford Dictionary of English (1998) edited by Judy Pearsall.

Oxford English Dictionary (1933 edited by James Murray *et al.*, 1989^2 edited by John Simpson and Edmund Weiner).

The New Shorter Oxford English Dictionary on Historical Principles (1993) edited by Lesley Brown.

Webster's Third New International Dictionary of the English Language (1961) edited by Philip Gove.

Monolingual learners' dictionaries

Cambridge Dictionary of American English (2000) edited by Sidney Landau.

Cambridge International Dictionary of English (1995) edited by Paul Proctor.

Collins COBUILD English Dictionary (1987, 1995^2, 2001^3) edited by John Sinclair.

Longman Dictionary of Contemporary English (1978 edited by Paul Proctor, 1987^2 edited by Della Summers and M. Rundell, 1995^3 edited by Della Summers).

Longman Language Activator (1993) edited by Della Summers.
Longman Lexicon of Contemporary English (1981) compiled by Tom McArthur.
Oxford Advanced Learner's Dictionary of Current English (1948 edited by A.S. Hornby, E.V. Gatenby and H. Wakefield; 1963[2] edited by A.S. Hornby, E.V. Gatenby and H. Wakefield; 1974[3] edited by A.S. Hornby, with A.P. Cowie and J. Windsor Lewis; 1989[4] edited by A.P. Cowie, 1995[5] edited by Jonathan Crowther; 2000[6] edited by Sally Wehmeier).

Thematic dictionaries

A Thesaurus of Old English (1995) compiled by Jane Roberts and Christian Kay, with Lynne Grundy.
Longman Dictionary of Scientific Usage (1979) compiled by A. Godman and E.M.F. Payne.
Longman Language Activator (1993) edited by Della Summers.
Longman Lexicon of Contemporary English (1981) compiled by Tom McArthur.
Roget's Thesaurus of English Words and Phrases (1852), Longmans, Green and Co. `
The Scots Thesaurus (1990), edited by Iseabail McLeod.

Abbreviations

In order to save space, dictionaries regularly cited will usually be referred to in the course of the book by the following abbreviations:

CCD – *Collins Concise Dictionary*
CED – *Collins English Dictionary*
Chambers – *Chambers English Dictionary*
CIDE – *Cambridge International Dictionary of English*
COBUILD – *Collins COBUILD English Dictionary*
COD – *Concise Oxford Dictionary*
ECED – *Encarta Concise English Dictionary*
LDEL – *Longman Dictionary of the English Language*
LDOCE – *Longman Dictionary of Contemporary English*
NODE – *New Oxford Dictionary of English*
OALD – *Oxford Advanced Learner's Dictionary*
OED – *Oxford English Dictionary*
SOED – *Shorter Oxford English Dictionary*
W3 – *Webster's Third New International Dictionary*.

Where the abbreviation is followed by a number, e.g. COD8, the number refers to the edition, i.e. *Concise Oxford Dictionary*, eighth edition.

1 Words

1.1 What is a word?

You take a dictionary off the shelf, or access a dictionary on your computer, and open it because you want to look up a 'word'. Dictionaries are the repositories of words. Words are arranged in dictionaries in alphabetical order, and as you look down the column in a print dictionary or the list in an electronic dictionary, you are reading a list of words. Or are you? Here is the list of the 25 'headwords' between *want* and *wardrobe* in COD10 (i.e. *Concise Oxford Dictionary*, tenth edition: see 'Dictionaries cited', p. ix):

> want, wanting, wanton, wapentake, wapiti, War., war, waratah, war baby, warble[1], warble[2], warble fly, warbler, warby, war chest, war crime, war cry, ward, -ward, war dance, warden, warder, ward heeler, ward of court, wardrobe.

A number of items in this list do not quite match our usual concept of what constitutes a word, which is − I suggest − 'a sequence of letters bounded by spaces'. Indeed, only 15 of the 25 items could be described in this way. Two of the remaining items are less than a full word: the abbreviation *War.* (for *Warwickshire*), and the suffix *−ward* (used to form words like *backward, skyward* − see Chapter 2). The other eight items all consist of more than one 'word': seven of them have just two words, and one has three (*ward of court*). You will also have noticed that one word (*warble*) is entered twice. So, just what is a 'word'?

The word before *want* in the COD10 list is *wannabe*. Is that a word, or is it three (*want to be*)? In our usual concept of a word, it is one, because it is a sequence of letters bounded by spaces. This conception of words comes, of course, from writing, the medium in which we are most conscious of words; and dictionaries are based on the written form of the language. In speech, though, words are composed of sounds and syllables, and they follow one another in the flow of speech without spaces or pauses. We make no more pause in saying *war baby* than we do with *wardrobe*, even though the first consists of two words in writing and the second of only one.

There is, clearly, a measure of confusion here that needs some sorting out in a book about words and dictionaries. Let us make the following distinction of terms:

orthographic word   a word in writing, a sequence of letters bounded by spaces
phonological word   a word in speech, a sequence of sounds (the boundaries of
      phonological words are determined by rules of syllable structure, stress, and
      the like)
lexeme   a word in the vocabulary of a language; it may occur as a headword in a
      dictionary.

A lexeme may, therefore, consist of more than one orthographic word, as *warble fly*, *war chest*, *ward of court*. Even though they are listed as headwords, we should exclude abbreviations and affixes (see 1.6 below) from the category of lexeme.

1.2 Same sound, same spelling, different word

We noticed that *warble* is entered twice in COD10. The compilers of this dictionary are following common practice and recognising two different lexemes with the same spelling (and, as it happens, the same pronunciation). The first *warble* is the verb that refers to birdsong; the second is a noun denoting 'a swelling or abscess beneath the skin on the back of cattle . . . caused by the presence of the larva of a warble fly'. However, the fact that the meanings of the two lexemes are completely unrelated is not the primary criterion for distinguishing them. Dictionaries usually operate with the criterion of etymology (see Chapter 10) for deciding that a single orthographic word represents more than one lexeme. If a single spelling can be shown to have more than one origin, then it constitutes more than one lexeme. In the case of *warble*, the 'birdsong' lexeme has its origin, according to COD10, in the Old Northern French word *werble*, which came into English during the Middle English period (1066–1500). The 'abscess' lexeme also originates in the Middle English period, but it has a different, according to COD10 'uncertain', provenance.

Lexemes that share the same spelling and pronunciation, but have a different etymology, are termed **homonyms** (a Greek word, meaning 'same (*homo*) name (*nym*)').

Another orthographic word with a double entry in the dictionary is *tear*. The first *tear* lexeme relates to 'pulling or ripping apart', the second denotes the drop of salty liquid that comes from the eyes when someone weeps. In this case, however, the same spelling has different pronunciations, i.e. phonological words. Since the dictionary is based on spelling, *tear* is entered twice. As might be expected, *tear* (rip) and *tear* (weep) also have different origins, both from Old English, the first from *teran* and the second from *tēar*. Lexemes that share the same spelling, but not the same pronunciation, are called **homographs** (from Greek, 'same' + 'writing'). There are not very many homographs in English, by comparison with the number of homonyms. Here are some further examples for you to figure out (or look up):

bow, curate, denier, irony, prayer, refuse, reserve, sow, supply, wind.

Much more common in English are the counterparts to homographs: lexemes that are pronounced the same, but spelled differently, e.g. *pale/pail*. These present no problem to a dictionary, since it is the spelling that takes priority; and each is entered as a headword at the appropriate place in the alphabetical sequence. Lexemes that share the same pronunciation, but not the same spelling, are called **homophones** (from Greek, 'same' + 'sound'). Here are some further homophone pairs in English:

bare/bear, gait/gate, haul/hall, leak/leek, miner/minor, paw/poor/pore/ pour, sew/sow, stake/steak, taught/taut

You will notice that most homophones arise because vowel sounds that used to be pronounced differently, as represented by the spelling, have in the course of historical sound changes come to be pronounced the same.

1.3 Lexemes and variants

If you look up *sung* in a dictionary, you will find a very brief entry along the lines of 'past participle of *sing*', which is a cross-reference to the entry for *sing*. If you look up the word *talked*, which is the past participle of *talk*, you will not find an entry. For both these words, the dictionary gives their description under a single entry: *sing* for *sung*, and *talk* for *talked*. You do not need a separate treatment of *sung* or *talked*, because what is said about *sing* or *talk* is equally applicable to them. They are merely 'variants' of the entry word; in effect they are the 'same word'.

The lexeme *sing*, for example, has the following variants: *sing, sings, sang, singing, sung*. The lexeme *talk* has one variant fewer: *talk, talks, talked, talking*. What we are looking at are the inflections of verbs in English:

base/present tense	*sing*	*talk*
third person singular/present tense	*sings*	*talks*
past tense	*sang*	*talked*
present participle	*singing*	*talking*
past participle	*sung*	*talked*

The verb *talk* represents the 'regular' paradigm, where the past tense and the past participle have the same form, with the *−(e)d* suffix. The verb *sing* is one of a number with 'irregular' inflections.

There is a sense in which *sing, sings, sang, singing* and *sung* are all the 'same word'; they are different manifestations of the same lexeme, variants chosen according to the grammatical context of the lexeme. For example, if the subject of a sentence is a 'third person singular' (equivalent to *he*, *she* or *it*) and the speaker/writer has chosen present tense, then the form of the verb will be *sings* or *talks*, with the 's' suffix marking the 'third person singular present tense' (e.g. 'until the fat lady/she sings') We need a further term to distinguish this type of 'word':

> *word-form* an inflectional variant of a lexeme

To illustrate word-forms we have chosen verbs, because verb lexemes have more inflections than any other type of lexeme in English. Two other types of lexeme regularly have inflectional variants and so more than one word-form: nouns and adjectives – though not every member of these classes, as is the case with verbs. Countable nouns (*biscuit*, *coin*), but not uncountable nouns (*dough*, *salt*), have a 'plural' inflection. Some nouns, mainly referring to animate beings, have a 'possessive' inflection. The word-forms for plural nouns have a –*(e)s* suffix as the regular inflection (*bananas*, *oranges*, *mangoes*). A small number of countable nouns form the plural irregularly, e.g. *feet*, *geese*, *mice*, *teeth*; *children*; *knives*, *loaves*; *nuclei*, *millennia*, *formulae*, *hypotheses*, *criteria*. The possessive inflection is normally marked in the singular noun by an apostrophe + *s* (e.g. *cat's*, *girl's*, *nephew's*), and in the plural noun by an apostrophe only, placed after the plural suffix (e.g. *cats'*, *girls' nephews'*). This, of course, applies to writing: in speech, the possessive singular adds –*(e)s*, and so is no different from the plural; and the plural possessive is the same as the normal plural, except where the plural is formed irregularly (e.g. *mice's*, *children's*, *women's*). Summarising, the word-forms of (some) noun lexemes are:

base/singular	*girl*	*child*
plural	*girls*	*children*
possessive singular	*girl's*	*child's*
possessive plural	*girls'*	*children's*

Note that the three inflected forms of *girl* (the 'regular' paradigm) have the same pronunciation.

Some adjective lexemes in English have a 'comparative' and a 'superlative' form. The adjectives concerned are 'gradable' (e.g. *long*, *quick*, *small*), rather than 'ungradable' (*daily*, *mortal*, *sterile*). Most gradable adjectives that are one-syllable in length can have these forms, as may most two–syllable gradable adjectives. The regular inflection for the comparative is –*er*, and for the superlative –*est* (e.g. *longer/longest*, *quicker/quickest*, *smaller/smallest*). There is a very small number of irregular forms: *good*, *better*, *best*; *bad*, *worse*, *worst*. An alternative way of expressing comparison, applied to some two-syllable adjectives and to nearly all gradable adjectives of three syllables or more, is with the adverbs *more* and *most* (e.g. *more/most skilful*, *more/most treacherous*). Summarising, the word-forms of (some) adjective lexemes are:

base	*slow*	*good*
comparative	*slower*	*better*
superlative	*slowest*	*best*

When one-syllable adjectives do not permit word-forms with *−er/-est*, it is usually because their pronunciation is somehow awkward (e.g. *sourer*, *wronger*).

1.4 War chests and wards of court

In the list from the COD10 in 1.1 we noted several lexemes composed of more than one orthographic word. A number of them have *war* as their first element: *war chest*, *war crime*, *war cry*, *war dance*. Two independent lexemes have come together to form a new lexeme with a specialised meaning, to denote some entity that is considered worth having its own 'name'. We call such lexemes **compounds** (see further Chapter 2). Sometimes compounds are written, as in the examples with *war*, with a space between the two elements. Other compounds are written as a single orthographic word (e.g. *warhead*, *warlord*, *warpath*, *warship*), while others have a hyphen joining the two elements (e.g. *war-torn*, *window-shop*, *world-class*). The current tendency is away from 'hyphenated compounds' towards either 'solid compounds' (one orthographic word) or 'open compounds' (two or more orthographic words).

The other multi-word lexeme in the list is *ward of court*, which is a phrase rather than a compound. **Phrasal lexemes** have a number of common structures, of which the 'noun + preposition + noun' of *ward of court* is one. Here are some further examples of this structure:

> age of consent, cash on delivery, chapel of rest, home from home, hostage to fortune, man about town, meals on wheels, place in the sun, rite of passage, skeleton in the cupboard.

A second phrasal structure consists of a noun in the possessive followed by another noun, e.g.

> athlete's foot, banker's card, collector's item, fool's paradise, hair's breadth, lady's finger, ploughman's lunch, potter's wheel, saint's day, smoker's cough, traveller's cheque, writer's block.

A third phrasal structure consists of two words of the same type (noun, verb, adjective) joined by the conjunction *and*. These are sometimes called 'binomials'. Here are some examples:

> bells and whistles, black and white, bow and scrape, down and out, fast and furious, hammer and tongs, nip and tuck, pins and needles, rock and roll, sweet and sour, ups and downs, you and yours.

There are also a few cases of 'trinomials', e.g. *hop, skip and jump*; *hook, line and sinker*. You will notice that a number of these items are used metaphorically: *hammer and tongs* has nothing to do with the literal instruments used by the blacksmith, but refers to the intensity or vigour with which something is done.

A fourth kind of phrasal lexeme consists of a verb + adverb (sometimes called a 'particle'), to form what are called 'phrasal verbs'. Here are some examples:

> break up, calm down, find out, give in, look over, pass out, show up, take off, waste away, wear out.

Some of these phrasal verbs have a literal or near-literal meaning, others are more-or-less figurative in meaning. In one of its meanings, *take off* is literal (e.g. referring to aircraft leaving the runway), in another it is figurative (in the sense of 'imitate').

A fifth kind of phrasal lexeme, if indeed we can count them as lexemes, are typically metaphorical or figurative in meaning. They are **idioms**, which have a range of structures from phrase up to whole sentence. An idiom has two essential characteristics: its meaning is more than the meaning of the sum of its parts, and usually figurative; and it has a relatively fixed structure. The idiom *a storm in a teacup* (American English equivalent *a tempest in a teapot*) has the figurative meaning of a 'fuss about nothing', and there is no possibility of substituting or adding anything to its structure. In *pull the wool over someone's eyes*, the meaning is figurative (i.e. 'deceive'), and the only substitution possibilities are appropriate inflections for the verb *pull* and an appropriate possessive noun or pronoun in the place of *someone's*. Idioms are all pervasive in language and show a diversity of form and meaning (see Fernando and Flavell (1981) for a fuller treatment). Here are a few more examples from English:

> know which side one's bread is buttered, at the drop of a hat, go against the grain, come to a pretty pass, take someone for a ride, spill the beans, throw the baby out with the bathwater, walk on eggshells.

You will notice that in some cases (e.g. *take someone for a ride*) a literal interpretation is also possible. Only the context will reveal whether the literal or the metaphorical (idiomatic) meaning is the intended one.

1.5 Classifying words

In talking about words, we often, as already in this chapter, need to refer to them by the conventional broad classification into 'parts of speech', or 'word classes' as the preferred term now is. Rather than assume that this is general knowledge, as most dictionaries do, we will devote a little discussion to it.

Although we have school-based definitions in our minds, such as 'a verb is a doing word', words are classified more rigorously largely on the basis of the roles they play in the structure of sentences. English has four large classes, into which most new words go, and four smaller, fairly static classes. The four large classes are:

- *nouns* are the largest class by far; they represent the animate and inanimate objects that are the participants in sentences as subjects, objects, etc. (*beauty, cat, leaf, niece, nonsense, water*)
- *verbs* represent the action, event or state that the sentence is about, and hold the pivotal position in the sentence, determining which other elements need to be present (*break, decide, fall, have, keep, love*)
- *adjectives* occur in front of nouns as descriptive words, as well as after verbs like *be* with a similar function (*feeble, gigantic, lazy, new, rough, vain*)
- *adverbs* are a diverse class, in part representing circumstantial information such as time (*again, always, sometimes, soon*) and manner (*clearly, efficiently, quickly, tentatively*), in part acting as modifiers of adjectives or other adverbs (*quite, somewhat, very*), in part forming connections between sentences (*however, moreover, therefore*).

The four smaller word classes, whose major function is to link the members of the larger classes together in sentence structure, are:

- *pronouns* stand for nouns and their accompanying words (noun phrases) to avoid unnecessary repetition, including personal pronouns (*I, you, he, she, it, we, they*), possessive pronouns (*mine, yours, hers*), reflexive pronouns (*myself, yourself, themselves*), relative pronouns (*who, whose, which*), indefinite pronouns (*someone, nobody, anything*)
- *determiners* accompany nouns and are subdivided into 'identifiers' and 'quantifiers'; identifiers include the articles (*a, the*), demonstratives (*this, that*) and possessives (*my, your, her, our, their*); quantifiers include the numerals (*two, five; second, fifth*) and indefinite quantifiers (*few, many, several*)
- *prepositions* combine with nouns or noun phrases primarily to form prepositional phrases (*at, for, from, in, of, on, over, through, with*)
- *conjunctions* are used to connect clauses or sentences, but also phrases and words; they include the co-ordinating conjunctions (*and, but, or*) and a larger number of subordinating conjunctions (*although, because, if, until, when, while*).

You should consult a grammar book if you need a more extensive explanation of the word classes.

1.6 Taking words to pieces

In the course of this chapter, we have mentioned terms like 'affix' and 'suffix', which are parts of words. This section looks at the analysis of words into their constituent elements and suggests some terms that will be useful in talking about word structure. First of all, we need a term to denote an element of a word: it is **morpheme**. Words are composed of morphemes. Many words, sometimes called 'simple' words, consist of only one morpheme:

> bed, dream, go, in, over, please, shallow, treat, usual, vote, whole, yellow.

Here are some words composed of more than one morpheme:

> bedroom, dreamy, going, live-in, overland, displease, shallowest, mistreat-ment, usually, voters, wholemeal, yellowish.

Each of these words has, as one of its morphemes, a 'simple' word from the earlier list, which forms the 'root', or in the case of compounds like *bedroom* one of the roots, of the word. The root morpheme is the kernel of the word, with the main meaning, which is modified by other morphemes in various ways.

Compounds are composed of two or more root morphemes: *bedroom, live-in, overland, wholemeal*. These compounds have a variety of structures in terms of the word class membership of the roots: noun + noun, verb + preposition, preposition + noun, adjective + noun. Many compounds are like *bedroom*, where the first part modifies the second and the word class of the compound is that of the second part, in this case a noun: a 'bedroom' is a kind of 'room'. The other three compounds are different: *live-in*, with a preposition as second part, is an adjective (as in *a live-in nanny*); *overland*, with a noun as second part is either an adjective (*an overland journey*) or an adverb (*we're travelling overland*); and *whole-meal*, again with a noun as second part, is an adjective (*wholemeal bread*).

The other words in the list are all composed of root + affix. 'Affix' is the general term for morphemes that cannot be used by themselves as simple words; they only occur 'bound' to another morpheme. If they occur before the root, and so are bound to the right, they are called 'prefixes' (e.g. *dis-* in *displease*). If they occur after the root, and so are bound to the left, they are 'suffixes' (e.g. *-ish* in *yellowish*). Note that, when writing affixes, the convention is to put a hyphen on the side where the affix is bound, i.e. to the right of prefixes and to the left of suffixes.

Some of the suffixes mark 'inflections' (see 1.3 above): *go-ing* (present participle), *shallow-est* (superlative), *voter-s* (plural). There are no inflectional prefixes in English. The resulting words are 'word-forms' (inflectional variants) of the root lexeme.

The other affixes represent 'derivations'. The addition of the affix creates a new, derived lexeme. We would expect it to be entered in a dictionary some-where, though, as we shall see (Chapter 8), dictionaries vary in how they treat derivations. The addition of a suffix usually changes the word class of the root, though a prefix rarely does:

> *dream* (noun) + *-y*   *dreamy* (adjective)
> *dis-* + *please* (verb)   *displease* (verb)
> *mis* + *treat* (verb)   *mistreat* (verb)

mistreat + *-ment*	*mistreatment* (noun)
usual (adjective) + *-ly*	*usually* (adverb)
vote (verb) + *-er*	*voter* (noun)
yellow (adjective) + *-ish*	*yellowish* (adjective)

Note that an inflectional suffix, e.g. the plural 's' on *voters*, is always the final suffix in a word.

We might conclude from our discussion of morphemes so far that roots are always 'free' (i.e. can occur as simple lexemes), and affixes are always 'bound' (i.e. they need a root to attach to). However, there is a certain set of words in English, mostly compounds, that have bound roots. Here are some examples:

> anthropomorphic, astronaut, bibliography, biology, neuralgia, synchrony, telepathy, xenophobia.

These lexemes are formed from (bound) roots that are taken from the classical languages (Greek and Latin) and put together to form, for the most part, new words that were unknown in classical Greek and Latin. They are known as 'neo-classical compounds', and their parts are called 'combining forms'. Our examples are formed as follows:

- *anthropo-* (human) + *-morphic* (in the form of)
- *astro-* (star) + *-naut* (sailor)
- *biblio-* (book) + *-graphy* (writing)
- *bio-* (life) + *-ology* (study)
- *neuro-* (nerve) + *-algia* (pain)
- *syn-* (same) + *-chrony* (time)
- *tele-* (distant) + *-pathy* (feeling)
- *xeno-* (foreigner) + *-phobia* (fear).

Some roots from the classical languages occur in derivations, when they are also bound, e.g. *chron-ic*, *graph-ical*, *naut-ical*, *neur-al*, *path-etic*.

To summarise:

> a word is composed of one or more morphemes
> a morpheme may function as a root or as an affix (prefix or suffix)
> a root morpheme is usually free, an affix is always bound
> bound roots are usually combining forms from Greek or Latin.

1.7 Further reading

You can find a fuller treatment of words and word structure in Jackson and Zé Amvela's *Words, Meaning and Vocabulary: An Introduction to Modern English Lexicology* (2000) and in Francis Katamba's *English Words* (1994).

2   Facts about words

In Chapter 1, we examined the ambiguity of the term 'word' and suggested a set of terms for resolving the ambiguity. We also outlined the morphology of the word in English and proposed terms for talking about the structure of words. This chapter makes a further contribution to the lexicology (study of words) of English, before we move on to the study of dictionaries (lexicography) in the next chapter.

2.1 Where English words came from

The vocabulary of English contains words from more sources than the vocabulary of any other language, as a consequence of its history and the contacts between its speakers and those of other languages. As far as its basic components are concerned, it is useful to view the vocabulary of English as being composed of a number of strata, rather like a rock formation in geology. The substratum of English is Anglo-Saxon, the collection of dialects that developed after the invading Germanic tribes, the Angles, Saxons and Jutes, colonised England following the departure of the Roman legions in the fifth century AD, driving the Celtic inhabitants to the fringes of the country in Wales and Cornwall. The language became known during this time as 'English', and we refer to the language during the period up to the mid-eleventh century as 'Old English'. The only significant influence on the language from outside during this period was from across the North Sea, the Viking invaders, who also spoke a Germanic language, Old Norse. For a time the country was divided, with 'Danelaw' on the eastern side of a line from Chester to the Wash. Old English and Old Norse were to a great extent mutually intelligible, and the influence of Old Norse on Old English was limited. The greatest linguistic legacy of the Vikings was in place names, e.g. ending in –*by* or –*thorpe*; but also many words beginning with *sk-* come from Old Norse, as do the third person plural pronouns (*they*, *them*, *their*). Even with these additions, the vocabulary of Old English was essentially Germanic, with a handful of words from Celtic, and a number of ecclesiastical terms taken from Latin following the introduction of Roman Christianity as a result of Augustine's mission in 597. (See Roberts *et al.* 1995 for a description of Old English vocabulary.)

The next stratum of vocabulary began to be laid with the Norman conquest in 1066. The influence of this event, and its political and social consequences, on English vocabulary was monumental, though it took a couple of centuries for its full effects to be worked out. The language of government, administration and the law became (Norman) French; English was not used for any official written purposes; in due course many people, especially in the rising merchant class, became bilingual in English and French. It is estimated that in excess of 10,000 words entered English from French between the twelfth and fourteenth centuries. French is a Romance language, with its origins in Latin; so a Latinate stratum was being overlaid on the Ango-Saxon substratum. Indeed, the substratum suffered considerable erosion, with a large proportion of the Old English vocabulary being replaced by words from the Latinate superstratum.

A further Latinate stratum was laid during the latter half of the sixteenth century and into the seventeenth, during the period that is called the 'Renaissance'. It was a period in which the classical civilisations of Greece and Rome were rediscovered, admired and celebrated; their literatures republished and extensively studied, translated and imitated. While words had been coming into English directly from Latin, as well as via French, for some centuries, the trickle now became a flood, and many thousands of Latin words were added to English, as well as Greek words, though these often came via Latin. The Renaissance also saw the beginnings of exploration, which developed in the eighteenth and nineteenth centuries into colonisation and empire; the contact with many different cultures and languages has enriched the vocabulary of English from a multitude of sources.

The substratum of English vocabulary is Anglo-Saxon, and the one hundred most frequently occurring words in both writing and speech are of Anglo-Saxon origin. Overlaid on this substratum is a stratum of Latinate vocabulary, mainly of French origin, from the medieval period: we do not recognise the vast majority of these words as foreign imports any more; they have become quite naturalised. Overlaid on this is a further Latinate stratum, taken directly from Latin during and after the Renaissance; many of these words still betray their origin, and they belong for the most part to the vocabulary of academic discourse and specialist jargon. Additionally, English has imported words from countless languages around the world, and continues to do so (see Crystal 1995: 126f.).

2.2 Making new words

There are two basic methods by which a language may increase its vocabulary. The first is to use the material (morphemes) available in the language already (see 1.6) and to recombine it in new ways. The other is to import a word from another language (mentioned in 2.1 above), a process called, rather curiously, 'borrowing' – there is, after all, no intention to return the borrowed item, which is termed a 'loanword'. Nearly all new words are added to the larger word classes (1.5), especially nouns, verbs and adjectives, with the majority being nouns.

2.2.1 Compounds

Compounds are formed by joining two or more root morphemes or (classical) combining forms (see 1.6) into a single lexeme. A new discovery, product, sensation or process is often suitably named by a compound, whose status as a lexeme is reinforced by usage and confirmed by inclusion in a dictionary. Compounds are often idiomatic in meaning, or at least not entirely transparent. For example, the meaning of *seat belt* – as a safety restraint in vehicles or aircraft – is not immediately obvious from the two parts of the compound. If you were unfamiliar with the object, you would need some explanation of the word. This is even more so in the case of neo–classical compounds, where a knowledge of Greek and Latin would be required for their interpretation; e.g. *calligraphy* ('beautiful' + 'writing'); *mastectomy* ('breast' + 'cut out'); *pachyderm* ('thick' + 'skin'), denoting a large mammal with a thick skin, such as an elephant; *stenothermal* ('narrow' + 'heat'), i.e. tolerant of only small changes in temperature.

Where a compound is composed of more than two roots, a structure is usually evident among the parts, which is sometimes reflected in how the compound is written. For example, *four-wheel drive* indicates that *four* and *wheel* belong together and relate as a unit to *drive*; whereas *golden handshake* indicates that *hand* and *shake* belong together and *golden* is then added to form the three-part compound.

An interesting compound is formed by the combination of two roots and the addition of the –*ed* suffix, to form an adjective. The –*ed* suffix looks like the past participle inflection of verbs (1.3), but there is no verb involved in this word formation. Here are some examples: *dark-haired, empty-handed, hard-nosed, jet-lagged, muddle-headed, open-minded, quick-witted, round-shouldered, sharp-tongued, warm-hearted.* They are mostly, but not exclusively, composed of 'adjective + noun-*ed*'.

A special type of compound is formed by blending two roots; the first root loses letters/sounds from the end and the second from the beginning, e.g. *break-fast +lunch > brunch, smoke + fog > smog, transfer + resistor > transistor.* Sometimes, one of the elements does not lose any material, e.g. *car + hijack > carjack, cheese + hamburger > cheeseburger;* or there are shared letters, e.g. *circle + clip > circlip, floppy + optical > floptical, twig + igloo > twigloo.*

2.2.2 Derivatives

The addition of a derivational prefix or suffix to a lexeme forms a derivative. The lexeme may be 'simple' (i.e. a single morpheme), or it may be a compound, or it may be a derivative already; e.g. *care-ful, landscape-(e)r, national-ity.* Some derivational affixes have their origin in Anglo–Saxon (e.g. *-ful, -er*), others have come from French or Latin (e.g. *-al, -ity*); and while there is a tendency to use Anglo–Saxon affixes with Anglo–Saxon roots and Latinate affixes with Latinate roots, some mixing does occur, e.g. *beauti-ful, preach-er* (Latin root + Anglo–Saxon suffix), *fals(e)-ity, ship-ment* (Anglo–Saxon root + Latin suffix).

Prefixes, of which usually not more than one is added to a root, do not normally change the word class of the item to which they are added. Common prefixes include those with a 'negative' or 'opposite' meaning, such as *dis-, in-* (and its variants *il-, im-, ir-*), *un-*, the 'again' prefix *re-*, the 'attitude' prefixes *pro-* and *anti-*, and the *self-* prefix. Here is an example of each: *dis-please, in-decision, il-legible, im-patient, ir-reversible, un-certain, re-read, pro-life, anti-freeze, self-addressed*.

Suffixes are numerous and usually change the word class of the item they are added to. Changing verbs to nouns are: *-er* (the 'doer'/'agent' suffix), *-(t)ion, -ment, -ance*; e.g. *bak(e)-er, educat(e)-ion, enjoy-ment, perform-ance*. Changing adjectives to nouns are: *-ity, -ness*; e.g. *sincer(e)-ity, smooth-ness*. Changing adjectives to verbs are: *-en, -ify, -ise*; e.g. *thick-en, solid-ify, internal-ise*. Changing verbs to adjectives are: *-able/-ible*; e.g. *avoid-able, collaps(e)-ible*. Changing nouns to adjectives are: *-al, -ful, -ly*; e.g. *cultur(e)-al, hope-ful, friend-ly*. And changing adjectives to adverbs is: *-ly*; e.g. *quick-ly, smooth-ly*. More than one derivational suffix may be added to a root, e.g. *friend-li-ness, recover-abil-ity, care-ful-ly, nation-al-is(e)-ation*.

A special type of derivation occurs which changes the word class of a lexeme but does not add a suffix. It is called 'conversion'. For example, *bottle* is primarily a noun, but it is used as a verb, with the sense 'put into a bottle', by conversion. A contrary conversion would be *catch*, where the verb can also be used as a noun. There are many cases of conversion (e.g. *dirty* (adjective to verb), *skin* (noun to verb), *spill* (verb to noun), *spoon* (noun to verb)) and it is still a productive process, especially from nouns to verbs, e.g. *doorstep, handbag, progress, showcase, text-message*.

A minor type of derivation is 'backformation', a kind of derivation in reverse, in which a supposed affix is removed from a word. This is how the verb *edit* was derived from the noun *editor*, by removing the supposed 'doer' suffix *-or* (compare *actor, advisor*). A similar backformation derived *babysit* from *babysitter*, *commentate* from *commentator*, *malinger* from *malingerer*, *scavenge* from *scavenger*. *Automate* was derived by backformation from *automation*, *destruct* from *destruction*, *enthuse* from *enthusiasm*, *greed* from *greedy*, *sedate* from *sedation*, *televise* from *television*.

2.2.3 Acronyms

A minor, but nevertheless much used word formation process takes the initial letters of a phrase and creates a word, called an acronym. Either the acronym is pronounced as a normal word (e.g. AIDS (Acquired Immune Deficiency Syndrome), UNESCO (United Nations Educational, Scientific and Cultural Organisation)), or the letters are spelled out (e.g. ATM (Automated Teller Machine), HIV (Human Immunodeficiency Virus)). Sometimes the two forms are combined, e.g. CD-ROM (Compact Disc – Read Only Memory). The acronym is usually spelt with capital letters, but a few acronyms no longer betray their origin in this way, e.g. *laser* ('light amplification by stimulated emission of radiation'). Here are some further examples, first of 'said' acronyms:

DAT (Digital Audio Tape), DWEM (Dead White European Male), MIDI (Musical Instrument Digital Interface), SIMM (Single In-line Memory Module); then of 'spelled out' acronyms (also called 'initialisms'): BSE (Bovine Spongiform Encephalopathy), CSA (Child Support Agency), FAQ (Frequently Asked Question), HTML (HyperText Markup Language), LMS (Local Management of Schools).

A further type of acronym is formed by taking the first syllable of the words of a phrase, e.g. *biopic* (biographical picture), *infotech* (information technology), *Ofsted* (Office of Standards in Education), *pixel* (picture element). In the case of *Ofsted*, the second element (*st*) does not consist of the full syllable, and an *x* has been added to *pixel* to join the two syllables. These 'syllabic acronyms' are a relatively rare formation.

2.2.4 *Loanwords*

When a word is 'borrowed' from another language and added to the vocabulary, it is a 'loanword'. Some loanwords continue to betray their origins, either in their spelling or their pronunciation, or both (e.g. *blitzkrieg* (German), *kibbutz* (Hebrew), *spaghetti* (Italian)); while others have become naturalised (e.g. *coach* (Hungarian), *gong* (Malay), *tycoon* (Japanese)).

Words have been borrowed into English for a number of reasons. After the Norman conquest, a new language was imposed on top of the English, and so, for example, *beef*, *mutton* and *pork* appeared alongside *cow*, *sheep* and *pig*. During the Renaissance, excessive admiration for Roman and Greek cultures and languages led to the borrowing of words from Latin and Greek to remedy what was felt to be a lack in English of erudite vocabulary; and so *abscond* was borrowed alongside *hide*, *calculate* for *count*, *emporium* for *shop*, *manuscript* for *book*, *protect* for *ward*, *transgress* for *sin*, *valediction* for *farewell*.

When the explorers and colonists went to new countries, experienced different foods, and came into contact with plants and animals they had never encountered before, they often took the words for these things from the local languages. So, we have *chipmunk* from Algonquian (in North America), *kookaburra* from Wiradhuri (in Australia), *kiwi* from Maori (in New Zealand), *chutney* from Hindi, *poppadom* from Tamil, *lychee* from Chinese, *sushi* from Japanese, *impala* from Zulu, *sherbet* from Turkish, and so on. Through the centuries, when a culture has been admired for its prowess in a particular area, English has borrowed its words for that topic; e.g. musical terms from Italian (*concerto*, *opera*, *soprano*, *tempo*), culinary terms from French (*casserole*, *fricassee*, *au gratin*, *purée*, *sauté*).

When a profession has sought an erudite vocabulary to mark off its supposed area of competence, it has usually looked to the classical languages for its jargon. The law, for example, has taken many terms from Latin, such as: *ad litem* ('in a lawsuit'), *bona fide* ('with good faith'), *corpus delicti* ('body of offence'), *ejusdem generis* ('of the same kind'), *in personam* ('against the person'), *lis pendens* ('a lawsuit pending'), *obiter dictum* ('a passing remark' – by a judge), *prima facie* ('at first impression'), *subpoena* ('under penalty' – i.e. to attend court), *ultra vires* ('beyond (one's legal) power'). Medicine, on the other hand, has tended to look more to Greek for its jargon: an inflammatory disease ends in *-itis* (*bronchitis*, *peritonitis*), a surgical removal ends in *-ectomy* (*hysterectomy*, *vasectomy*), the medical care of particular groups ends in *-iatrics* (*geriatrics*, *paediatrics*).

English continues to enhance its vocabulary by taking in loanwords from languages around the world. Some recent borrowing includes: *balti* (Urdu), *ciabatta* (Italian), *gite* (French), *intifada* (Arabic), *juggernaut* (Hindi), *karaoke* (Japanese), *nouvelle cuisine* (French), *ombudsman* (Swedish), *paparrazi* (Italian), *perestroika* (Russian), *salsa* (Spanish), *tikka* (Punjabi).

2.3 Word meaning

One of the most important tasks of a lexicographer is to capture the 'meaning' of a word in a 'definition' (see Chapter 8). We need to determine first of all what constitutes the 'meaning' of a word, which is the purpose of this section of the chapter. The suggestion is that the meaning of a word is composed of a number of features: its relation with the real world, the associations that it carries with it, its relations with other words in the vocabulary, and the regular company that it keeps with other words in sentence and text structure.

Many words have more than one meaning; they manifest 'polysemy'. Ascertaining how many meanings, or 'senses', a lexeme has, and in what order to arrange them are difficult decisions for a lexicographer to make, and dictionaries may differ quite markedly in their analysis. Our immediate discussion, however, is concerned with the general factors that may apply to any lexeme or sense of a lexeme.

2.3.1 Reference

The primary feature of meaning is the relation of reference between a lexeme and the entity – person, object, feeling, action, idea, quality, etc. – in the real world that the lexeme denotes. The exact nature of the reference relation has exercised the minds of linguists and philosophers over many centuries (Lyons 1977). We use words to talk about and make reference to the world we live in, our experience of that world, our speculation about what might have been or could be, our imagination of other possible worlds and possible scenarios. Our worlds are inhabited by humans and other creatures, by natural objects and artefacts, by our ideas, opinions and beliefs, which possess characteristics that we describe, and which interact in a myriad ways. We can talk about all these things and communicate about them with other people who speak the same language, because we have a shared vocabulary and grammar. In particular, we agree about which word refers to which aspect of reality or our experience of it.

The reference of some words is both more obvious and more easily described. This is the case especially for tangible objects (*bicycle*, *trumpet*) and for physical actions (*jump*, *spill*). For words that denote more abstract entities, the reference relation is less clearly discernible. This is the case for many abstract nouns (*deference, solitude*), for verbs expressing mental and emotional states and processes (*think, worry*), and for adjectives generally, especially where they are gradable (*long, warm*) or evaluative (*ridiculous, superb*). For some words, belonging to the smaller, grammatical classes (1.5), a relation of reference may be scarcely discernible (*about, this*).

What we are often interested in, including lexicographically, is how words that have a similar reference differ from each other. For example, how do *happen, occur, befall, transpire* and, perhaps, *materialise* differ? They all denote 'come about' or 'take place' (LDEL2: 718). The differences are subtle and may have little to do with reference as such, and more to do with context: *occur* would be found in a more formal context than *happen*; *befall* has an old-fashioned ring to it; *transpire* and *materialise* are, perhaps, particular kinds of 'come about'. We cannot isolate a word either from the typical contexts in which it occurs or from its relationships with other words.

2.3.2 *Connotation*

A distinction is often drawn between the 'denotation' of a word and its 'connotation'. While the denotation is the straightforward, neutral relation between a word and its referent, the connotation brings in the, often emotive, associations that a word may have for a speaker or a community of speakers. For many English speakers, the word *champagne*, while denoting a sparkling wine from a particular region of France, has the connotation of celebration or expensive living.

Some words spread particular negative or positive connotations (semantic prosodies) across the phrases or sentences in which they occur. For example, *fundamentalist* or *fundamentalism*, which denote 'adherent/adherence to the fundamental teachings of a movement or religion', are usually used in a negative context and with a connotation of a fanaticism that should be disapproved of. On the other hand, *inspire*, denoting 'creating the desire to do or feel something', usually has a positive connotation and spreads a positive semantic prosody, occurring typically with nouns like *confidence, enthusiasm* or *loyalty*.

Such connotations are widely shared and may be or become intrinsic to the contexts in which the users of a language generally situate the words. Connotations may be more restricted in scope, to a particular generation (e.g. *blitz* to those who lived through World War II), or to a particular group (e.g. *safe* to those who have hazardous occupations), or even to an individual. A connotation that is shared by a large proportion of speakers can be considered as a contributory feature to the meaning of a lexeme.

2.3.3 *Sense relations*

A third contributory factor to the meaning of a lexeme or a sense of a lexeme is the semantic relations it contracts with other lexemes in the vocabulary, often termed 'sense relations'. They include: sameness or similarity of meaning (synonymy), oppositeness of meaning (antonymy), the 'kind of' relation (hyponymy), and the 'part of' relation (meronymy).

Synonymy is a widespread relation in English, in large part because there are words with similar meaning from more than one of the strata that make up the vocabulary (2.1). For example, *begin* has an Anglo-Saxon origin, while its synonym *commence* entered English from French during the medieval period; similarly with *keep* and *retain*, *leave* and *depart*, *tell* and *inform*, *live* and *reside*, *share* and *portion*, and so on. Equally, synonym pairs exist that derive, on the one hand, from French in the medieval period, and on the other, from Latin during the Renaissance: *complete* and *plenary*, *join* and *connect*, *sign* and *portent*, *taste* and *gustation*, *vote* and *plebiscite*. There are, even, synonym triplets from each of the three strata of vocabulary; e.g. *end, finish, terminate*; *hatred, enmity, animosity*; *kingly, royal, regal*; *sin, trespass, transgression*. In general, as the examples cited confirm, the synonym from the Latinate strata tends to be used in more formal contexts than the one from the Anglo-Saxon substratum.

The other major source of synonym pairs is dialect difference, either between national varieties (e.g. British and American English) or between dialects within a national variety. The major differences between British and American English are in vocabulary, rather than in grammar, e.g. (BrE word followed by AmE word) *biscuit, cookie*; *car park, parking lot*; *drawing pin, thumbtack*; *flannel, washcloth*; *lorry, truck*; *single (ticket), one-way*; *waistcoat, vest*; and many more. Here are some synonym pairs for Scottish English and English English: *birl, whirl*; *dree, endure*; *fankle, entangle*; *kirk, church*; *lum, chimney*; *neep, turnip*; *outwith, outside*; *vennel, alley*.

Antonymy is a less frequently occurring sense relation than synonymy. It is most prevalent among gradable adjectives, where the antonyms represent the opposite ends of a scale, e.g. *big, small*; *wide, narrow*; *beautiful, ugly*; *quick, slow*. Other word classes also show antonymy: verbs *begin* and *end*, nouns *bottom* and *top*, prepositions *into* and *out of*, adverbs *above* and *below*. Not all antonymy is of the same type. In the case of gradable antonyms, the words are in a 'more/less' relation: *wide* and *narrow* cover overlapping parts of a spectrum, and an object is *wide* or *narrow* in relation to some norm. In contrast some antonyms have an 'either/or' relation: *win* and *lose* are mutually exclusive, you do either one or the other. A third type of antonym shows a 'converse' relation: *buy* and *sell* are the converse of each other; if X sells some goods to Y, then Y buys them from X.

Hyponymy relates words hierarchically, with a superordinate word (hypernym) having a more general meaning than the subordinate word (hyponym). The hyponyms are in a 'kind of' relation to the hypernym. For example, *knife, fork* and *spoon* are kinds of *cutlery*; so, *cutlery* is the superordinate word, with general meaning, and *knife, fork* and *spoon* are its hyponyms, with more specific meaning. These is turn may be superordinate words to their hyponyms; *spoon*, for example, has the hyponyms *teaspoon, tablespoon, dessertspoon, ladle*. A large part of vocabulary can be viewed as being related by hyponymy, but, as with language generally, there is no neat system of hyponymy relations organising the whole vocabulary of English.

Meronymy is like hyponymy in that it relates words hierarchically, but the relation is a 'part of' relation. The meronyms of a superordinate word represent the parts of that word. For example, *ball*, *heel* and *instep* are meronyms of *foot*; *hub*, *rim* and *spoke* are meronyms of *wheel*; *flower*, *root* and *stalk* are meronyms of *plant*. Together, hyponymy and meronymy serve to group words into semantic sets, known as 'lexical fields', in which the lexemes all refer to the same area of meaning (see further Chapter 12).

2.3.4 Collocation

The sense relations between words are 'paradigmatic' relations: a synonym, antonym, hyponym or meronym would substitute for its counterpart in some slot in the structure of sentences. The meaning of a word is also determined by its 'syntagmatic' relations, specifically by its collocation, the other words that typically accompany it in the structure of sentences and discourses. For example, the noun *ban* is typically modified by the adjective *total* or *complete*, is associated with the verbs *impose* and *lift*, and is followed by the preposition *on*. In a sentence with the verb *spend*, the Object would typically consist of either an amount of money (*two hundred pounds*) or a period of time (*last weekend*). The adjective *flippant* typically associates either with a noun referring to something said (*remark*, *answer*, *comment*) or with the noun *attitude*.

The word 'typically' occurs in all these statements about collocation, because collocation is a matter of the statistical probability or likelihood that two words will co-occur. One of a pair may exercise a stronger attraction than the other; for example, *wine* is more likely to co-occur with *red* than *red* is with *wine*, because *red* can co-occur with many nouns, while *wine* occurs with only a small number of adjectives. Description of collocation is most reliably based on the analysis of large computer corpora of texts, which can yield appropriate statistical data.

To summarise, the components of (the sense of) a lexeme's meaning are: its relations with the 'real world' in the form of its denotation and connotation; its relations with other (senses of) lexemes in the vocabulary; its relations with the other lexemes that typically accompany it in the structure of sentences.

2.4 Describing words

In this concluding section of the chapter, we shall examine what constitutes the description of a lexeme; in other words, what information about words a lexicographer needs to take account of in framing a dictionary entry. Following Hudson (1988), 'lexical facts' include: the form of a word, its structure, its meaning, its grammar, its usage, and its origin.

By the 'form' of a word is meant its pronunciation (phonology) and spelling (orthography). The description of pronunciation specifies what sounds (phonemes) a word has, if it has more than one syllable how they are each stressed, and if the pronunciation is subject to any variation in connected speech (e.g.

vowel reduction or change in stress). The description of spelling specifies the letters that make up the word, any variant spelling, and possibly where the word may be broken at the end of a line.

The structure of a word refers to its composition in terms of morphemes (1.6), how the roots relate to each other in a compound word, what prefixes and suffixes the word has and how they modify the meaning of the root. The description of structure also needs to indicate if there are any pronunciation or spelling changes, either in the root or in an affix, as a result of joining morphemes together to form the word. For example, *clear* changes pronunciation and spelling when the suffix *-ify* is added (*clarify*), as does *discreet* with the suffix *-ion* (*discretion*); *bake* loses an 'e' when *-er* is added to form *baker*, as does *debate* with suffix *-able* (*debatable*). The suffix *-able* alternates with *-ible* (*discernible*), with no difference in pronunciation, depending on which Latin root it is added to.

The meaning of a word was discussed quite fully in 2.3. Both the reference relation and any other relevant semantic relations (sense relations, collocation) need to be described for an adequate account of meaning.

The description of grammar has two aspects: the inflections that a word has, and how a word fits into the syntax of sentences. For inflections, the description specifies which inflections the word may have (1.3), how they are pronounced and spelled, and any changes to the form of the root that result from their addition. For example, the addition of plural suffix *-(e)s* changes *hoof* to *hoov-es*, *city* to *citi-es*, the addition of the past tense/past participle suffix *-(e)d* changes *cry* to *cri-ed*, *slap* to *slapp-ed*. If a word has an irregular form (e.g. of plural or past tense), this too will be specified, e.g. *foot – feet, appendix – appendices, criterion – criteria, buy – bought, tell – told, see – saw*.

The description of the syntactic operation of words begins with their assignment to a word class (1.5), which is an initial specification of where the word may be used in the structure of sentences. Any deviation from the normal expectation needs to be specified, e.g. if an adjective is restricted to one of the three possible positions for adjectives (i.e. 'attributive' – before nouns (*the brown suit*), 'postpositive' – after nouns (*time enough*), and 'predicative' – after a verb like *be* (*the suit is brown*)). For example, *awake* occurs as predicative (*the baby is awake*) but not as attributive, and *chief* occurs as attributive (*our chief concern*) but not as predicative; *galore, emeritus* and *extraordinaire* occur only in postpositive position. For verbs, the specification of syntactic operation is even more complex, including not only whether a verb may take an Object, Complement, etc., but also what type of Object (e.g. noun phrase, nominal clause) and so on.

The description of usage specifies whether a word, or any of its senses, is restricted to particular contexts. The restriction could be geographical (a national variety or a dialect), it could be time-bound (an obsolete or archaic meaning), it could be the formality of the situation or the word's status in the language (e.g. slang or taboo). The restriction could be linked with the expression of the speaker's or writer's attitude, to indicate disapproval or an insult, or to be appreciative. Or a word may be restricted in its usage because to use it would be offensive to a particular group of people.

Finally, the description of a word includes a specification of its origin, if it belonged to Anglo-Saxon or if it has been 'borrowed', from which language and when. 'Origin' is sometimes taken to mean the 'ultimate' origin, as far as this can be ascertained; for example, a word taken from French during the medieval period may have its origin traced back through older French to Latin. This part of the description may also chart the history of changes in the form (spelling and pronunciation) and in the meaning of the word.

These are the features of words, their lexical description, that lexicographers must grapple with and from among which they must choose what to include in their lexicographical descriptions, which are published in dictionaries.

2.5 Further reading

For many of the topics of this chapter, see: Jackson and Zé Amvela's *Words, Meaning and Vocabulary* (2000) and David Crystal's *The Cambridge Encyclopedia of the English Language* (1995), especially Part II.

On new words, see: John Ayto's *Twentieth Century Words* (1999) and Elizabeth Knowles and Julia Elliott's *The Oxford Dictionary of New Words* (1997).

Sense relations are discussed fully by D.A. Cruse in his *Lexical Semantics* (1996).

See Dick Hudson's article in *IJL* (1988) for a 'Checklist of Lexical Facts'.

3 The dictionary

How many times have you heard someone say, or have you said yourself, 'I'll look it up in the dictionary'? The assumption behind such a comment is that 'the dictionary' is a single text, perhaps in different versions, rather like the Bible. Every household is assumed to have one; children are taught how to consult the dictionary in school; there is one in every office. Lawyers quote the dictionary in court, teachers and lecturers appeal to it, politicians and preachers argue from its definitions. The dictionary is part of the cultural fabric of our society; each major new edition warrants a review in the daily press. And we all take what the dictionary says as authoritative: if the dictionary says so, then it is so. Life would be impossible if the dictionary was not the final arbiter in our linguistic disputes.

Yet, walk into any bookshop and cast your eye over the shelf where the dictionaries are, pick a few up and examine them, read the blurb on the dust jacket, and you will soon notice that they are all different. They are all recognisably dictionaries, with a more or less alphabetical list of words and information about them, but they have different formats, highly variable numbers of pages, a variety of page layouts, and so on. Compare some of the entries, and you soon realise that the notion of 'the dictionary' as a single text is wide of the mark. What distinguishes them is more notable than what they have in common.

3.1 What is a dictionary?

A dictionary is a reference book about words. It is a book about language. Its nearest cousin is the encyclopedia, but this is a book about things, people, places and ideas, a book about the 'real world', not about language. The distinction between dictionary and encyclopedia is not always easy to draw, and there are often elements of one in the other. But they do not share the same headword list – you would be unlikely to find *resemble* in an encyclopedia – and they do not provide the same information for the headwords that they do have in common. Compare the following entries for *toad*:

> **toad** Any of the more terrestrial warty-skinned members of the tailless amphibians (order Anura). The name commonly refers to members of the

genus Bufo, family Bufonidae, which are found worldwide, except for the
Australian and polar regions.

Toads may grow up to 25 cm/10 in. long. They live in cool, moist places
and lay their eggs in water. The eggs are laid not in a mass as with frogs, but
in long strings. The common toad B. bufo of Europe and Asia has a rough,
usually dark-brown skin in which there are glands secreting a poisonous
fluid which makes it unattractive as food for other animals; it needs this
protection because its usual progress is a slow, ungainly crawl.

(*Hutchinson New Century Encyclopedia*)

toad/təʊd/*n*. **1** any froglike amphibian of the family Bufonidae, esp. of the
genus Bufo, breeding in water but living chiefly on land. **2** any of various
similar tailless amphibians. **3** a repulsive or detestable person. **toadish** *adj*.
[Old English *tadige, tadde, tada*, of unknown origin]

(COD9)

Dictionaries are usually arranged in alphabetical order of the headwords. Indeed
the expression 'dictionary order' is synonymous with 'alphabetical order'. But
there are word books that are arranged by topic or theme, rather than by alphabet
(see Chapter 12), and they have a long history (Hüllen 1999; McArthur 1986).

Dictionaries are reference books. People consult them to find out information about words. We must assume that compilers of dictionaries – lexicographers – include information that they know or expect people will want to look
up. What we cannot assume, however, is that lexicographers will exclude information that they might expect users will not want to look up. A dictionary is
more than just a reference book; it is also a (partial) record of the vocabulary of
a language. Any dictionary contains entries and information that few, if any,
users will want to access, either because they know it already, or because it is of
no interest to them. It would be the rare user who would consult a dictionary
for information on the word *the*, and yet no dictionary would be without an
entry for *the*. However, anyone serious about discovering the subtleties of the
definite article in English would be more likely to consult a grammar book than
a dictionary.

If the dictionary is distinguished, as a reference book, from the encyclopedia
on the one hand, it is distinguished, as a linguistic description, from the grammar book on the other. A grammar book, as the description of the grammatical
system of a language, deals with the general rules and conventions for the structure of sentences and tends to deal with words as classes or subclasses. A dictionary describes the operation of individual lexical items, including, where relevant,
how they fit into the general patterns of grammar. Grammar and dictionary are
complementary parts of the description of a language, and a dictionary will use
terms that are defined by the grammar. The point at which grammar and dictionary converge in their treatment of words concerns primarily the so-called
'grammatical' words, like the definite article, which play a crucial and often
complex role in grammar.

Who, then, are the users of dictionaries, and for what purposes do they use them? We readily think of students and learners, academics, word game and crossword puzzle buffs as regular, if not frequent, users of dictionaries. Most people probably have occasion to consult a dictionary from time to time, and many of us have a fascination with words and dictionaries, as the long-running television series *Call My Bluff* and *Countdown* demonstrate. Sometimes we just want to establish the existence of a word, perhaps a derivation that we're not sure of. Or we want to check the spelling of a word. Or we look up a word that we have met and with which we are not familiar, and whose meaning we need to ascertain. These, surveys have shown, are the main uses that people make of dictionaries. Occasionally, someone may wish to find out the pronunciation of a word that they have encountered only in writing, or for the sake of general interest look up a word's etymology.

The upshot of this is that any dictionary contains a vast amount of information that is unlikely to be consulted by any of its users. It is there because of the dictionary's recording function, its description of the lexical resources of the language. The fulfilment of its recording function may, though, be in conflict with the dictionary's reference function, to provide useful information in an easily accessible manner. We shall explore some of these issues further in Chapter 7.

3.2 Dictionaries, not 'the dictionary'

If there is no such publication as 'the dictionary', what is the range of publications that are called 'dictionary'? First, we should distinguish between those dictionaries that treat a single language from those that treat more than one, usually two languages: the former are 'monolingual' dictionaries and the latter are 'bilingual' dictionaries. Although, as we shall see in Chapter 4, bilingual dictionaries have the longer pedigree and they contain in part similar information to monolingual dictionaries, they are performing a quite different function and have a number of crucial distinctives. In particular, bilingual dictionaries have two sections, an A-language to B-language section (e.g. English–German), and a B-language to A-language section (e.g. German–English); and in bilingual dictionaries the definitions of words are the translation equivalents in the other language. This book is concerned only with monolingual dictionaries.

Second, we should distinguish among monolingual dictionaries between those whose purpose is primarily historical and those that seek to describe the vocabulary at a particular point or period of time. The primary historical dictionary for English is the multi-volume *Oxford English Dictionary*, and its abbreviated two-volume offshoot, the *Shorter Oxford English Dictionary*, which aim to chart the birth, death, and developments in form and meaning of words that have constituted the vocabulary of English since 1150 for the OED and since 1700 for the SOED. The 'synchronic' dictionary, by contrast, takes a snapshot of the vocabulary at some point in time. Such a dictionary might chart the vocabulary of Old English (Roberts *et al.* 1995) or of Middle English (e.g. Kurath and Kuhn

Table 3.1 Comparison of the *Collins* range

	CED4	CCD4	CPED4
Page size	187 × 260 mm	152 × 234 mm	107 × 151 mm
No. of pages	1785 + xxxvii	1740 + xxi	632 + vii
'References'	180,000	no claim	no claim
'Definitions'	196,000	no claim	44,500
Price (2001)	£29.99	£16.99	£7.99

1954), or, most usually, of the contemporary language. While we devote a chapter (5) to the OED, because of its importance in the development of lexicography, we are mostly concerned in this book with dictionaries charting the contemporary vocabulary.

Even among dictionaries of the contemporary language there is a bewildering variety. Dictionaries vary according to size, from desk-size, through concise, to pocket and smaller, with varying dimensions, numbers of pages, and coverage. All dictionaries present a selection from contemporary vocabulary, but it is very difficult to make comparisons, because of the confusingly different methods of counting the contents (Jackson 1998). Table 3.1 provides a rough estimate of the relative sizes.

Dictionaries also vary according to their intended audience or user group. Some dictionaries are aimed at young users at various stages in their growth and educational development; they are characterised by an appropriate selection of vocabulary, limited amounts of information for each entry, and often the use of pictures and colour. There is a range of monolingual English dictionaries that is aimed at learners of English as a second or foreign language, which take into account the particular needs of this group of users. The 'monolingual learners' dictionaries' (MLDs) are an interesting set of reference works, and they have been associated with some of the most exciting lexicographical innovations. They are discussed in more detail in Chapter 11. The dictionaries aimed at the native speaker adult user might be termed the 'general-purpose' dictionary (Béjoint 2000: 40). They are the dictionary that most people own, and they are the focus of much of the discussion in this book.

Besides the general-purpose dictionary, a wide variety of 'specialist' dictionaries is published. Some specialist dictionaries focus on an aspect of lexical description: there are dictionaries of pronunciation (e.g. Jones 1997; Wells 2000), dictionaries of spelling (e.g. West 1964), and dictionaries of etymology (e.g. Weekley 1967). Other specialist dictionaries focus on the vocabulary of a topic or subject-matter, e.g. Dictionary of Economics (Pearce 1992), Dictionary of Lexicography (Hartmann and James 1998). Such dictionaries define the terminology that is crucial for talking about the subject; they exclude some lexical information (e.g. pronunciation, grammar, etymology); and they tend towards the encyclopedic, both in the extent of their definitions or explanations, and in their inclusion of entries for people who have made a significant contribution to the development of the subject.

The term 'dictionary' is thus applied to a diverse range of reference publications. Our focus will be on the general-purpose dictionary of desk and concise size, with some consideration of historical dictionaries and those for learners.

3.3 What is in a dictionary?

From the perspective of its 'macro-structure', there are potentially three parts to a dictionary: the front matter, the body, and the appendices. Some dictionaries do without appendices, but most have front matter, however brief. The front matter usually includes an introduction or preface, explaining the innovations and characteristics of the edition concerned, together with a guide to using the dictionary, which may consist of a single-page diagram or some lengthier account. Other front matter might be an explanation of the transcription system used for indicating pronunciation, a list of abbreviations used in the dictionary, and an essay on some relevant topic, such as the history of the language or varieties of English around the world. Appendices may be various and even non-lexical; here is a selection: abbreviations, foreign words and phrases, ranks in the armed forces, counties of the UK and states of the US, weights and measures, musical notation, Greek and Cyrillic alphabets, punctuation, works of Shakespeare.

The body of a dictionary contains an alphabetical list of 'headwords'. Each headword is accompanied by a number of pieces of information, which together with the headword constitute the 'entry'. The headword is usually printed in bold type and hangs one or two spaces to the left of the other lines. Entries are presented in two columns on each page, though there may be three columns in some, usually larger dictionaries (e.g. NODE, W3, but also ECED).

The headwords represent the particular selection of vocabulary and other items that the editors have decided merit inclusion, given the size and purpose of the dictionary. General-purpose dictionaries will all tend to share a headword list that encompasses the core vocabulary; where they differ will be in the amount of technical and specialist, as well as colloquial, slang and dialect vocabulary they include. Editors will be concerned to be up-to-date, especially in socially and culturally significant areas such as computing, medicine, the environment, fashion, and so on. The inclusion of the latest vocabulary in such areas is often used as a selling point for a new edition.

If you examine the headwords in a general-purpose dictionary, you will find that it includes more than just lexemes. In terms of lexemes, it will include: 'simple' lexemes (1.6); compounds, possibly all, but at least those written solid (without a hyphen); and derivatives whose meanings are considered to need a separate definition from their roots. Other derivatives are contained within the entry for the root, as 'run-ons', usually in bold type but without a definition. The headword list will usually include inflected forms where these are 'irregularly' formed (1.3) and are alphabetically some distance from the citation form (e.g. *bought* in relation to *buy*): the entry will contain just a cross-reference to the citation form. The list may also include items that are not lexemes, especially derivational affixes and combining forms (1.6), and abbreviations. In some dictionaries (e.g. CED, NODE) the headword list includes names of places and people, introducing geographical and biographical entries, e.g.

Birmingham/'buhming(h)em/2nd largest British city, in the W Midlands of England; a major industrial, service, and transport centre with growing high-tech and light industries; home of two universities, a symphony orchestra, and the National Exhibition Centre; est. pop. 998,200 (1987)

(LDEL2)

Angelou/'anʤəlu:/, Maya (b.1928), American novelist and poet, acclaimed for the first volume of her autobiography, *I Know Why the Caged Bird Sings* (1970), which recounts her harrowing experiences as a black child in the American South.

(NODE)

Some headwords will be entered more than once. This applies to homonyms (1.2), e.g. *spell*, with four entries in COD9, and to homographs, e.g. *bow*, with one entry pronounced /bəʊ/ and two entries pronounced /baʊ/. In some dictionaries (e.g. LDEL) each word class that a headword belongs to will occasion a separate entry; for example, *rear* has four entries in LDEL2, one each for the verb, noun, adjective and adverb uses of the headword.

The 'micro-structure' of a dictionary refers to the arrangement of the information within the entries. The range and type of information within an entry will vary according to the kind of headword, but will typically include some or all of the following (compare 2.4):

- *Spelling:* the headword indicates the normal spelling, but any variations will follow.
- *Pronunciation:* within rounded ( ) or slash // brackets, together with any variations.
- *Inflections:* if these are formed irregularly or occasion some spelling adjustment such as doubling of consonants, dropping of 'e' or changing 'y' to 'i'.
- *Word class:* usually indicated by conventional abbreviations, 'n' for noun, 'adj' for adjective, etc.; verbs are also marked for 'transitive' (vt) or 'intransitive' (vi).
- *Senses:* where a lexeme has more than one meaning, each sense is usually numbered; where a sense, or group of senses belong to a different word class or subclass, this is indicated before the sense(s) concerned.
- *Definition:* each sense is given a definition, which is an explanation of its meaning.
- *Examples:* where the elucidation of a sense benefits from an illustrative phrase or sentence, usually given in italic type.
- *Usage:* where a sense is restricted in its contexts of use, an appropriate label precedes the sense concerned; if the restriction applies to all the senses of a lexeme, the label precedes any of the senses.

- *Run-ons:* undefined derivatives (with a word class label), idioms, phrasal verbs (if they are not included as headwords), usually in bold type.
- *Etymology:* conventionally in square brackets as the final item in the entry.

Some dictionaries include additional information, for example on collocation or the syntactic operation of words. Learners' dictionaries, especially (see Chapter 11), contain detailed information on these topics, as well as other additional material. By way of illustration, here is the entry for *drink* from COD9:

> **drink**/drɪŋk/ *v. & n. v.* (past **drank**/dræŋk/; past part. **drunk**/drʌŋk/) **1 a** *tr.* swallow (a liquid). **b** *tr.* swallow the liquid contents of (a container). **c** *intr.* swallow liquid, take draughts (*drank from the stream*). **2** *intr.* take alcohol, esp. to excess (*I have heard that he drinks*). **3** *tr.* (of a plant, porous material, etc.) absorb (moisture). **4** *refl.* bring (oneself etc.) to a specified condition by drinking (*drank himself into a stupor*). **5** *tr.* (usu. foll. by *away*) spend (wages etc.) on drink (*drank away the money*). **6** *tr.* wish (a person's good health, luck, etc.) by drinking (*drank his health*). *n.* **1 a** a liquid for drinking (*milk is a sustaining drink*). **b** a draught or specified amount of this (*had a drink of milk*). **2 a** alcoholic liquor (*got the drink in for Christmas*). **b** a portion, glass, etc. of this (*have a drink*). **c** excessive indulgence in alcohol (*drink is his vice*). **3** (as **the drink**) *colloq.* the sea. **drink deep** take a large draught or draughts. **drink in** listen to closely or eagerly (*drank in his every word*). **drink off** drink the whole (contents) of at once. **drink to** toast; wish success to. **drink a person under the table** remain sober longer than one's drinking companion. **drink up** drink the whole of; empty. **in drink** drunk. **drinkable** *adj.* [Old English *drincan* (*v.*), *drinc(a)* (*n.*), from Germanic]

We examine the micro-structure and the information contained in dictionary entries in more detail in Chapters 8, 9 and 10.

3.4 Compiling a dictionary

No lexicographer of English starts with a blank sheet of paper, but rather stands in a tradition of dictionary making that reaches back more than six centuries (Green 1996: 39), a history that we shall begin to trace in the next chapter. While some lexicographers find themselves revising and updating an existing dictionary to produce a new edition, others take on the challenge of innovation and hack a fresh path for lexicography. Even then, they build on the work of previous generations of lexicographers, both in determining the headword list and in deciding what kinds of information to provide.

Briefly, we may identify three aspects to dictionary compilation: the selection of headwords, the sources of data, and the writing of the entries. Any dictionary contains a selection from the total vocabulary of English, which is difficult to estimate but probably lies between one and two million words (Crystal 1995). Dictionaries do not usually reveal their headword count, which would be

Table 3.2

CED4	NODE
gl.	GLA
glabella	glabella
glabrescent	glabrous
glabrous	glacé
glacé	glacé icing
glacial	glacial
glacial acetic acid	glacial period
glacialist	glaciated
glacial period	glaciation
glaciate	glacier
glacier	Glacier Bay National Park
glacier cream	glaciology
glacier milk	glacis
glacier table	glad^1
glaciology	glad^2
glacis	gladden
glacis plate	gladdon
glad	glade
Gladbeck	glad eye
gladden	glad–hand
gladdon	gladiator
glade	gladiolus
glad eye	glad rags
glad hand	Gladstone
gladiate	Gladstone bag
gladiator	Glagolitic
gladiatorial	
gladiolus	
glad rags	
gladsome	
Gladstone	
Gladstone bag	
Glagolitic	

unreliable in any case, as it depends on what items are included as headwords (e.g. affixes and abbreviations) and how compounds and derivatives are treated. A desk–size dictionary probably contains no more than 100,000 headwords; the CD-ROM version of COD10 gives the headword count as 64,679. Headword lists in similar size dictionaries differ only at the margins: the core vocabulary is standard, judgements are made about specialist and non-standard (slang, dialect) lexemes. Compare the brief lists of headwords between *gl-* and *glag-* in CED4 and NODE, both published in 1998 shown in Table 3.2.

   The lexicographers' data comes from a number of sources. First of all, they have access to previous dictionaries, which can be mined both for the headword list and for lexical information. It is not unusual to find the same definition reproduced in successive editions of a dictionary. Second, dictionary publishers

keep a 'citation file', which records the results of the publisher's reading programme in identifying new words together with examples of their contexts of
use, usually in the form of complete sentences. Some citation files go back a
long way, Oxford's, for example, to the mid-nineteenth century, when citations began to be collected for what became the OED (see Chapter 5). Third,
and of increasing importance, lexicographers have access to computer corpora,
large collections of texts in electronic form. Oxford and Longman lexicographers use the *British National Corpus*, a 100 million-word corpus of both spoken
and written English; Collins lexicographers use the *Bank of English*, a growing
corpus, developed at the University of Birmingham, now of more than 400
million words, originally put together for the pioneering COBUILD learners'
dictionary (see Chapter 11).

A computer corpus can be searched rapidly and efficiently. It can be used for
checking information, or for seeking answers to specific queries. But, more
significantly, it can provide the raw data for the construction of dictionary
entries. Using a 'concordance' program, a lexicographer can perform a KWIC
(Key Word in Context) search and obtain a list of all the occurrences of a
lexeme in a corpus, together with a specified amount of context for each. The
results of the search suggest to the lexicographer how many senses to identify for
the lexeme and provide examples of use.

The third aspect of compiling a dictionary, identified earlier, was writing the
entries. It is rare that a dictionary is the work of a single lexicographer. A team
is more usual, with some members specialising in particular aspects of lexical
description. Many dictionaries have a pronunciation specialist, for example, or
an etymology specialist, as well as consultants for technical areas of vocabulary
or for other varieties of English. Lexicographers write the definitions, and editorial staff coordinate the input of all the contributors. Dictionaries are nowadays compiled on computer, so that all members of a team can have simultaneous
access to the developing dictionary text. This makes rigorous editorial checking, always a necessity, even more important, before a dictionary is released for
publication. We pursue the topic of dictionary compilation in Chapter 13.

3.5　Evaluating a dictionary

Dictionaries are commercial publications; publishers invest considerable sums
of money in their development; and they are tailored to perceived market needs.
Like any other book publication, they are subjected to review in newspapers,
magazines and professional journals. Newspaper reviews of dictionaries tend
towards the trivial, focusing on 'newsworthy', often idiosyncratic features, such
as who has been included and excluded from the biographical entries, or supposed modish, usually slang, lexical items. However, dictionaries are not just
commercial publications; they are also linguistic descriptions and so they are of
interest to language and linguistics scholars, who subject them to academic
scrutiny and criticism. Indeed, a specialist branch of linguistic studies has developed whose concern is specifically lexicography: it has its scholarly associations

(e.g. EURALEX – the European Association for Lexicography), its own journals (e.g. *International Journal of Lexicography*), a three-volume encyclopedia devoted to it (Hausmann *et al.* 1989), and its own courses and research projects.

Academic lexicography, or 'metalexicography' (Béjoint 2000: 8n), is concerned, among other things, with the business of 'dictionary criticism' (Osselton 1989), which proposes methods and criteria for reviewing and evaluating dictionaries. The reviewing of dictionaries is not like that of other books. It would, for example, be impossible for a reviewer to read the whole text of a dictionary: CED4 claims to have 3.6 million words of text, and NODE 4 million. Dictionary reviewers must find other methods, such as sampling, or having a carefully selected checklist of items and features to investigate.

One approach is to take the claims that a dictionary makes about itself, in the blurb on the cover or book-jacket or in the front matter, and check these against the practice of the dictionary as reflected in its content, as well as against the accumulated insights and judgements of the scholarly community. An alternative approach establishes a set of criteria that arise from the academic study of lexicography and applies these to the dictionary under review. It is often useful to have a team of reviewers, each of whom takes a separate aspect for critical scrutiny, e.g. the treatment of pronunciation, of grammar, of meaning, of etymology (compare Higashi *et al.* 1992).

A further consideration in dictionary criticism is the perspective from which the review is conducted. The academic metalexicographer's primary focus is probably on the adequacy of a dictionary as a lexical description. An alternative focus might be that of the user, particularly where accessibility and comprehensibility of the information could be an issue, as with a learners' dictionary, or where a specific set of users is being targeted, as with a children's dictionary.

Dictionary criticism is an important activity. It not only provides informed reviews of dictionaries for potential users, it also contributes to advances in lexicography and to improvements in dictionaries. We explore it further in Chapter 14.

Summarising, this chapter has sought to distinguish dictionaries from encyclopedias and grammars, to show that dictionaries are the products of a tradition of lexicography, to suggest some of the range of reference works with the 'dictionary' title, to survey the content of general-purpose dictionaries, to raise some of the issues in dictionary compilation, and to introduce the business of dictionary criticism. We have set the agenda for the remainder of the book, beginning with an account of the history of dictionary making in English.

3.6 Further reading

A good overview is Sidney Landau's *Dictionaries: The Art and Craft of Lexicography* (originally 1989, now in a second edition, 2001). Also recommended is Henri Béjoint's (1994) *Tradition and Innovation in Modern English Dictionaries*, Clarendon Press Oxford, republished in paperback, with only minor updating, in 2000 as *Modern Lexicography: An Introduction*, Oxford University Press.

4   The beginnings

This chapter and the next two trace the history of dictionary making in English up to the present time. This chapter takes us up to Samuel Johnson's dictionary in the mid-eighteenth century, the next is devoted to the *Oxford English Dictionary*, and Chapter 6 first recaps on the American practice and then brings the story up to date.

4.1 Bilingual beginnings

The beginnings of English lexicography go back to the Old English period (2.1), specifically to the introduction (from 597) of the Roman form of Christianity and the development of monasteries. The language of the Roman Church was Latin; its priests and monks needed to be competent in Latin in order to conduct services, and to read the Bible (Jerome's 'Vulgate' version) and other theological texts. The monasteries were the institutions of education for the clergy in the language of the church, as well as in the doctrines and practices of the faith. Many monasteries also developed extensive libraries of theological and other manuscripts (printing was still 750 years in the future), which would have been written in Latin, and which became objects of study and commentary. As English monks studied these Latin manuscripts, they would sometimes write the English translation above (or below) a Latin word in the text, to help their own learning, and as a guide to subsequent readers. These one-word translations, written between the lines of a manuscript, are called 'interlinear glosses'; they are seen as the beginnings of (bilingual) lexicography (Hüllen 1989).

In due course, and to aid in the teaching and learning of Latin, these glosses were collected together into a separate manuscript, as a glossary, which may be regarded as a prototype dictionary. The words in the glossary were then ordered, either alphabetically, in early glossaries only by the first letter, then by second and subsequent letters, or topically (Chapter 12). One of the best known topical glossaries was compiled by Ælfric, who was the Abbot of the monastery at Eynsham, near Oxford, during the first decade of the eleventh century. Ælfric was well known as an educator: he wrote a grammar of Latin, as well as a number of other instructional works. His glossary, known as 'The London Vocabulary', is found appended to a number of extant copies of his Grammar.

The glossary is a list of Latin words, arranged by topic, together with an Old English equivalent for each of them. Ælfric's topics encompassed a wide range of vocabulary, from 'God, heaven, angels, sun, moon, earth, sea' to 'herbs' and 'trees', to 'weapons' and 'metals and precious stones' (for full, but slightly differing lists, see McArthur 1986: 75, Hüllen 1999: 64 – reproduced in 12.2).

Latin continued as the language not only of the church but also of education and learning generally throughout the medieval period. It was the language of instruction for all subjects in the medieval universities (Oxford dates from 1167, Cambridge from 1230), and scholarly publication was in Latin, the European lingua franca of education. Academics were expected to be able to both speak and write fluently in Latin. When schools were founded in order to prepare students for entry to the universities, they concentrated on teaching Latin – the origin of the 'grammar' school. There thus developed a considerable demand for instructional material for the teaching and learning of Latin grammar and vocabulary. Dictionaries were compiled to meet this demand, both Latin–English (e.g. the *Hortus Vocabulorum*, 'garden of words', of around 1430) and English–Latin (e.g. the *Promptorium Parvulorum*, 'storeroom for young scholars', of 1440). Both of these dictionaries appeared in due course in printed form, the *Hortus* in 1500, and the *Promptorium* in 1499.

Latin took on a new significance during the period of the Renaissance (2.1), as scholars rediscovered the literature of Roman authors and made their works known, both through publication in the original language and through translations into English. It is the latter that are of particular significance. When translators came across a Latin word for which they could not find a ready equivalent in English, a common solution would be to 'borrow' the Latin word into English. Since Latin had been for so long the common language of academic discourse, this practice seemed the most convenient to many translators. However, since many readers would not be as familiar with Latin, some translators appended a glossary of such 'borrowed' words to their translations. Philemon Holland, for example, who published a translation of Plutarch's *Moralia* in 1603, appended 'An explanation of sundry tearmes somewhat obscure, in this translation of Plutarch, in favour of the unlearned Reader; after the order of the Alphabet'. The 'unlearned' reader was one who did not know Latin. As it happens, Holland's translation was the last to contain such a glossary, because of a significant development in lexicography.

Before we come to that, let us note that the Renaissance period saw not only the revival of the classical languages of Rome and Greece, but also a burgeoning interest in the vernacular languages of Europe. This interest, prompted by increasing travel, resulted in a number of bilingual dictionaries: for French and English, John Palsgrave's *Esclarcissement de la langue francoyse* (1530) and Randle Cotgrave's *A Dictionarie of the French and English Tongues* (1611); for Italian and English, John Florio's *A Worlde of Wordes* (1598); for Spanish, English and Latin, Richard Percyvall's *Bibliotheca Hispanica* (1591). Dictionaries for English and Latin also continued to be published, e.g. Richard Huloet, *Abecedarium Anglo-Latinum* (1552), Thomas Thomas, *Dictionarium Linguae Latinae et Anglicanae* (1587).

4.2 'Hard' words

The first monolingual English dictionary is considered to be Robert Cawdrey's *A Table Alphabeticall* of 1604, which contained in fuller book form the kind of list that Philemon Holland had appended to his translation of Plutarch. The title page of Cawdrey's dictionary proclaims it to be:

> A Table Alphabeticall, conteyning and teaching the true writing, and understanding of hard, usuall English wordes, borrowed from the Hebrew, Greeke, Latine, or French, &c.
>
> With the interpretation thereof by plaine English words, gathered for the benefit & helpe of Ladies, Gentlewomen, or any other unskilfull persons.
>
> Whereby they may the more easilie and better understand many hard English wordes, which they shall heare or read in Scriptures, Sermons, or elsewhere, and also be made able to use the same aptly themselves.

'Unskilful' persons, like Holland's 'unlearned reader', would be those without a knowledge of the classical languages, especially Latin; and since girls and young women did not enjoy the same educational opportunities as boys and young men – the 'public' schools and the universities were exclusively male preserves – this applied to all women, apart from those with parents enlightened and wealthy enough to have provided them with private tutoring.

Cawdrey's *A Table Alphabeticall* begins a tradition of 'hard word' dictionaries. You will have noticed that Cawdrey uses the word 'hard' twice on his title page. A 'hard' word was a loanword, usually of recent borrowing, whose use was not yet widespread and which was not readily comprehensible to 'uneducated' readers. Despite his inclusion of Hebrew in his list of languages of origin and the '&c' (i.e. etc.) after 'French', Cawdrey marks only words of Greek origin (with 'g' or 'gr') and words of French origin (with '§'), the unmarked ones being assumed to have a Latin origin. Cawdrey's book, despite its recognition as the first monolingual dictionary, is not entirely original; in 1596 *The English Schoole Master* by Edmund Coote had appeared, which contained a grammar, the catechism, prayers, and a vocabulary, and it is this last that Cawdrey mined for his work – even the title pages have similar wording. Cawdrey, though, has twice as many words as Coote, and he used other sources as well.

Cawdrey's first edition contained around 2500 'hard' words, and it went through four editions, the last published in 1617, but there was little augmentation of the word list. Each word in the dictionary is provided with a synonym or explanatory phrase in 'plaine English words'. Here are the first few words of Cawdrey's *A Table Alphabeticall*:

> § ABandon, cast away, or yeelde up, to leave, or forsake
> Abash, blush
> abba, father
> § abbesse, abbatesse, Mistris of a Nunnerie, comforters of others

§ abbettors, counsellors
aberration, a going a stray, or wandering
abbreviat,) to shorten, or make short
§ abbridge,)
§ abbut, to lie unto, or border upon, as one lands end meets with another
abecedarie, the order of the Letters, or hee that useth them . . .
Apocrypha (g), not of authoritie, a thing hidden, whose originall is not
    knowne

Cawdrey's pioneering work was followed in 1616 by John Bullokar's *An English Expositor*, whose title page proclaimed:

An English Expositor: Teaching the Interpretation of the hardest words
    used in our Language.
With Sundry Explications, Descriptions, and Discourses.
By I.B. Doctor of Physicke.

Besides having more entries than Cawdrey – it contained 'sundry olde words now growne out of use, and divers termes of art, proper to the learned' – Bullokar also provides more expansive explanations, e.g.

Heretike. He that maketh his owne choice, what points of religion he will beleeve, and what he will not beleeve.

Hereditarie. That which commeth to one by inheritance.

Heriot. The best living beast which a Tenant hath at his death, which in some Mannors is due to the lord of whom the land is holden.

Hermaphrodite. Of both natures: which is both man and woman.

Hermite. One dwelling solitarie in the wildernesse attending onely to devotion.

By his death in 1641, the *Expositor* had reached its third edition with little revision. A radical revision and expansion of the *Expositor* in 1663 by someone who styled themself 'A Lover of the Arts' greatly increased its popularity and it continued to be republished until 1731.

Part of the expansion of Bullokar's *English Expositor* in 1663 involved extensive borrowing from a third hard-word dictionary, which had been first published in 1623, Henry Cockeram's *The English Dictionarie*, and the first to use 'dictionary' in its title. On the title page of one of the first editions, though not subsequently repeated, Cockeram acknowledged his debt to Cawdrey and Bullokar:

The English Dictionarie: or, An Interpreter of hard English Words.
    Enabling as well Ladies and Gentlewomen, young Schollers, Clarkes, Merchants, as also Strangers of any Nation, to the understanding of the

more difficult authors already printed in our Language, and the more speedy attaining of an elegant perfection of the English tongue, both in reading, speaking and writing.

Being a Collection of the choicest words contained in the *Table Alphabeticall* and *English Expositor*, and of some thousand of words never published by any heretofore.

Cockeram's target audience is wider than Cawdrey's, even extending to the foreign learner of English ('Strangers of any Nation'). Moreover, Cockeram's *Dictionarie* has three parts: the first is the list of hard words, together with their glosses and explanations (more in the style of Cawdrey than of Bullokar); the second is a list of 'vulgar' words together with their 'refined or elegant' equivalents, as an aid to writing with good style; and the third, following the practice of some Latin–English dictionaries, is a list of 'Gods & Goddesses'. The 1663 revision of Bullokar's *Expositor* included the second and third parts of Cockeram's *Dictionarie*. Cockeram's work went through twelve editions, the last, a substantially revised one, in 1670.

The scope of the hard-word dictionary had already widened since the publication of *A Table Alphabeticall*. It was widened further with the publication in 1656 of Thomas Blount's *Glossographia*, whose title page declared:

Glossographia: or a Dictionary, Interpreting all such Hard Words, Whether Hebrew, Greek, Latin, Italian, Spanish, French, Teutonick, Belgick, British or Saxon; as are now used in our refined English Tongue.

Also the Terms of Divinity, Law, Physick, Mathematicks, Heraldry, Anatomy, War, Musick, Architecture; and of several other Arts and Sciences Explicated.

With Etymologies, Definitions, and Historical Observations on the same. Very useful for all such as desire to understand what they read.

Blount, lawyer by profession, borrowed extensively from other dictionaries, both monolingual and bilingual, but he also included words that he had come across in his reading or that he had heard spoken around him in London. Blount's definitions vary in length, from single words to extensive explanations, but his singular innovation was the introduction of etymologies and 'historical observations'. The etymology consists of the word in the original language in brackets after the headword, e.g.

Deprehend (deprehendo) to take at unawares, to take in the very act.

Depression (depressio) a pressing or weighing down.

The 'historical observations' are included in the explanation and are sometimes rather fanciful, e.g.

> *Hony-Moon*, applyed to those marryed persons that love well at first, and decline in affection afterwards; it is hony now, but it will change as the moon.

Blount is also notable for giving his sources, or citing his authorities, an issue that would become increasingly important. For example:

> *Depredable* (depredabilis) that may be robbed or spoiled. *Bac.*

The '*Bac.*' refers to Francis Bacon (1561–1626), the philosopher and scientist, Blount's source for this word. Blount is more comprehensive than any of his predecessors, but the focus is still on the 'hard' words, with the addition of the technical terms of 'arts and sciences'.

Hard word dictionaries continued to expand: Edward Phillips' *The New World of English Words* of 1658 contained around 11,000 entries, which had increased to 17,000 by the fifth edition in 1696, the year of Phillips' death. Elisha Coles' *An English Dictionary* of 1676 expanded his headword list to 25,000, largely by adding dialect words, old words from Chaucer and Gower, and canting terms. The canting terms were thieves' slang words, and Coles justifies their inclusion as follows:

> 'Tis no Disparagement to understand the Canting Terms: It may chance to save your Throat from being cut, or (at least) your Pocket from being pick'd.

Coles' dictionary represented the state of the art in lexicography at the end of the seventeenth century. However, it still did not contain the everyday vocabulary of English. A truly comprehensive dictionary was still to come.

4.3 Completeness

The monolingual English dictionary had started life at the beginning of the seventeenth century as a modest list of loanwords. As the century progressed the word list expanded, mostly in the direction of the more unusual type of lexeme. Etymology began to be attended to, and before the century ended two etymological dictionaries had appeared: Stephen Skinner's *Etymologicon Linguae Anglicanae*, published four years after the author's death in 1671; and the anonymous *Gazophylacium Anglicanum* in 1689, which took much of its material from Skinner.

The beginning of the eighteenth century brought a new focus to the monolingual English dictionary, with the publication in 1702 of *A New English Dictionary*, whose author is identified only by the initials 'J.K.' It is widely supposed that the author is John Kersey, who revised Edward Phillips' *New World of English Words* in 1706 and who published a dictionary under his full name in 1708, the *Dictionarium Anglo-Britannicum*. J.K.'s dictionary proclaims itself to be:

A New English Dictionary: Or, a Compleat Collection Of the Most Proper and Significant Words, Commonly used in the Language; With a Short and Clear Exposition of Difficult Words and Terms of Art.

The whole digested into Alphabetical Order; and chiefly designed for the benefit of Young Scholars, Tradesmen, Artificers, and the Female Sex, who would learn to spell truely; being so fitted to every Capacity, that it may be a continual help to all that want an Instructor.

Most of J.K.'s 28,000 headwords had never before appeared in a dictionary. Its aim is to be 'compleat' and to identify the 'proper' words of the language; its target audience includes the increasingly literate tradesmen and craftsmen; and its primary purpose is to aid its users in correct spelling. Many of the current school textbooks contained spelling lists; J.K. incorporates this feature into his dictionary and thus brings into the dictionary the words of everyday vocabulary. Many of the headwords in *A New English Dictionary* have only the scantiest of definitions or explanations, e.g.

An *Apron*, for a Woman, &c.

An *Arm* of a man's body, of a tree, or of the sea.

An *Elephant*, a beast.

May, the most pleasant Month of the Year.

Little serious attention was paid to etymology; at best, the language from which a loanword was borrowed is indicated.

The two principles, of completeness and etymology, came together in Nathaniel Bailey's *An Universal Etymological English Dictionary* of 1721, which promised both a larger scope and a wider group of users than its predecessors:

An Universal Etymological English Dictionary: Comprehending The Derivations of the Generality of Words in the English Tongue, either Antient or Modern, from the Antient British, Saxon, Danish, Norman and Modern French, Teutonic, Dutch, Spanish, Italian, Latin, Greek, and Hebrew Languages, each in their proper Characters.

And Also A Brief and clear Explication of all difficult Words . . . and Terms of Art . . .

Together with A Large Collection and Explication of Words and Phrases us'd in our Antient Statutes . . . and the Etymology and Interpretation of the Proper Names of Men, Women, and Remarkable Places in Great Britain; Also the Dialects of our Different Counties.

To which is Added a Collection of our most Common Proverbs, with their Explication and Illustration.

The whole work compil'd and Methodically digested, as well as for the Entertainment of the Curious, as the Information of the Ignorant, and for the Benefit of young Students, Artificers, Tradesmen and Foreigners.

Bailey's 40,000 words were culled from a wide variety of sources and encompass both the everyday and the less usual. For the first time proverbs were included (some ninety in all), and serious attention was paid to etymology, e.g.

> *Emerald*, (*Esmeraude*, F. *Esmeralda*, Span. *Smaragdus*, L. of Σμαραγδος, Gr.) a precious Stone.

Bailey's dictionary (see Simpson 1989) proved enormously popular, dominating the eighteenth century, and reaching its thirtieth edition in 1802, by when the word list had expanded to around 50,000 items. It was aimed at the 'curious' as well as the 'ignorant', at the 'young student' as well as the 'foreigner'; and its known users included the Prime Minister of the day, William Pitt the Elder.

In 1730, however, Nathaniel Bailey published a further dictionary, with the title *Dictionarium Britannicum*. It is important not least because it was used by Samuel Johnson as the basis for his dictionary (see 4.5 below). The title page included the statements:

> Dictionarium Britannicum: Or a more Compleat Universal Etymological English Dictionary than any Extant.
>
> Containing Not only the Words, and their Explications; but their Etymologies . . .
>
> Also Explaining hard and technical Words, or Terms of Art, in all the Arts, Sciences, and Mysteries following. Together with Accents directing to their proper Pronunciation, showing both the Orthography and Orthoepia of the English Tongue . . .

> Collected by several Hands, The Mathematical Part by G. Gordon, the Botanical by P. Miller. The Whole Revis'd and Improv'd, with many thousand Additions, by N. Bailey.

The 48,000 items did not include the proverbs, though they were reinstated in greater numbers in the second edition of 1736. The proper names, apart from those from myths and legends, are removed to an appendix. Noteworthy here is the inclusion of 'Orthoepia', i.e. pronunciation, as least as far as the stressing (Accent) of polysyllabic words is concerned. Note, too, that Bailey acknowledges the assistance of specialists in mathematics and botany. The second edition, which increases the entries to 60,000, to better fulfil the title claim of 'universal', also notes the contribution of 'T. Lediard, Gent. Professor of the Modern Languages in Lower Germany' to the etymologies, to pay attention to that part of the title. Lediard's hand is evident, as the following examples show:

Littoral (*litoralis*, of *litus*, L. the sea shore)

Little (*litel*, *lytel* or *lytle*, Sax. *litet* and *liten*, Su. *lidet* or *lille*, Dan. *luttel*, Du. *lut*, L.G.)

(Note: the language label follows the form: L = Latin, Sax = Saxon, Su = Swedish, Dan = Danish, Du = Dutch, L.G. = Low German.)

A number of 'compleat' dictionaries followed Bailey's two during the first half of the eighteenth century, but they were largely derivative of his, or indeed reverted to earlier types.

4.4 Ascertaining and fixing

To appreciate the next developments in lexicography, we need to understand some of the debates about language that exercised scholars and authors in the eighteenth century. There was deep concern about the state of the English language. The wholesale importation of words, from Latin especially, as a result of the Renaissance, and arising from the translation of classical authors into English, had provoked the 'inkhorn' controversy. Some authors, and translators in particular, were accused of borrowing Latin words, even though an equivalent already existed in English, merely in order to sound more erudite. People looked back to a 'golden age' of the English language – the Elizabethan period, when Shakespeare was writing – and saw only a degeneration in English since that time. The question was how to arrest the decay, how to 'fix' the language so that it would not degenerate any further, and how to effect improvements that would help restore the language to a former glory.

Some looked across the Channel admiringly and enviously, as it seemed that the French had cracked the problem. In 1635, Cardinal Richelieu, Louis XIII's chief minister, had founded the Académie française, whose chief purpose was to codify the French language and to pronounce on what was and was not acceptable French – as it has continued to do to this day. One of the instruments for achieving its aim was a dictionary. Begun in 1639, the *Dictionnaire de l'Académie française* was finally published fifty-five years later, in 1694, followed by a second edition in 1718. Voices in Britain were raised in favour of an English Academy to achieve the same purpose. Among them was that of the author Daniel Defoe (1660–1731), who, in his *Essay on Projects* of 1698, suggested that such an institution should have as its purpose: 'to encourage polite learning, to polish and refine the English tongue, and advance the so much neglected faculty of correct language, to establish purity and propriety of style'. Others opposed the establishment of an academy, among them Samuel Johnson, who did not regard this as the British way of doing things.

An alternative suggestion was that a group of suitable persons should be assembled to undertake the task of looking at the language. The Royal Society had formed a committee in 1664 'for improving the English tongue', but nothing seems to have come of it. The suggestion was taken up by Jonathan Swift

(1667–1745), the author of *Gulliver's Travels*, who wrote a pamphlet in 1712, addressed to the Earl of Oxford, the Lord Treasurer of England, with the title *A Proposal for Correcting, Improving and Ascertaining the English Language*. In it, Swift proposes that a group should be assembled 'of such Persons, as are generally allowed to be best qualified for such a Work'; they would 'have the Example of the *French* before them', though they are to 'avoid their mistakes'. 'They will', says Swift, 'find many Words that deserve to be utterly thrown out of our Language; many more to be corrected, and perhaps not a few, long since anti-quated, which ought to be restored, on Account of their Energy and Sound.' He continues:

> But what I have most at heart, is that some Method should be thought on for *Ascertaining* and *Fixing* our Language for ever, after such alterations are made in it as shall be thought requisite. For I am of Opinion, that it is better a Language should not be wholly perfect, than that it should be perpetually changing; and we must give over at one Time or other, or at length infal-libly change for the worse.

Change is the great enemy of language. The language must be 'ascertained' (with the eighteenth-century meaning of 'fix, determine, limit' – SOED) and 'fixed'.

Swift had both grammar and vocabulary in view in his *Proposal*, but as far as vocabulary was concerned, a crucial question was how to determine, in 'fixing' the language, which words should be regarded as legitimate and 'proper' words of English. The solution to this problem was seen in the appeal to 'authorities', those regarded as representing English at its best. Joseph Addison (1672–1719), one of the founders of *The Spectator*, had begun collecting quotations for the purpose of contributing to the compilation of a dictionary, but a summons by the king to public service brought this to a halt. In 1717, the following adver-tisement appeared in the newspapers:

> Just printed, Proposals for the Publication of a compleat and standard Dic-tionary of the whole English Language, as it is written in all its various Idioms and Proprieties, by the most authentick Orators and Poets, from Chaucer to Shaftesbury, whose Authorities shall be quoted throughout: According to the Method of the celebrated one of the French Academy. In 4 Vols. Fol.

There is, however, no evidence that the dictionary announced in this proposal ever saw publication. Like Addison, the poet Alexander Pope (1688–1744) was interested in contributing to a dictionary; he drew up lists of the prose authors from whose works he thought citations for a dictionary should be collected, and on the question of 'authority' he comments:

In most doubts, whether a word is English or not, or whether such a particular use of it is proper, one has nothing but authority for it. Is it in Sir William Temple, or Locke, or Tillotson? If it be, you may conclude that it is right, or at least won't be looked upon as wrong.

Such were the concerns of the eighteenth century about the state of English. The dictionary would be an instrument in achieving the aims of 'ascertaining' and 'fixing' the language. Of these concerns, and of the expected role of the dictionary, Samuel Johnson was aware as he planned his monumental work.

Before Johnson's dictionary appeared, another work was published that purported to address many of these concerns: Benjamin Martin's *Lingua Britannica Reformata* of 1749. Its title page promises much:

Lingua Britannica Reformata: Or, A NEW ENGLISH DICTIONARY, Under the Following TITLES, *VIZ*.

I. UNIVERSAL; Containing a Definition and Explication of all the Words now used in the English Tongue, in every *Art*, *Science*, *Faculty* or *Trade*.

II. ETYMOLOGICAL; Exhibiting and Explaining the true Etymon or Original of Words from their respective Mother-Tongues, the *Latin*, *Greek*, *Hebrew*, and *Saxon*; and their Idioms, the *French*, *Italian*, *Spanish*, *German*, *Dutch*, &c.

III. ORTHOGRAPHICAL; Teaching the True and Rational Method of Writing Words, according to the Usage of the most Approved Modern Authors.

IV. ORTHOEPICAL; Directing the True Pronunciation of Words by Single and Double Accents; and by Indicating the Number of Syllables in Words where they are doubtful, by a Numerical Figure.

V. DIACRITICAL; Enumerating the Various Significations of Words in a Proper Order, *viz. Etymological*, *Common*, *Figurative*, *Poetical*, *Humorous*, *Technical*, &c. in a Manner not before attempted.

VI. PHILOLOGICAL; Explaining all the Words and Terms, according to the Modern Improvements in the Various Philological Sciences, *viz. Grammar*, *Rhetoric*, *Logic*, *Metaphysics*, *Mythology*, *Theology*, *Ethics*, &c.

VII. MATHEMATICAL; Not only Explaining all Words in *Arithmetic*, *Algebra*, *Logarithms*, *Fluxions*, *Geometry*, *Conics*, *Dialling*, *Navigation*, &c. according to the Modern *Newtonian Mathesis*; but the Terms of Art are illustrated by Proper Examples, and Copper-Plate Figures.

VIII. PHILOSOPHICAL; Explaining all Words and Terms in *Astronomy*, *Geography*, *Optics*, *Hydrostatics*, *Acoustics*, *Mechanics*, *Perspective*, &c. according to the latest Discoveries and Improvements in this Part of Literature.

To which is prefix'd, An INTRODUCTION, containing A Physico-Grammatical Essay On the Propriety and Rationale of the ENGLISH TONGUE.

Martin was more famous as a scientist and advocate of Newtonian mathematics than as a lexicographer, but the plan of his dictionary is impressive in its organisation and attention to detail, and in the concern to reflect up-to-date scholarship. But, as Green (1996: 218) observes, Martin's practice does not quite live up to the promise. His 'Physico-Grammatical Essay', which runs to 108 pages, is its major innovation. In that essay, though, he does make some perceptive remarks about 'fixing' the language:

> The pretence of fixing a standard to the purity and perfection of any language . . . is utterly vain and impertinent, because no language as depending on arbitrary use and custom, can ever be permanently the same, but will always be in a mutable and fluctuating state; and what is deem'd polite and elegant in one age, may be accounted uncouth and barbarous in another.

Johnson, who proved to be the better lexicographer, would come to similar conclusions.

4.5 Samuel Johnson (1709–84)

When Johnson's *Dictionary of the English Language* appeared in 1755, nine years had elapsed since he had signed the contract with the group of booksellers who had approached him to compile it. The agreement had been for a delivery date of three years, and for a sum of 1500 guineas (£1575), which was in part meant to defray the expenses of the six assistants that he was intended to employ. First, Johnson prepared his *Plan of a Dictionary of the English Language*, which was published in 1747. Johnson was prevailed upon to address his *Plan* to the Earl of Chesterfield, who had a position in government and who was known to be interested in language matters, in the hope of obtaining his patronage, if not his financial support. In the event, neither was forthcoming, apart from an initial grant of £10, and Johnson later justified his address to the Earl on the grounds that it enabled him to buy more time with his booksellers.

The *Plan* is a fascinating document (reproduced in Wilson 1957), which shows considerable thought and reflection on his task by the beginning lexicographer. Johnson addresses himself to the methodological issues in the light of the contemporary concerns about the state of the language. He begins with the problem of 'selection', which words to include. 'The chief intent', he says, of the dictionary, 'is to preserve the purity and ascertain the meaning of our English idiom.' That would seem to suggest that 'the terms of particular professions . . . with the arts to which they relate' should be excluded, because 'they are generally derived from other nations'. But account must be taken of what the users of the dictionary will expect and require: foreign words cannot, then, be excluded, because people most often consult dictionaries to find 'terms of art':

> It seems necessary to the completion of a dictionary design'd not merely for critics but for popular use, that it should comprise in some degree the peculiar words of every profession.

He proposes to make a distinction between loanwords that are still considered to be foreign and those that have been 'incorporated into the language', by printing the former (which he calls 'aliens') in italics. He then discusses whether the common words should be included, and he argues for their inclusion on two grounds: it is not possible to 'fix the limits of the reader's learning'; and such words will need 'their accents . . . settled, their sounds ascertained, and their etymologies deduced'. In any case, he would prefer his readers to find more than they required rather than less.

After 'selection', Johnson turns his attention in the *Plan* to 'orthography', about which 'there is still great uncertainty among the best critics'. He proposes to make no changes from present practice, where this is clear, and to have good reason for introducing innovation. In respect of 'pronunciation' – 'the stability of which is of great importance to the duration of a language, because the first change will naturally begin by corruptions in the living speech' – he proposes to 'determine the accentuation of all polysyllables by proper authorities', and to 'fix the pronunciation of monosyllables, by placing them with words of correspondent sound'.

In respect of 'etymology', Johnson proposes a distinction between 'simple' and 'compound' words, and for 'simple' words between 'primitive' and 'derivative'. Primitive words will be traced to their language of origin, and no word will be admitted unless its original can be determined. Thus 'we shall secure our language from being over-run with *cant*, from being crouded with low terms, the spawn of folly or affectation'. After 'etymology' comes 'analogy', by which Johnson means the inflections of words: 'our inflections . . . admit of numberless irregularities, which in this dictionary will be diligently noted'. As for 'syntax', 'the syntax of this language is too inconstant to be reduced to rules, and can be only learned by the distinct consideration of particular words as they are used in the best authors'; for example, we say 'die of' but 'perish with'. Similarly, he will note 'phraseology', where a word is used in combination 'in a manner peculiar to our language'; he cites the example of *make* in expressions such as 'make love', 'make a bed', 'make merry'.

'The great labour is yet to come': 'interpretation' (i.e. definition) – 'the labour of interpreting these words and phrases with brevity, fulness and perspicuity', made the more difficult 'by the necessity of explaining the words in the same language'. He proposes to distinguish the separate senses of polysemous words, and to present the senses in a rational order: the 'natural and primitive signification' first, then the 'consequential meaning', then metaphorical sense, followed by the 'poetical', the 'familiar', the 'burlesque' senses. Finally, Johnson will deal with the 'distribution' of words 'into their proper classes', by which he means to distinguish words in general use from those used mainly in poetry, those that are obsolete, those used only by particular writers, those used only in burlesque writing, and 'words impure and barbarous'. Obsolete words will be included only if they occur in authors living since the accession of Elizabeth (1558), 'from which we date the golden age of our language'.

All Johnson's observations will be supported by 'citations':

> In citing authorities, on which the credit of every part of this work must depend, it will be proper to observe some obvious rules, such as of preferring writers of the first reputation to those of an inferior rank, of noting the quotation with accuracy, and of selecting, when it can be conveniently done, such sentences, as, besides their immediate use, may give pleasure or instruction by conveying some elegance of language, or some precept of prudence, or piety.

Additionally, Johnson intends to give the name of the author who first introduced a word or phrase, or who last used an obsolete word or phrase:

> By this method every word will have its history, and the reader will be informed of the gradual changes of the language, and have before his eyes the rise of some words, and the fall of others. But observations so minute and accurate are to be desired rather than expected, and if use be carefully supplied, curiosity must sometimes bear its disappointments.

Indeed, Johnson anticipates here the work that would lead to the *Oxford English Dictionary* over a century later. In any case, Johnson's restriction of his citations to a particular range of 'writers of the first reputation' precludes his attainment of this goal.

Johnson concludes his *Plan* with an address to the Earl of Chesterfield:

> This, my Lord, is my idea of an English Dictionary, a dictionary by which the pronunciation of our language may be fixed, and its attainment facilitated; by which its purity may be preserved, its use ascertained, and its duration lengthened. And though perhaps to correct the language of nations by books of grammar, and amend their manners by discourses of morality, may be tasks equally difficult; yet it is unavoidable to wish, it is natural likewise to hope, that your Lordship's patronage may not be wholly lost; that it may contribute to the preservation of the antient, and the improvement of modern writers.

Whether Johnson believed his own rhetoric at this point, or whether he was pandering to what he assumed were the Earl's opinions, is uncertain. By the time he had finished his dictionary, he was far less sanguine about its effects on 'fixing' the language, as he tells us in the *Preface* to the *Dictionary* (reproduced in Wilson 1957):

> Those who have been persuaded to think well of my design, will require that it should fix our language, and put a stop to those alterations which time and chance have hitherto been suffered to make in it without opposition. With this consequence I will confess that I flattered myself for a while; but now begin to fear that I have indulged expectation that neither reason nor experience can justify. When we see men grow old and die at a certain time one after another, from century to century, we laugh at the elixir that promises to prolong life to a thousand years; and with equal justice may the lexicographer be derided, who being able to produce no example of a nation that has preserved their words and phrases from mutability; shall imagine that his dictionary can embalm his language, and secure it from corruption and decay, that it is in his power to change sublunary nature, and clear the world at once from folly, vanity, and affectation.

What can then be done?

> If the changes that we fear be thus irresistible, what remains but to acquiesce with silence, as in the other insurmountable distresses of humanity? It remains that we retard what we cannot repel, that we palliate what we cannot cure. Life may be lengthened by care, though death cannot ultimately be defeated: tongues like governments have a natural tendency to degeneration; we have long preserved our constitution, let us make some struggles for our language. In the hope of giving longevity to that which its own nature forbids to be immortal, I have devoted this book, the labour of years, to the honour of my country.

Let us look at that 'labour of years', which Johnson mentions. They extended from June 1746, when he signed the contract with the booksellers, to April 1755, when the *Dictionary* was finally offered for sale. Johnson suffered many vicissitudes, not least in his personal life, including the London earthquake of 1750, the long illness and eventual death of his wife Tetty in 1752, as well as his financial problems, which required him to take on other work, among which was starting *The Rambler*. At no time did he have the full complement of six assistants working for him. And it seems that after a year or so of working on the dictionary, Johnson decided that he needed to revise his method and start over again (see Reddick 1990). His method consisted essentially in the following procedure.

Using an interleaved version of Bailey's *Dictionarium Britannicum* as his basis, Johnson undertook an extensive supplementary reading programme. Having selected a writer whom he admired, he would select a volume of his works, and when he found some word that he thought correctly used, he underlined it in pencil and marked the surrounding passage that he wanted copied. After he had gone through the book and marked everything that he thought could be used, he passed the book to one of his assistants, who copied out the marked passages onto blank sheets of paper or in blank books. They were then cut, or 'clipped', into separate slips and deposited in a bin. Subsequently, the large number of slips were sorted alphabetically by headword; Johnson decided which were repetitious or superfluous and so to be rejected, and which ones he would use. Sometimes he would revise the quotations to fit his purpose. In total, 114,000 quotations were used in the *Dictionary*. They were ready for Johnson to use by the summer of 1749, and he had then to decide how many senses to recognise for each word, write the definitions, and provide their etymologies. Pages were sent off to the printer bit by bit, and then the printed sheets were returned to Johnson for revision.

By April 1753, the first volume (A–K) was in final form, and a year later most of the *Dictionary* was printed. It awaited Johnson's prefatory essay on the history of the language. It is also possible that Johnson was playing for time, awaiting the award of an honorary MA degree from Oxford University, which was eventually granted in February 1755. So the title page cites the author as 'Samuel Johnson, A.M.'. When it appeared in April 1755, the two-volume folio *Dictionary* sold for £4.10s (i.e. £4.50) and sold around 2,000 copies. Further editions followed, on which Johnson worked, but it is the fourth edition of 1773 that represents a major revision, incorporating all the corrections to the mistakes and inconsistencies that Johnson was aware of from the first edition. Johnson's remained the foremost dictionary of the English language for a century, and its author was acclaimed as the one who had done for English single-handedly what it had taken forty French academicians to do for their language.

Johnson not only produced a monumental dictionary by a method, involving the collection of evidence (citations) and using the evidence to construct the entries, which became standard lexicographical procedure, but he also reflected, in the *Plan* and the *Preface* in particular, on the nature of the dictionary compiler's task and the issues that face lexicographers. Most of them represent questions that lexicographers have to struggle with still.

4.6 Further reading

The history of lexicography is entertainingly told in Jonathon Green's *Chasing the Sun* (1996).

Dictionaries before Cawdrey's are described in Gabriele Stein's *The English Dictionary before Cawdrey* (1985). Those from Cawdrey up to (but not including) Johnson are treated in De Witt T. Starnes and Gertrude E. Noyes' *The English Dictionary from Cawdrey to Johnson 1604–1755* (1946), republished in a version edited by Gabriele Stein (1991).

Johnson's story is told in Andrew Reddick's *The Making of Johnson's Dictionary 1746–1773* (1990).

5   *The New English Dictionary*

The popularity of Samuel Johnson's *Dictionary* continued into the nineteenth century, when it was joined by a rival, Charles Richardson's *A New Dictionary of the English Language*, published in 1836/7. Richardson's dictionary is significant for its extensive use of illustrative quotations, and its adherence to the rather bizarre 'philosophical philology' proposed by Horne Tooke (1736–1812). In *The Diversions of Purley* (1786, 1805), Tooke had put forward the notion that all words could be traced to primary nouns, or verbs, with a single meaning. His classic example was the word *bar*, which has the basic meaning of 'defence'; and he finds this meaning included in words such as *barn, baron, barge, bargain, bark*. Tooke's reductionist ideas enjoyed a measure of popularity, and they influenced Richardson's etymologies, which, needless to say, have much of the fanciful about them. By mid-century both leading dictionaries were considered to be wanting in their coverage of English vocabulary; the observation came from the newly formed Philological Society.

5.1 The Philological Society

The Society had been formed in May 1842, 'for the investigation of the Structure, the Affinities, and the History of Languages; and the Philological Illustration of the Classical Writers of Greece and Rome'. The concern about the lack of coverage by existing dictionaries was expressed in 1857 and related to the vocabulary of the earlier history of English. The Society formed a committee to collect 'unregistered words', and instituted the recruitment of volunteer readers to undertake a reading programme for the purpose. The aim was to publish a supplement to existing dictionaries. However, in November of that year, the Society heard two papers by one of the members of its Unregistered Words Committee (the other two members were Herbert Coleridge and Frederick Furnivall), the Dean of Westminster, Richard Chenevix Trench, which were later published under the title *On Some Deficiencies in Our English Dictionaries*. Dean Trench identified some seven deficiencies and proposed that 'the only sound basis' for a dictionary was 'the historical principle', by which he meant the new, 'scientific' comparative philology that had been developed especially in Germany, where Jakob and Wilhelm Grimm were already working on an historical dictionary of German, the *Deutsches Wörterbuch*.

5.2 The first edition

Trench's papers struck a chord with the Philological Society, and in January 1858 the Society resolved that 'a New Dictionary of the English Language be prepared under the Authority of the Philological Society'. In the following year, the Society published a 'Proposal for the Publication of a New English Dictionary by the Philological Society', calling for a comprehensive treatment of English vocabulary from the end of the thirteenth century, stating:

> The first requirement of every lexicon is that it should contain every word occurring in the literature of the language it professes to illustrate. In the treatment of individual words the historical principle will be uniformly adopted.

Herbert Coleridge was appointed as the first editor, and steps were taken to recruit voluntary readers to peruse the works of English literature for suitable citations. Coleridge drew up a set of working rules for editing the dictionary, which were published in 1860 as the *Canones Lexicographici*. He died the following year at the age of 31, from consumption, made worse by a chill resulting from sitting in damp clothes at a long Philological Society meeting.

Coleridge was succeeded as editor by Frederick Furnivall, the third member of the Unregistered Words Committee. Furnivall was a colourful and energetic character, with great organisational abilities, but he had fingers in many pies. He appointed sub-editors for the dictionary, whose job was to collect the slips from readers and organise them before sending them on to the editor. Furnivall also began to recognise how enormous the task was that the Philological Society had set itself, and he issued a fresh call in 1862 for voluntary readers. He proposed that a concise dictionary be prepared as a precursor to the main dictionary, but it became apparent that it would require almost as much work, so it came to nothing. Furnivall recognised that some of the earlier texts of English literature were not available in published form; so he founded the Early English Text Society in 1864, which concentrated on making available in printed form texts from before 1558 that had not been published previously. They provided an invaluable and necessary resource for the dictionary. In due course, Furnivall's other interests began to take over, and while he attempted to encourage his sub-editors, their efforts and those of the readers slackened, so that in his annual report to the Society of 1872, he notes that 'the progress in the Dictionary has been so slight that no fresh report in detail is needed'. Furnivall was looking for a new editor to take over the project. After two abortive approaches, he contacted a teacher at Mill Hill School in North London, who was a member of the Council of the Philological Society: James Murray.

The dictionary was in want not only of an editor, but also of a publisher. Furnivall made it his aim to secure both. Negotiations with Macmillan, who were known to be interested in publishing a dictionary, failed; but Furnivall continued to cultivate Murray for the editorship, while having approaches made to Cambridge and Oxford university presses. In due course, in 1878 Murray was appointed editor and on 1 March 1879 the Philological Society and Oxford University Press signed a contract to publish the dictionary. The contract agreed a four-volume, 7000-page dictionary to be completed in ten years. The first task was to retrieve all the materials that were still in the hands of the sub-editors and readers. This was done, and Murray built a corrugated iron structure in the garden of his Mill Hill home, which he called the 'Scriptorium', to house the material.

While still a full-time teacher, Murray set about his task as editor. Sorting the material that Furnivall had passed on to him, amounting to some 2 million slips, Murray realised that not only were there still many gaps in the evidence needed to compile the dictionary, but much of what he had received was not adequate. So he initiated a fresh reading programme, calling for 1000 readers for a period of three years: around 800 volunteered in the UK and between 400 and 500 in North America. One of the most prolific and devoted was an American surgeon, Dr W.C. Minor, who suffered from paranoid schizophrenia and was incarcerated in the Broadmoor Asylum for the Criminally Insane, after he had killed a man in London (his fascinating story is told in Winchester 1999). Murray issued the readers with clear instructions on what to look for (quotations that might indicate the birth of a word, or those that might define a word or were unusual in some way), to be sent in on 6 inch by 4 inch slips of paper, with the word in the top left-hand corner and full bibliographical details. He also offered to refund the postage that a reader incurred in sending the slips in to him. When he received the slips, Murray, with the help of his assistants, including his children (he had eleven in all), sorted them and put them into their appropriate pigeon holes in the Scriptorium. The three-year programme yielded around a million slips, and some 5 million were eventually collected in all for the first edition of the dictionary.

As well as collecting the essential data for the dictionary, Murray was also working on the principles that would underlie the editing of the dictionary, the appearance of the entries, and so on. In February 1884, the first part of the dictionary appeared, covering the letters A to Ant. It was clear that if faster progress was to be made on the dictionary – the ten-year goal was already receding – then Murray would have to devote more of his time to the project, and he would need help. In 1885, Murray became full-time editor and moved to Oxford to be near the point of publication; a new Scriptorium was built in the grounds of his house at 78 Banbury Road. A second editor was appointed, Henry Bradley, as well as a number of assistants.

In 1888, the first volume of the dictionary was published, covering the letters A and B. Murray explains in the Preface why it was taking so long to compile the dictionary:

The preparation of this volume has taken a much longer time than any of the promoters of the work anticipated. The time has been consumed chiefly in two directions: first, with the larger articles, as those on AT, BY, BUT, BE, BEAR, BREAK, the construction of which has occupied many days, sometimes even weeks. The mere study of the result, arranged in some degree of order, gives little idea of the toil and difficulties encountered in bringing into this condition what was at first a shapeless mass of many thousand quotations. And in this part of the work there was practically no assistance to be got from the labours of our predecessors; the attempt has never been made before to exhibit such a combined logical and historical view of the sense-development of English words. Our own attempts lay no claim to perfection; but they represent the most that could be done in the time and with the data at our command. The other direction in which much time has been consumed is the elucidation of the meaning of obscure terms, sometimes obsolete, sometimes current, belonging to matters of history, customs, fashions, trade, or manufactures . . . The difficulty of obtaining firsthand and authoritative information about these has often been immense, and sometimes insurmountable.

The Preface acknowledges the help of numerous people, including the sub-editors, who had given of their time voluntarily, as well as many scholars whom Murray had occasion to consult. He also lists all the readers who had contributed more than a thousand quotations. And he concludes the Preface with this comment:

> After all the help which has been received, and which has contributed so much to the completeness of the Dictionary, the element of time still remains inexorable; it is still, as in the days of Dr. Johnson, imperative that limits be set to research, in order that the work may 'in time be ended, though not completed'. Accordingly, since the close of Volume I, it has been the aim of the Editor and his staff to maintain such a regular rate of progress as will ensure the production of one Part a year. As Mr. Henry Bradley (whose co-operation in the present volume is mentioned above) is now at work independently, with a staff of assistants, on a third volume, there is reasonable ground to expect that the production of the work henceforth will be twice as rapid as it has been hitherto.

Murray was perhaps being optimistic: it would be another 40 years before the Dictionary was finally completed. A third editor, William Alexander Craigie, was appointed in 1901, though he had been working in Bradley's team since 1897; and a fourth editor, Charles Talbut Onions, was appointed in 1914, having worked for the Dictionary since 1895.

   The outbreak of World War I in 1914, the year in which Volume VIII was published, hindered progress, as members of the Dictionary staff volunteered for service in the armed forces. In 1915, James Murray, who had been knighted in 1908, died at the age of 78. The previous year he had been treated for cancer

Table 5.1 A New English Dictionary on Historical Principles founded mainly on the materials collected by The Philological Society

Volume	Letters	Date of publication	Editors
I	A & B	1888	Murray
II	C	1893	Murray
III	D & E	1897	Murray, Bradley
IV	F & G	1901	Murray, Bradley
V	H – K	1901	Murray
VI	L – N	1908	Murray, Bradley, Craigie
VII	O & P	1909	Murray
VIII	Q – Sh	1914	Murray, Bradley, Craigie
IX, Part I	Si – St	1919	Murray, Bradley, Craigie, Onions
IX, Part II	Su – Th	1919	Murray, Bradley, Craigie, Onions
X, Part I	Ti – U	1926	Murray, Bradley, Craigie, Onions
X, Part II	V – Z	1928	Murray, Bradley, Craigie, Onions

and had recovered enough to work on the letter T, but he contracted pleurisy soon afterwards and on 26 July went to his Maker, whom he had served for so long in working for his beloved Dictionary. Henry Bradley did not see the completion of the Dictionary either; he died in 1923, five years before the final volume reached publication.

The completed *New English Dictionary* contained 15,487 pages, more than twice the 7000 originally envisaged. James Murray edited nearly half of the entire work, some 7207 pages. Out of the 5 million quotations amassed, 1,861,200 were used in the Dictionary. It contained 252,200 entries, with 414,800 definitions. It had taken 44 years since the publication of A–Ant in 1884, and 70 years since the Philological Society had first proposed a 'New Dictionary of the English Language'.

In 1933 the Dictionary was republished under the title *Oxford English Dictionary*, in twelve volumes, together with an 866-page supplement, edited by Craigie and Onions, the two surviving editors. The supplement included words and senses that had been added to the language in the previous fifty years. Readers had continued to send in quotation slips even for words in volumes of the Dictionary already published. The supplement encompasses among other things: words of modern origin that had been omitted, either intentionally or accidentally, from the original dictionary; a large number of words from the arts and sciences; an expansion of the colloquial and slang vocabulary; a more generous inclusion of proper names; and American usages (Craigie was editing an historical dictionary of American English, which was published in 1936–44).

5.3 What the OED contains

Before we take the history of the OED any further, let us examine the content of what James Murray and his fellow-editors put together. In the Preface to Volume I, Murray expresses the aims of the Dictionary as follows:

> The aim of this Dictionary is to furnish an adequate account of the mean-
> ing, origin, and history of English words now in general use, or known to
> have been in use at any time during the last seven hundred years. It endeav-
> ours (1) to show, with regard to each individual word, when, how, in what
> shape, and with what signification, it became English; what development
> of form and meaning it has since received; which of its uses have, in the
> course of time, become obsolete, and which still survive; what new uses
> have since arisen, by what processes, and when: (2) to illustrate these facts
> by a series of quotations ranging from the first known occurrence of the
> word to the latest, or down to the present day; the word being thus made
> to exhibit its own history and meaning: and (3) to treat the etymology of
> each word strictly on the basis of historical fact, and in accordance with the
> methods and results of modern philological science.

The OED aims to do what Johnson had aspired to over a century earlier: present
a history of the entire vocabulary, beginning with words that were in current
use in 1150, all supported by a series of quotations that would illustrate the
changes and developments in meaning, as well as the birth and death of words
and senses of words. Even so, the OED is not totally inclusive in its coverage.
While it took a descriptivist (record what is there) stance, there were Victorian
sensibilities to be observed, so some of what today would be labelled 'coarse
slang' vocabulary is missing, as well as some scientific and technical vocabulary,
some of which was only being coined as the dictionary was being compiled.
After all, when Murray went to see Dr Minor in Broadmoor for the first time in
November 1896, he travelled by train from Oxford to Crowthorne and then by
horse-drawn carriage from the station to the Asylum. The coverage may also be
affected by the reliance on volunteer readers and their varying ability to spot
what was needed in the material that they read. Murray's instructions may not
have helped either, as he himself later acknowledged (Mugglestone 2000a:8):

> Make a quotation for *every* word that strikes you as rare, obsolete, old-
> fashioned, new, peculiar, or used in a peculiar way.

That said, the evidence from readers was frequently supplemented by the editors' own researches, as well as by those of other scholars who were approached
for information, especially on rare or technical words.
    Murray aimed to include all the 'common words' of the language, but, as he
makes clear in the 'General Explanations' that preface Volume I of the dictionary, this is a fluid category:

> the English Vocabulary contains a nucleus or central mass of many thou-
> sand words whose 'Anglicity' is unquestioned; some of them only literary,
> some of them only colloquial, the great majority at once literary and collo-
> quial, – they are the *Common Words* of the language. But they are linked on
> every side with other words which are less and less entitled to this appellation,

and which pertain ever more and more distinctly to the domain of local dialect, of the slang and cant of 'sets' and classes, of the peculiar technical-ities of trades and processes, of the scientific terminology common to all civilised nations, of the actual languages of other lands and peoples. And there is absolutely no defining line in any direction: the circle of the English language has a well-defined centre but no discernible circumference. Yet practical utility has some bounds, and a Dictionary has definite limits: the lexicographer must, like the naturalist, 'draw the line somewhere', in each diverging direction. He must include all the 'Common Words' of literature and conversation, and such of the scientific, technical, slang, dialectal, and foreign words as are passing into common use, and approach the position or standing of 'common words', well knowing that the line which he draws will not satisfy all his critics. For to every man the domain of 'common words' widens out in the direction of his own reading, research, business, provincial or foreign residence, and contracts in the direction with which he has no practical connexion: no one man's English is *all* English. The lexicographer must be satisfied to exhibit the greater part of the vocabulary of *each* one, which will be immensely more than the whole vocabulary of *any* one.

Murray acknowledges that the Dictionary extends its reach 'farther in the do-main of science and philosophy . . . than in that of slang or cant', on the basis that words in the former are likely to pass into literature, while those in the latter remain in the spoken language only.

The OED divides words into three classes: 'Main' words, 'Subordinate' words, and 'Combinations'. Main words include all single words, either simple or derived (1.6), as well as compounds which 'from their meaning, history, or importance, claim to be treated in separate articles'. Subordinate words are 'variant and obsolete forms of Main Words, and such words of bad formation, doubtful existence, or alleged use, as it is deemed proper, on any ground, to record'; e.g.

Afforse, obs. variant of AFFORCE

Afforst, obs. variant of ATHIRST

Affrait, -ly, see AFFRAYITLY, AFRAID.

Main and Subordinate words are headwords in the alphabetical series of the dictionary, with Subordinate words printed in smaller type than Main words. Combinations are those (derivatives and compounds) that either require no definition or which can be 'briefly explained in connexion with their cognates'; they are dealt with under the Main word that constitutes their first element. If a word belongs to more than one distinct word class, it is entered separately for each class (e.g. *brass* as noun and as verb).

The entry for a Main word consists of four sections: the Identification, the

Morphology, the Signification, and the Illustrative Quotations. The Identification section begins with the spelling: the headword gives the usual current form, in bold type and with initial capital letter. Any alternative current spellings follow, e.g. **Jowl, jole**. Words that are thought to be obsolete are preceded by a dagger symbol (†), e.g. †**Kask** (meaning 'active', 'vigorous'). Some words are preceded by a '||' symbol, which relates to their 'citizenship in the language'. In these terms, words are classified as: 'naturals', 'denizens', 'aliens', or 'casuals'. The class of 'naturals' includes all 'native' words (with their origin in Anglo-Saxon) and all 'fully naturalised' loanwords, which no longer betray their origin in spelling, pronunciation or inflection (e.g. *gas*, *street*). The class of 'denizens' includes loanwords that are naturalised as far as their use in the language is concerned, but which betray their origin in their spelling, pronunciation or inflection (e.g. *crèche*, *locus*). The class of 'aliens' comprises loanwords for objects, titles, etc. which are in common use but for which there is no English equivalent (e.g. *intifada*, *Knesset*). 'Casuals' are like aliens, except that they are not in common use and may be found, for example, in travel books. Denizens, aliens, and casuals tending towards aliens are marked with '||', e.g. ||**Hemiplegia**, ||**Kursaal**.

Following the headword and any alternative spellings comes the pronunciation, in rounded brackets. 'The pronunciation is the actual living form or forms of a word, that is, *the word itself*, of which the current spelling is only a symbolization', writes Murray in the General Explanations. The OED predates the International Phonetic Alphabet, and Murray took great pains, as well as scholarly advice, to develop an accurate transcription system to represent the sound of words. Pronunciation is followed in the entries by 'grammatical designation', i.e. word class or part of speech. Where a word belongs unequivocally to the class of nouns it is not given a label, otherwise the label '*sb.*' (i.e. 'substantive' – an older word for 'noun'). After the word class label, a 'specification' label may be given, if a word belongs to a particular domain or subject area (e.g. *Mus.* for 'Music'). Another label that may occur, then, is a 'status' label, such as *Obs.* (obsolete), *arch.* (archaic), *colloq.* (colloquial), *dial.* (dialect, i.e. 'now only dialect, whereas formerly in general use' – as dialect words are normally not included in the dictionary), and *rare*.

Where a word has changed its spelling or had previous alternative spellings, earlier spellings are given, and if there are a number they are introduced by the label 'Forms', e.g.

> **Housing** Forms: 5 howsynge, husynge, 7 howzen, 7–9 howsing, 7-housing.

The numbers refer to the centuries, so '5' = fifteenth century, '7–9' = seventeenth to nineteenth centuries, and so on. '1' is reserved for 'Anglo-Saxon', pre-twelfth century. The final piece of information under Identification is 'inflexions', for nouns and verbs, where these are not formed regularly.

The 'Morphology' section of the entry charts the 'form-history' of the word, including its etymology (i.e. its language of origin), any subsequent changes of form in English, and any other miscellaneous facts about its history. All this is enclosed in 'heavy square brackets'; e.g.

> *Knave* [OE. *cnafa* = OHG. *knabo, chnabe* (MHG. and G. *knabe*):— OTeut. **knabon*-. The relation between this and the synonymous *cnapa*, KNAPE (q.v.) is not clear. OHG. had also *knappo* (MHG. and G. *knappe*): on the supposed relationship between this and *knabo*, see Streitberg *Urgerm. Gram.* p. 151.]

(Note: OE = Old English, OHG = Old High German, MHG = Middle High German, G = German, OTeut = Old Teutonic, *Urgerm. Gram.* = *Urgermanische Grammatik* (i.e. 'Proto-Germanic Grammar'), :— = 'descended from', * = 're-constructed form'.)

Knave is a 'native' word, from Old English (Anglo-Saxon). Here is an example of the Morphology of a borrowed word:

> **Hurcheon** [a. ONF. *herichon*, OF. *heriçun* (12th c. in Littré), mod.F. *hérisson* (in Hainault *hirchon, hurchon*, Picard *hérichon, irechon*) :— pop.L. **hēricion-em*, f. *hēricius*, late form of *ēricius* hedgehog. See also URCHIN.]

(Note: a. = 'adopted from', ONF = Old Northern French, OF = Old French, mod.F = Modern French, pop.L = popular Latin, f. = 'from'; 'Littré' refers to a nineteenth-century historical French dictionary edited by Émile Littré and one of Murray's models.)

Hurcheon is a word for a hedgehog, though noted by the OED as now (1901) limited to Scottish and Northern English dialects. Note the cross-reference to *urchin*, another dialect word for 'hedgehog'.

If the Morphology section of an entry shows the 'form-history' of the word, the Signification section shows the history of its meanings. Where a word has more than one meaning or 'sense', they are numbered in arabic numerals (1, 2, 3, etc.) straight through the entry from beginning to end. Sometimes a word develops more than one 'branch' of meaning independently; the branches are then numbered with Roman numerals (I, II, III, etc.), but the sense numbers follow on sequentially in the second branch from those in the first. Should a sense be subdivided, the divisions are marked by lower-case letters of the alphabet (a, b, c, etc.). Obsolete senses, like obsolete words, are preceded by the dagger (†) symbol. Senses that represent incorrect and confused uses of the word are preceded by the '¶' symbol. For example, the headword *idea* has five branches:

> **I.** General or ideal form as distinguished from its realization in individuals; archetype, pattern, plan, standard. (Senses 1 to 6)
> **II.** Figure, form, image. (Sense 7)
> **III.** Mental image, conception, notion. (Senses 8 and 9)
> **IV.** Modern philosophical developments. (Senses 10 and 11)

V. (Sense 12, '*attrib.* and *Comb.*', i.e. 'attributive uses and in combinations')

Each sense has its own definition, followed by the Quotations relevant to that sense, arranged in chronological order. The first quotation records the earliest discovered use of the word in that sense, and the last, if the word has become obsolete, the last discovered use. The aim was to include approximately one quotation for each century during which the sense of a word was known to have been in the vocabulary of English. As an example, here are the quotations for the first sense of *behaviour* ('Manner of conducting oneself in the external relations of life; demeanour, deportment, bearing, manners'):

> **1490** CAXTON *Eneydos* xxxi. 120 For hys honneste behauoure [he] be-gan to be taken with his loue. **1530** BALE *Thre Lawes* 53 In clennes of lyfe and in gentyll behauer. **1601** SHAKS. *Twel.N.* iii.iv.202 The behauiour of the yong Gentleman, giues him out to be of good capacity, and breeding. **1754** CHATHAM *Lett. Nephew* v.32 Behaviour is of infinite advantage or prejudice to a man. **1797** GODWIN *Enquirer* I.xiii.III Their behaviour is forced and artificial. **1862** H.SPENCER *First Princ.* II.i. § 36 Special directions for behaviour in the nursery, at table, or on the exchange. **1875** JOWETT *Plato* (ed.2) IV.226 His courage is shown by his behaviour in battle.

Whatever its shortcomings, the OED represents a monumental achievement in lexicography, given the resources available to James Murray, his fellow-editors and staff in the late nineteenth and early twentieth centuries. It has served well the generations of students of the English language, who have mined its contents for all manner of scholarly endeavours. But things have not stood still with the OED, though it seemed for many years as if the 1933 edition represented the completion of the work.

5.4 The supplements and the second edition

The 1933 supplement, however, made only a selection of the materials then available for adding to the earlier parts of the dictionary in particular. In the 1950s, Oxford University Press decided that work should begin on a new supplement, not only to fill out the existing contents of the dictionary, but also to take account of the increase in vocabulary since the dictionary's publication. In 1957, the year in which W.A. Craigie died, a new editor was appointed to oversee the work of the supplement: Robert Burchfield, born in New Zealand in 1923, but who had been working at Oxford University since 1950, where he formed a friendship with C.T. Onions, who pointed him in the direction of lexicography.

Burchfield's supplement was to incorporate and replace the 1933 supplement, and it was originally envisaged as a one-volume publication, to be completed in seven years. This was later, in 1965, revised to a three-volume publication. In the event it became four volumes, and the publication spanned the years 1972 to 1986:

    1972 Volume 1, A–G
    1976 Volume 2, H–N
    1982 Volume 3, O–Scz
    1986 Volume 4, Se–Z

In 1957 Burchfield instituted a fresh reading programme, and in the Preface to the first volume he notes that one-and-a-half million quotations had been extracted 'from works of all kinds written in the period since 1884'. The reading programme also spread its net rather wider than that of the original OED:

> We have made bold forays into the written English of regions outside the British Isles, particularly that of North America, Australia, New Zealand, South Africa, India, Pakistan. We have endeavoured to extract from textbooks and journals the central enduring vocabulary of all major academic subjects, including newish disciplines like Sociology, Linguistics, Computer Science.

Burchfield also noted the inclusion of 'a wide range of colloquial and coarse expressions referring to sexual and excretory functions'.

The OED's distinction between 'main' and 'subordinate' words is abandoned in the supplement, though the system of labelling words as 'archaic', 'obsolete', and so on is retained. However, the use of subject labels is considerably extended, in view of the expanding and specialised vocabulary of science, and in view of the fact that 'the complexity of many scientific subjects is such that it is no longer possible to define all the terms in a manner that is comprehensible to the educated layman'. The supplement volumes contained over 69,000 entries in all, with more than half-a-million quotations.

As Burchfield's work on the supplement drew towards its conclusion in the early 1980s, Oxford University Press decided to take the next step in the development of the OED. In 1984, the New Oxford English Dictionary Project was founded, with the aim of transferring the dictionary to the electronic medium. It was proposed to integrate the OED and Burchfield's supplement into a single electronic text, which would form the basis for future revision and extension of the dictionary, as well as result in a second edition of the OED in print form. Overseeing this development were Edmund Weiner, appointed editor in 1984, and John Simpson, appointed co-editor in 1986.

The transfer of the dictionary and its supplement to electronic form was a massive undertaking, which required the cooperation of several organisations on both sides of the Atlantic Ocean: the International Computaprint Corporation in Fort Washington, Pennsylvania; the University of Waterloo in Canada; and IBM United Kingdom Ltd; as well as the Oxford University Press. The project employed more than 120 keyboarders to input the text – the complexity and variety of the fonts and typefaces precluded the use of a scanning device – and some 50 proofreaders checked their work. Edmund Weiner and John Simpson, with a staff of lexicographers in Oxford corrected and edited the electronic dictionary, and they added around 5,000 new words, to form the second edition of the OED. One other major change was to abandon Murray's transcription system for pronunciation and to use the International Phonetic Alphabet, which has become the standard system for dictionaries.

OED2 was published in a print version in March 1989, on schedule – the first time that any part of the OED had appeared on time. It comprises 20 volumes, runs to 21,730 pages, with 59 million words of text. It defines over half-a-million words, and includes 2.4 million quotations. It takes up over a metre of shelf space. A number of electronic versions of the first and second editions of the dictionary followed, including a magnetic tape, for use on mainframe computers, and a CD-ROM, for use on personal computers. A definitive single CD-ROM of OED2 was released in 1992, with a second version in 1999.

Not only is the CD-ROM version of the OED more portable, it allows the dictionary to be searched in ways that would be impossible with the print version. For example, any of the following parts of entries may be searched independently: headwords, definitions, etymologies, quotations. And the quotations may be searched separately under 'date', 'author', 'work' and 'text'. A search under 'etymologies' can reveal all the words that have their origin in a particular language, or more accurately, all those words that have the language mentioned, for one reason or another, in their etymology: the search for 'Russ' (i.e. Russian) gives 473 results. A search under 'date' will give all the quotations from works published in a particular year, under 'author' all the quotations taken from that author's works, under 'work' all the quotations from a particular publication. However, searching the OED in this way is not straightforward, and it shows up many inconsistencies in the coding, arising no doubt from the timescale over which it was compiled and the number of editors and sub-editors who worked on it. If, for example, you wanted to find all the quotations from Shakespeare's *Hamlet*, you would need to know that the title is usually abbreviated as *Ham.*; when you search for *Ham*, you find that you also have some extraneous results, such as for the 'B'*ham* Daily Post'. Nevertheless, electronic searching opens up many more uses of the OED as a scholarly tool for research on the English language and its history. Many inconsistencies and inaccuracies, though, remain to be ironed out. And that is the purpose of the next phase of the New OED Project.

5.5 Third edition

Since 1993, the OED team, a staff of some 120, has been undertaking a thoroughgoing revision of the whole dictionary, with the aim of publishing a third edition in 2010. This involves the examination of every word in the dictionary, to revise definitions where needed, to check pronunciations, to review etymologies in the light of modern scholarship, and to reassess the quotations, including searching for earlier citations. It is also anticipated that many thousands of new words will be added to the dictionary's list. Some three volumes of 'Additions' have been published in print form. Besides in-house checking and research, the dictionary staff are in touch with scholars around the world, often by means of email (or 'e-mail' – both spellings are given in OED2), and they regularly issue 'appeals' for information in their regular newsletters and on their internet website <oed.com>. The 'Chief Editor' of OED3 is John Simpson, and Edmund Weiner is the 'Principal Philologist'.

Meanwhile, the OED has been on-line since March 2000, and as revisions are made in preparation for OED3, they are displayed on-line. Beginning with the letter 'M', around 1000 revised entries per quarter are incorporated, and subscribers can compare the OED3 entry for a word with its OED2 version. The editors have found that the revision process virtually doubles the size of the dictionary text. A 'Preface to the Third Edition' already exists on-line and explains principles and procedures that are being followed for this edition. One of the major areas of work is in updating and augmenting the quotations. Many words are found to have an earlier citation than previously thought, sometimes significantly so; for example, *Magnificat* is now known to have existed in Old English, instead of Middle English; and *macaroon* is found in Middle English, instead of Early Modern English. New data comes into the editorial offices from four major reading programmes, covering UK and North American sources from the nineteenth and twentieth centuries, texts from the early modern period up to the nineteenth century, scholarly articles on the analysis of English vocabulary, material from other dictionary projects, as well as that assembled by private contributors. Moreover, electronic sources, such as on-line editions of newspapers and full-text databases of literary and other works, are searched for useful material. Efforts are also being made to enhance the coverage of varieties of English across the world, as well as giving due regard to scientific terminology.

Simpson concludes his Preface by exploding a number of 'myths' about the OED:

> There are a number of myths about the *Oxford English Dictionary*, one of the most prevalent of which is that it includes every word, and every meaning of every word, which has ever formed part of the English language. Such an objective could never be fully achieved. The present revision gives the editors the opportunity to add many terms which have been overlooked in the past, but it should be fully understood that fully comprehensive coverage of all elements of the language is a chimera. That said, the content of the Dictionary is certainly comprehensive within reasonable bounds.

It is often claimed that a 'word' is not a 'word' (or is not 'English') unless it is in 'the dictionary'. This may be acceptable logic for the purposes of word games, but not outside those limits. Proponents of this view expect dictionaries to include 'proper' English, whereas dictionaries in fact include many slang, informal, technical, and other words which such people might not consider to be 'proper', typically labelled according to the register of the language to which they belong. It may be added here that the question 'How many words are there in the English language?' cannot be answered by recourse to a dictionary.

> Another myth about the Dictionary, and about dictionaries in general, is that they provide a comprehensive analysis of each word treated. Again, this cannot be the case in a finite text. But more important, philosophically, is that any dictionary attempts to provide information in a manner which is accessible to the reader . . . The reader should . . . regard the Dictionary as a convenient guide to the history and meaning of the words of the English language, rather than as a comprehensive and exhaustive listing of every possible nuance.

The OED has come a long way since the Philological Society resolved to commission a 'New English Dictionary on Historical Principles' in 1858. It continues to develop and be enhanced as an historical record of English vocabulary by exploiting the new electronic media, and by incorporating the insights of recent scholarship and research. The third edition promises to fulfil James Murray's dream to a level of accuracy and consistency that he was unable to achieve with the resources at his disposal. But it continues as a legacy to his vision above all others.

5.6 Further reading

The OED website <oed.com> is an excellent resource on all aspects of the dictionary, including its history and current development. The website offers a tour of the *OED Online*: <oed.com/tour>.

James Murray's story is told in an account by his granddaughter, K.M. Elizabeth Murray, in *Caught in the Web of Words* (1977). His friendship with Dr W.C. Minor is described by Simon Winchester in *The Surgeon of Crowthorne* (1999).

An explanation of the second edition of the OED is given by Donna Lee Berg in *A Guide to the Oxford English Dictionary* (1993). A collection of scholarly articles on the OED can be found in *Lexicography and the OED* (2000) edited by Lynda Mugglestone.

6   Up to the present

In our review of the development of the English dictionary we are now going to backtrack a little and cross the Atlantic, to pick up the story as it unfolded in America. The American colonies achieved their independence from Britain in 1776. As the new nation instituted its own system of government, investigated its own flora and fauna, developed contacts, both friendly and hostile, with speakers of native American languages, and absorbed large numbers of immigrants from Europe and elsewhere speaking a wide diversity of languages, the vocabulary of English in America incorporated a whole new set of words unknown to the speakers of English in Britain. At the same time, there were trends, driven by the desire to assert the identity of the infant nation, to establish an American language, as distinct from the English language. And there was resistance to these trends.

6.1 Noah Webster (1758–1843)

One of the major advocates in the fledgling nation of the American language was Noah Webster, 'a schoolmaster, spelling reformer, lawyer, lecturer, journalist, crusader for copyright legislation, and the unlikely author of a two-volume work entitled the *History of Pestilential Diseases*, which was considered the standard work in the field' (Morton 1994: 40). While a schoolmaster, Webster, dissatisfied with the available textbooks, had published in 1783 *A Grammatical Institute of the English Language*, which included a spelling book, as well as a grammar and a reader. In due course, the spelling book was detached from the rest and published as the *Elementary Spelling Book*. The 'Blue-Back Speller', as it was called, was not the first such work, but it became the standard work used by every child growing up in America; it sold around 100 million copies during the century of its publication.

Webster was an ardent advocate of spelling reform. He was not the first, either in Britain or America, and he has certainly not been the last. But Webster argued for spelling reform on political and patriotic grounds. In his *Dissertations on the English Language* (Boston 1789), Noah Webster put forward his argument as follows (cited in Green 1996: 256):

A capital advantage of this reform in these States would be that it would make a difference between the English orthography and the American. This will startle those who have not attended to the subject; but I am confident that such an event is an object of vast political consequence. The alteration, however small, would encourage the publication of books in our own country. It would render it, in some measure, necessary that all books should be printed in America. The English would never copy our orthography for their own use; and consequently the same impressions of books would not answer for both countries. The inhabitants of the present generation would read the English impressions; but posterity, being taught a different spelling, would prefer the American orthography.

Besides this, a national language is a band of national union. Every engine should be employed to render the people of this country national; to call their attachments home to their own country; and to inspire them with the pride of national character.

In the event, the spelling reforms that were adopted in American English were only a limited subset of those proposed by Webster: the 'or' spelling for 'our' in words like *favour*; the 'er' for 're' in words like *theatre*; and the single consonant, where British English has a double, in words like *traveller*.

Another 'engine' that would further the sense of a national American language would be a dictionary of American English. Webster's first attempt was *A Compendious Dictionary of the English Language*, published in 1806. It was not particularly original, being based, as Webster acknowledges, on John Entick's *New Spelling Dictionary of the English Language*, published in Britain in 1764 and imported into America. However, Webster claims to have added 5000 new words that he had collected from his reading and that reflected life in America. He also added a 52-page appendix with a variety of 'encyclopedic' information, such as foreign currency conversions, weights and measures, a list of local post offices, and 'Chronological Tables of Remarkable Events and Discoveries'. In the introduction, Webster takes Johnson to task for his failings and claims that he – Noah Webster – will be recognised as the most influential lexicographer of the time; moreover, what he would compile would be an American dictionary.

The truly American dictionary, for which the *Compendious Dictionary* was just a precursor, did not appear for another two decades. In 1828, Webster published a two-volume work entitled *An American Dictionary of the English Language*, containing some 70,000 entries. A small minority of these represented words that were to be found exclusively in American English (e.g. *bobsled, gerrymander, moccasin, pretzel, squash, wigwam*), and while he preferred citations from American authors over British ones, they by and large illustrated a common language. The most admired feature of Webster's dictionary has been his definitions: '[he] wrote definitions that were more accurate, more comprehensive, and not less carefully divided and ordered than any previously done in English lexicography' (Friend 1967, quoted in Morton 1994: 43). James Murray, the editor of the OED, called him 'a born definer of words'. The weak point of the *American Dictionary* was its etymologies. Webster ignored the new philological research coming from Germany and pursued his own idiosyncratic path, based on his reading of the Bible, by which he thought all post-Flood languages could be traced back to an original Chaldee. The etymologies would eventually be revised, after Webster's death, in an edition edited by C.A.F. Mahn, a German scholar, and published in 1864 as the 'Webster–Mahn' dictionary.

6.2 Dictionary wars

Webster's view that America should distinguish itself linguistically from Britain and develop its own norms and standards of language was not shared by all his fellow-Americans. Some continued to look towards the mother country for guidance on lexicographic and linguistic matters. Such a one was Joseph Worcester (1784–1865), who edited a new edition of *Johnson's English Dictionary, as Improved by Todd, and Abridged by Chalmers; with Walker's Pronouncing Dictionary, Combined*, which was published in America in 1827. In 1829, Worcester made an abridgement of Webster's *American Dictionary*, from which he omitted many of the etymologies and citations, and which he augmented with terms that he had come across while editing *Johnson*. Webster did not like Worcester's revision. In 1830, Joseph Worcester published his own dictionary, the *Comprehensive Pronouncing and Explanatory Dictionary*; he added some new words, pitched his spelling somewhere between Johnson and Webster, excluded etymology, and paid particular attention to pronunciation, his speciality.

In 1834, Noah Webster, by now in his mid-seventies, wrote an article in which he accused Worcester of plagiarism. Webster's accusation appears to have been intended to discredit Worcester, whose dictionary had become a serious competitor to his own. In lexicography, plagiarism is a difficult accusation to sustain, because all dictionaries borrow from their predecessors. Webster had done so himself, as Worcester pointed out in his rebuttal, which also highlighted the innovations and differences of the *Comprehensive Dictionary*. This exchange began a twenty-year 'dictionary war', in which Worcester's dictionaries represented a conservative and Anglocentric approach to lexicography, and Webster's championed the distinctiveness of American English and the necessity for America to set its own linguistic standards. A second edition, 'corrected and enlarged', of Webster's *American Dictionary* was published in 1841, but it made no impression on the Worcester share of the market. Worcester responded with his *Universal and Critical Dictionary of the English Language* in 1846. By this time, Webster had died (in 1843, at the age of 85), and the rights to reprint and revise his dictionary had been bought from his heirs by George and Charles Merriam, who were printers and booksellers in Springfield, Massachusetts, and who carried on the fight on Webster's behalf. They set about revising and expanding the *American Dictionary*, publishing it in a single volume at half its original price in 1847, which greatly increased its sales, despite the family's fears that their royalty income would be reduced.

The next salvo in the 'war' was fired by Worcester, who brought out a substantially new work in 1860, the *Dictionary of the English Language*, and it soon became recognised on both sides of the Atlantic as the best available dictionary. But Webster was to triumph in the end. A thoroughgoing revision of the *American Dictionary* was undertaken by the editor, Noah Porter, with Carl Mahn, from Berlin, bringing the etymologies into line with modern scholarship. This is the edition that was known as the 'Webster–Mahn', though the publishers used the term 'Unabridged'; it contained 114,000 words. Published in 1864, it became the dictionary of preferred use in education, the law and printing presses. Joseph Worcester died a year later, and the 'war' was effectively over. Webster's dictionaries, published by G. and C. Merriam Company, went from strength to strength, with a new edition in 1890 called *Webster's International Dictionary*, which claimed 175,000 entries, and the *New International* in 1909, which claimed in its Preface:

> The book has been entirely remade: the previous material has been sifted and rearranged; a radical change in the construction of the page has been introduced; the definitions have been treated with nicer discrimination and a more historic method; and in every department there has been an enlargement of the vocabulary and an enrichment with new information. Its salient features in comparison with its predecessor are: A more full and scholarly treatment of the whole field of the English language; a great addition of words and definitions; a greatly increased amount of encyclopedic information; a more exhausting and discriminating treatment of synonyms; a greater comprehensiveness in the illustrations; and an arrangement of material that makes the dictionary much easier of consultation. In short, the New International is essentially a new book.

The dictionary claimed over 400,000 'words printed in bold-faced type, together with the inflected forms that appear in small capitals'.

The numbers game continued to be played. Funk and Wagnalls claimed 450,000 entries in their *New Standard Dictionary* of 1913. *Webster's Second New International Dictionary* of 1934 claimed 600,000, though it is no longer clear exactly what is being counted, certainly not just headwords (see 3.4). This second edition of the *New International*, edited by William Allan Neilson, achieved a dominance among American dictionaries, and 'still figures in the minds of many middle-aged and elderly Americans as the dictionary par excellence' (Landau 1989: 64). But preparations were already being made for a third edition.

6.3   *Webster's Third New International Dictionary*

A systematic reading programme for the third edition was begun by editorial staff at G. and C. Merriam in 1936, but the chief editor to see the project through was not identified until 1951. He was Philip B. Gove, who had been on the staff of the dictionary since 1946. He was supported by a number of associate and assistant editors, and they called upon more than 200 specialist outside consultants, on everything from Iranian etymology to pipe organs. It was published in 1961, and it was, claimed Gove in the Preface, 'a completely new work, redesigned, restyled, and reset; every line of it is new'. The reading programme amassed some four-and-a-half million citations, to add to those already on file, as well as to those available in the OED and other historical dictionaries. The dictionary was the eighth in line from Webster's *American Dictionary* of 1828, and it aimed to be 'a prime linguistic aid to interpreting the culture and civilization of today, as the first edition served the America of 1828'.

W3 claims a vocabulary of 450,000 words. It also claims to have included 100,000 new words that were not in the second *New International*. So, it must have removed 250,000 items that were in W2. W3 has no appendices, all entries are contained within the main alphabetical sequence. Gove claimed continuity with Merriam–Webster tradition, though his critics did not always see it like that. In respect of definitions, though, there was innovation:

> The primary objective of precise, sharp defining has been met through development of a new dictionary style based upon completely analytical one-phrase definitions throughout the book . . . Defining by synonym is carefully avoided.

Here is the definition of the first sense of *pantomime*:

> a solo dancer of imperial Rome acting all the characters of a story (as of tragic love) usu. from myth or history by means of steps, postures, and gestures alone with the help of changes of mask and costume, a chorus singing the narrative usu. in Greek, an orchestra, and sometimes an assistant.

It was in the overall policy that the Merriam–Webster traditions were honoured:

> In continuation of Merriam–Webster policy the editors of this new edition have held steadfastly to the three cardinal virtues of dictionary making: accuracy, clearness, and comprehensiveness. Whenever these qualities are at odds with each other, accuracy is put first and foremost, for without accuracy there could be no appeal to *Webster's Third New International* as an authority. Accuracy in addition to requiring freedom from error and conformity to truth requires a dictionary to state meanings in which words are in fact used, not to give editorial opinion on what their meanings should be.

It was this policy – to state meanings in which words are in fact used – that was seen by critics of the dictionary as innovative and, moreover, damaging. If people could no longer look to their Webster's dictionary for an authoritative pronouncement on what the meaning ought to be, how words ought to be pronounced, spelled and used, then they were adrift in a linguistic sea without any chart or compass.

The American public has generally looked to their dictionaries as uncontestable and reliable authorities in matters of language usage, more so than the British public. W3 was widely considered to have abrogated its cultural role by succumbing to the influence of modern structural linguistics and its 'descriptivist' stance. Here is a typical reaction, from a review in the *Chicago Daily News*, October 1961 (reproduced in Sledd and Ebbitt, 1962: 81):

> In this new edition, it turns out that good English ain't what we thought it was at all – good English, man, is whatever is popular. This is a nifty speak-as-you-go dictionary. Not like that moldy fig of a Second Edition, which tried to separate 'standard English' from slang, bastardized formations, colloquialisms, and all the passing fads and fancies of spoken English.
>
> What's the point in any writer's trying to compose clear and graceful prose, to avoid solecisms, to maintain a sense of decorum and continuity in that magnificent instrument, the English language, if that peerless authority, Webster's Unabridged, surrenders abjectly to the permissive school of speech?

Many reviewers counselled their readers to hang on to their second edition. The one item that was cited more than any other as evidence of this new permissiveness was the entry for *ain't*. Some reviewers implied that it was new to W3, even though it had been entered in Webster's dictionaries since 1890. Others inferred that W3 approved of *ain't*, or at least did not condemn it sufficiently. The first edition of the *New International* (1911) had the following entry for *ain't*:

> Contr. for *are not* and *am not*; also used for is not. *Colloq.* or *illiterate*.

The entry in the third edition is more extensive, and the comments on its usage are more differentiated:

> **1 a:** are not <you ~ going> <they ~ here> <things ~ what they used to be> **b:** is not <it ~ raining> <he's here, ~ he> **c:** am not <I ~ ready> — though disapproved by many and more common in less educated speech, used orally in most parts of the U.S. by many cultivated speakers esp. in the phrase *ain't I* **2** *substandard* **a:** have not <I ~ seen him> <you ~ told us> **b:** has not <he ~ got the time> <~ the doctor come yet>

Even though the comment on the *am/is/are not* contraction implied a 'colloquial' restriction, and the *has/have not* contraction was labelled 'substandard', the critics missed the condemnation contained in 'illiterate'.

Not all reaction to *Webster's Third* was hostile, and the dictionary continues in print, with successive impressions augmented by an 'Addenda Section' of new words and phrases. A fourth edition is said to be in preparation (Béjoint 2000: 45).

6.4 Collegiate dictionaries

Although American dictionaries range in size from the 'unabridged' dictionaries like W3 to 'pocket' dictionaries, there is most competition in the 'college' dictionary market. The college, or 'collegiate', dictionary is a desk size dictionary, aimed at the lucrative upper secondary ('high') school and undergraduate ('college') sector, as well as the learner of English as a second language (Hartmann and James 1998). All the main publishers have a dictionary of this type, including:

- *Merriam Webster's Collegiate Dictionary* (tenth edition, 1995)
- *Random House Webster's College Dictionary* (second edition, 1997)
- *American Heritage Dictionary of the English Language* (fourth edition, Houghton Mifflin, 2000).

By comparison with their British counterparts (see below), American dictionaries have tended to be more 'encyclopedic' in their scope. They have routinely included biographical and geographical entries, as well as more extensive scientific and technical information. Diagrams and line drawings also intersperse the text. The college dictionary is much more of an all-purpose reference work. On the other hand, they tend to contain limited information on etymology, and they pay little attention to other varieties of English than the American (Béjoint 2000). Spelling and pronunciation are almost uniformly American. Some of the practices of American lexicography, including numbered definitions and biographical and geographical entries, have been imitated by some British dictionaries.

6.5 British dictionaries

The British equivalent, in terms of size, of the American collegiate dictionary is the 'desk' dictionary, represented by:

- *Collins English Dictionary* (fourth edition, 1998)
- *New Oxford Dictionary of English* (1998)
- *Longman Dictionary of the English Language* (second edition, 1991)
- *Chambers English Dictionary* (1988).

British publishers also have a long tradition of producing 'concise' dictionaries, the most famous of which is the *Concise Oxford Dictionary*, first published in 1911, under the editorship of F.W. and H.G. Fowler, and now in its tenth edition (1999), edited by Judy Pearsall.

Each dictionary has its own particular characteristics. When CED appeared in its first edition in 1979, it introduced into British dictionaries the American practice of numbered definitions and the inclusion of biographical and geographical entries. Its definitions of scientific and technical terms also tend towards the encyclopedic, including the Latin terms for flora and fauna. As an example, here is the definition of *elephant*:

either of the two proboscidean mammals of the family *Elephantidae*. The **African elephant** (*Loxodonta africana*) is the larger species, with large flapping ears and a less humped back than the **Indian elephant** (*Elephas maximus*), of S and SE Asia.

In terms of vocabulary coverage, CED excels in its attention to the specialist terms of a variety of subject areas, its inclusion of words from the main national Englishes around the world, as well as from British English dialects.

For Oxford University Press, whose flagship general-purpose dictionary had been the *Concise*, NODE was a significant innovation. Not only was it Oxford's first desk size dictionary, it also pioneered a departure in the treatment of the meanings of words, since followed by the tenth edition of the *Concise*. NODE recognises at a general level the 'core' sense(s) of a word, for each of which 'subsenses' may be identified. For example, the noun *grain* has six numbered core senses in NODE, as against twenty-three numbered senses in CED4. Like CED, NODE includes biographical and geographical entries. It is also notable, not only for having three columns per page, but more especially for the clarity of the layout of its entries to aid accessibility (Chapter 7).

The first edition of LDEL in 1984 was based on Webster's Collegiate Dictionary, but the text underwent significant revision and augmentation for the second (1991) edition. As its origin would suggest, it contains biographical and geographical entries. Also significant is the practice of a separate entry for each word class that a lexeme may belong to; for example, *puncture* has a noun entry and a verb entry, *purple* has an adjective, a noun and a verb entry. The other notable feature of LDEL is the boxed synonym essays explaining the, often subtle, differences between words with similar meanings; for example, under *danger* is a box discussing the differences between *danger, peril, jeopardy, hazard* and *risk*.

Chambers English Dictionary has a long history, going back to the publication of the first edition of *Chambers Twentieth Century Dictionary* in 1901. It is something of a relic of an earlier tradition, with its extensive nesting of compounds and derivatives under the root lexeme, the absence of numbering of its definitions, and its appendices for foreign phrases and abbreviations (included by most modern dictionaries in the main body). While consciously including words from other national varieties of English, including those of Australia, South Africa and the Caribbean, it also aims to encompass the vocabulary of Shakespeare, Spenser and Milton. Its coverage of Scottish English words is unrivalled, as befits its publishing origin. And it continues the Johnsonian tradition of the occasional amusing definition; one that has persisted in Chambers is that for *éclair*:

a cake, long in shape but short in duration, with cream filling and chocolate or other icing.

Chambers 21st Century Dictionary, first published in 1996, is a radical departure, bringing Chambers more into line with current lexicographical practice.

6.6 Learners' dictionaries

Perhaps the most interesting and innovative sector of British lexicography over the past quarter of a century and more has been that devoted to the development of the 'monolingual learner's dictionary', coinciding with the growth of the English-as-a-foreign-language industry. Beginning with A.S. Hornby's *Advanced Learner's Dictionary* of 1948, which remained unrivalled for three decades, the market now has four major dictionaries:

* *Oxford Advanced Learner's Dictionary* (sixth edition, 2000)
* *Longman Dictionary of Contemporary English* (third edition, 1995)
* *Collins COBUILD English Dictionary* (third edition, 2001)
* *Cambridge International Dictionary of English* (1995).

Since the first edition of LDOCE in 1978 to rival the OALD, then in its third, but not significantly different, edition, the developments in learners' dictionaries have been remarkable, as each has sought to gain the edge in providing a dictionary that will both meet the particular needs of this user group and make the information as readily accessible as possible.

Learners' dictionaries are discussed in some detail in Chapter 11. Let us just note here that they have not been limited to the A-to-Z format of the four listed above. Tom McArthur's *Longman Lexicon of Contemporary English* (1981) arranges the vocabulary it covers by topic (lexical field), so that the learner can both perceive the words available for an area of meaning and learn the differences in meaning between them. In 1993, the *Longman Language Activator* announced itself as 'the world's first production dictionary'. Intended as a supplement to the traditional learner's dictionary, the *Activator* aims to help learners choose the appropriate word for a given context by arranging the vocabulary under around one thousand 'key words'. Both these dictionaries are further discussed in the context of Chapter 12.

6.7 Electronic dictionaries

A number of dictionary publishers have made their dictionaries available in the electronic medium. We have already mentioned the availability of the OED both on-line and on CD-ROM (Chapter 5). Before the advent of CD-ROM technology, the third edition of *Collins English Dictionary* was produced on 3.5″ floppy disks, but quite a number of dictionaries are now available in CD-ROM format, including:

* *Oxford English Dictionary*, second edition
* *Oxford Talking Dictionary*, a version of the *Shorter Oxford English Dictionary* with pronunciations, published by The Learning Company
* *Concise Oxford Dictionary*, ninth edition
* *Concise Oxford Dictionary*, tenth edition

- *New Oxford Dictionary of English*
- *Longman Dictionary of the English Language,* packaged with 'Infopedia UK', published by SoftKey
- *Encarta World English Dictionary 2001*
- *Oxford Advanced Learner's Dictionary*
- *Longman Interactive English Dictionary,* a version of LDOCE
- *Collins COBUILD English Dictionary*
- *Cambridge International Dictionary of English.*

The electronic medium opens up a number of possibilities for dictionaries that are not presented by the print versions. We will now review these possibilities and how they have been exploited by some of the current CD-ROM dictionaries.

At its simplest level, a CD-ROM dictionary allows you to look up a word, just as in a print dictionary; except that, instead of turning pages to find the word, you enter it in a box and press the 'Enter' key or click on a 'Search' or 'Find' icon to initiate the electronic search. The entry for the word is then displayed in a larger frame, while the headword list with the selected word highlighted is displayed in a smaller frame. It is then usually possibly by one means or another to scroll forward and backward through the headwords and their associated entries. This is the limit of the possibilities allowed by the 'Infopedia' LDEL, except that the CD-ROM contains a number of reference works that can all be searched together, thus providing an integrated information system.

The electronic medium allows considerably more sophisticated exploitation of a dictionary text. The COD10 on CD-ROM, for example, gives an initial choice between a 'Quick' search and a 'Full' search. The Quick search relates to the headword list, and the Full search to the complete text of the dictionary. The screen is divided into a headword list on the left and the dictionary entry on the right. The Quick search allows:

- a straightforward lookup, by typing the headword in the search box, whose place will be found in the headword list and its entry displayed in the larger righthand window; you can scroll through the dictionary in either direction by moving the cursor from item to item in the headword list.
- a lookup using 'wildcards', where, as is now the convention, '?' stands for a single letter, and '*' stands for any number of letters; a search for '?a?e' will find all four-letter words having 'a' as their second letter and 'e' as their fourth; '*ist' will find all the words ending in 'ist'; the results of the search are displayed in the lefthand box, together with the total number of items found (180 for '?a?e', 291 for '*ist').

The 'hypertext search' facility enables an instant cross-reference to any word in an entry, simply by positioning the cursor over the word and clicking on it. Thus, if you do not understand a word used in a definition, you can immediately consult the entry for that word by this means. Some entries have words specifically marked (highlighted in red) for cross-reference.

The Full search facility has three boxes, in which items can be typed, connected by 'Boolean' operators (*and, or, not*). Any number of the boxes may be utilised for a search of the full text of the dictionary. Some of the possibilities are:

- search for a word, by typing it in the first box: *fabric* will find all the (317) entries that contain this word, including those whose definitions indicate that the word denotes a type of fabric; *russ* will find all the (123) words that are marked as being of Russian origin (though you need to know that *Russ* is used in the etymologies as the abbreviation of *Russian*).
- search for a phrase, by typing it in the first box: *time of year* will find the nine items (six of them including *season*) that contain this phrase in their definitions; *musical instrument* finds 81 items, some of which are types of musical instrument.
- search for two or three words to occur simultaneously in an entry, though not necessarily as a phrase, by using the operator *and* to join them: '*flower* and *petal*' finds seven items; '*greek* and *roman* and *art**' finds *classical, classicism* and *muse*.
- search for two alternative forms: '*complementary* or *complimentary*' finds 36 entries containing these words, all but four with the first of them.
- search for one (or two) forms but excluding a second (or third): '*colour* not *pigment*' finds 444 entries, '*pigment* not *colour*' finds 71 (and, incidentally, '*colour* and *pigment*' finds 19).

The Full text searches in the electronic COD10 are powerful and certainly beyond what could be achieved using the print version of the dictionary. But they are quite undiscriminating, finding a search item anywhere in the dictionary text.

The electronic COD9, by contrast, allows for more discriminating full-text searching. It achieves this by allowing the user to switch on one or more of a number of 'filters', which restrict the search to: headwords, definitions, idioms, phrasal verbs, etymology. By switching on the 'etymology' filter, for example, and selecting *Russian* as the search term, it will find this term only in the etymology field of an entry. By switching on the 'phrasal verbs' filter and asking it to search for '* & *up*', it will find all the phrasal verbs that are formed with *up* as their adverb particle. The 'idioms' filter enables you to search for all the idioms containing a particular word, e.g. *time*. Selecting the 'headwords' filter also allows the search to be restricted by word class, by means of a 'part-of-speech' filter. Switching on the 'headwords' filter, selecting 'adjective' from the 'part-of-speech' filter, and then searching for '*able/*ible' finds all the adjective headwords and run-on derivatives ending in this suffix. The 'definitions' filter covers everything else, including any restrictive labelling (Chapter 9): so, to find all the words labelled 'derogatory' in COD9, you switch on the 'definitions' filter and search for *derog* (once you have discovered that this is the abbreviation used by COD9).

For lexical research purposes, the electronic COD9 is a more flexible and sophisticated tool than its later counterpart. Moreover, the COD9 CD-ROM contains all the front and back matter of the print dictionary, including the preface, the guide to using the dictionary, and the very useful 'style guide'. It also provides a 'standard British pronunciation' of every word, which is activated by double-clicking on the phonetic transcription.

Using the search facilities opened up by the medium is not the only way in which publishers have sought to exploit CD-ROM based dictionaries. The CD-ROM version of NODE, for example, has the more limited search facilities of COD10, but it is intended to match with other Oxford reference titles to form a seamless integrated electronic library. The *Oxford Talking Dictionary*, developed by The Learning Company, takes the text of *The New Shorter Oxford English Dictionary* (1993), 'a historical dictionary of modern English' (Preface, p. vii), including its quotations, and adds a number of other features: pronunciation, a proper name dictionary, a thesaurus, maps and pictures – to produce a searchable encyclopedic dictionary and thesaurus.

These are the beginnings of the exploitation of the electronic medium for dictionary purposes, but, apart from searching of various degrees of sophistication and integration with other reference works, publishers have done little more than transfer the print dictionary to the electronic medium (Pruvost 2000). There are more imaginative possibilities, and some of the CD-ROM versions of the learner's dictionaries have begun to take them, as we shall see when we discuss them in Chapter 11.

6.8 The future

Are electronic dictionaries the future? Do they spell the end of the print dictionary? It is probably too early to write the print dictionary's obituary. For the majority of lookups that we make day-to-day (Chapter 7) – checking a spelling, seeing if a word exists, finding out the meaning of an unusual word – it is the print dictionary that we will continue to reach for. The information we need is limited, and the print version is to hand, portable and convenient. However, when we are sitting at the computer, writing a letter or a report or an essay, we will naturally use the electronic dictionary on our hard drive, because it is only a click away and is, in any case, linked into our word processing software. We may also choose to power up the computer if we have a particular problem that we think the electronic dictionary can solve, such as using the wildcard function to find the possible words that might go into the crossword puzzle that we're struggling with.

Certainly, if we are students and scholars of language, the electronic versions open up to us possibilities for the exploitation of dictionary texts that the print versions could not begin to offer. Similarly, if we are professionally involved with language, for examples as translators or writers or teachers, the electronic dictionaries, with their still unrealised potential for development, provide a superior resource to the print dictionary. As we noted in Chapter 5, the potential for the great *Oxford English Dictionary*, both in its development and in its use, is substantially enhanced by the electronic medium. Indeed, it is debatable whether a print version of the OED will ever again be economically viable.

The electronic revolution has had and is having a profound effect both on the compilation of dictionaries (Chapter 13) and on the ways in which they can be and are being used. But print dictionaries are not in terminal decline; they are still likely to be around for some considerable time to come.

6.9 Further reading

Chapters 10 and 11 of Jonathon Green's *Chasing the Sun* (1996) trace the history of lexicography in America. The controversy surrounding W3 is told in Herbert C. Morton's *The Story of Webster's Third* (1994), and James Sledd and Wilma R. Ebbitt's *Dictionaries and THAT Dictionary* (1962) contains a fascinating collection of contemporary reviews of W3.

Dictionary typology is discussed in Chapter 5 of Reinhard Hartmann's *Teaching and Researching Lexicography* (2001), and in Chapter 1 (pp. 32ff) of Henri Béjoint's *Modern Lexicography* (2000).

Material on electronic dictionaries is still sparse. American English dictionaries on CD-ROM are reviewed by Creswell (1996); Nesi (1999) looks at electronic dictionaries for language learners (more applicable to Chapter 11); and Pruvost (2000) reports on a colloquium that discussed the transferring of print dictionaries to the electronic medium.

7 Users and uses

In Chapter 3, we noted the important place that 'the dictionary' holds in our culture. The education system makes extensive use of them. They are objects of discussion and review in the media. We are a 'dictionarate' society (Ilson 2001). Most people own one, have some idea about what it contains, consult it from time to time. In this chapter, we are going to consider who uses a dictionary and for which purposes. We look first at how dictionaries conceive of their aims, then at the uses people make of dictionaries and how the structure of dictionaries aids or hinders access to the information that users seek. Finally, we ask whether dictionaries have two sets of conflicting and incompatible aims.

7.1 Dictionary aims

In the Preface to W3, the editor, Philip Gove, wrote of the aims of the dictionary as follows:

> G. and C. Merriam Company now offer *Webster's Third New International Dictionary* to the English-speaking world as a prime linguistic aid to interpreting the culture and civilization of today, as the first edition served the America of 1828.
>
> This edition has been prepared with a constant regard for the needs of the high school and college student, the technician, and the periodical reader, as well as of the scholar and professional . . . The dictionary more than ever is the indispensable instrument of understanding and progress.
>
> This new Merriam–Webster unabridged is the record of this language [English] as it is written and spoken. It is offered with confidence that it will supply in full measure that information on the general language which is required for accurate, clear, and comprehensive understanding of the vocabulary of today's society.

Gove identifies the groups of users whose needs have especially been considered in the course of compiling the dictionary, and he specifies what those needs are: interpreting today's culture and civilisation, understanding the vocabulary of today's society. 'Interpreting' and 'understanding' (hard words) were the aims of Robert Cawdrey's first monolingual dictionary in 1604 (see Chapter 4). But W3 has an aim that Cawdrey did not have, and it in large part explains the difference between them: to be the 'record' of the language. What it is exactly that dictionaries are recording has been touched on briefly in Chapter 3, and it will be examined in more detail in Chapters 8 to 10.

All dictionaries make a selection from the one to two million words of current English. Gove acknowledges this in respect of the 450,000 words chosen for W3. So, when a dictionary claims to provide 'the most comprehensive coverage of current English' (NODE), or to be 'the world's most comprehensive dictionary' (CED4), we must interpret those statements as meaning 'of large content or scope; wide-ranging' rather than 'including or dealing with all or nearly all elements or aspects of something' (definitions from NODE). All dictionaries aim for comprehensiveness in the 'wide-ranging' sense, for, as Samuel Johnson noted in his *Plan*, 'it is rather to be wished that many readers should find more than they expect, than that one should miss what he might hope to find'. NODE claims to have 'targeted previously neglected fields as diverse as computing, complementary medicine, antique collecting, and winter sports' and to have undertaken 'a detailed and comprehensive survey of plants and animals throughout the world, resulting in the inclusion of hundreds of entries not in any other one-volume dictionary' (Preface). CED4's claim to comprehensiveness rests on its coverage of 'the whole spectrum of general language from formal and archaic to slang and informal expressions', its inclusion of 'the language of an enormous range of general subjects, from art to television, and specialist subjects, from aeronautics to zoology', as well as 'varieties of English from all over Britain and around the world' (Foreword). Comprehensiveness ranges, then, along the dimensions of formality, topic, and dialect.

Chambers, which also claims to have 'enjoyed long acceptance as the most comprehensive single-volume dictionary of the English language' (dust jacket), notes that dictionaries 'must be faithful recorders of the language' (Preface). In fulfilling this obligation, they need to reflect changes in society and their effects on the vocabulary, and this, in turn influences the selection of the words to include. However, *Chambers* is mindful that, as well as being 'of unrivalled value to . . . students, scholars, writers, journalists, librarians and publishers' and 're-plete with words of technical importance to scientists, lawyers, accountants and people in business', it is also 'the treasure chest for all word-game players and word lovers' (dust jacket). For this reason, *Chambers* includes 'unusual and archaic words' for such users. *Chambers* also numbers among its users those who 'read it simply for pleasure' (Preface). The dictionary has an extensive range of users and their needs to satisfy.

And they, like all dictionary users, need to be able to find their way around the dictionary and access efficiently the information that they are seeking. Dictionaries aim to be 'accessible'. NODE claims 'maximum accessibility – with a revolutionary new entry style' (dust jacket). CED4 claims that 'in 1979 Collins English Dictionary revolutionised the way English dictionaries were presented . . . by the simple but, at that time, radical approach of considering the user's needs' (Foreword). *Chambers* claims to be 'the most accessible of reference books' (dust jacket). Accessibility is about how a user gets at the particular piece of information about the word or phrase that they are consulting the dictionary for. In a reference work of the scale and density of a desk size or concise dictionary, this is clearly an important issue, since users are not usually prepared to peruse a considerable amount of material in order to locate the sought-for nugget of enlightenment. We discuss below the factors that contribute to accessibility; here, we merely note that it is an aim of dictionaries to be accessible.

We can conclude that dictionaries have two fundamental aims: coverage, and accessibility. Coverage includes the aim to be 'comprehensive', representing an up-to-date and wide-ranging selection of vocabulary, and the aim to be a 'faithful record' of the lexical resources of the language. Both aims can be viewed as user-oriented: ensuring that what a user wants to know is made available, and enabling the user to get at it by the most straightforward means. But do we know what users consult their dictionaries for?

7.2 Dictionary uses

What kind of reliable evidence is there about what users look up in a dictionary? What methodologies are there for finding out? Most of the surveys that have been done (referenced in Béjoint 2000: 141) have involved the use of a questionnaire, in which users (mainly students) report on their own dictionary use. Self-reporting does not always produce the most reliable data; besides a tendency to overstate or underplay, according to question asked and the personality of the respondent, questions such as 'How often do you consult a dictionary?' are notoriously difficult to gauge accurately. Nevertheless, results from questionnaires on the use of native speaker dictionaries all agree that the top two reasons for consulting a dictionary are:

1   to discover the meaning of a word
2   to check the spelling of a word.

The first of these may involve either looking up a word that is unknown and whose meaning cannot be deduced from the context in which it has been met (a 'hard' word), or checking the meaning of a word about which the user may be confused (perhaps, for example, *aggravate*).

A questionnaire administered to French students of English on their use of monolingual English dictionaries (including learners' dictionaries) revealed that looking up the meaning of words was also the top use for this group of users (Béjoint 1981). Checking spelling came joint fourth with checking pronunciation. Reflecting their use of dictionaries for writing tasks, including translation (see 6.5 below), the second and third most frequent occasions of lookup for these students were: to check the syntactic patterns that a word could enter; and to discover a synonym for a word. What Béjoint also discovered was that most of the respondents had not read the front matter of their dictionary, in particular the guide to using the dictionary, and so were unaware of the wealth of information that the dictionary contained.

Despite a hundred or more studies of dictionary use, we are still far from understanding either the range of uses for which dictionaries are consulted or the strategies that are used to access dictionary information (Hartmann 2001). Most of the studies have focused on students, and many of them on students engaged in tasks associated with foreign language learning – translation, writing in the foreign language, and so on. And most of them have used a questionnaire as the study instrument, which does not necessarily produce an authentic picture of dictionary use, as expressed by Hatherall (1984: 184):

> Are subjects saying here what they do, or what they think they do, or what they think they ought to do, or indeed a mixture of all three?

An alternative method of investigating dictionary use is the 'protocol' or diary, when a respondent is asked to record their lookup each time they use a dictionary in the course of a specific task (e.g. Nuccorini 1992). Again, this involves self-reporting, but it requires recording procedures as they are being undertaken or immediately on completion, so the resulting data may well turn out both to be more authentic and to provide greater insight into the dictionary lookup process and the reasons for it. A method that does not involve self-reporting would be direct observation of subjects, which would only be possible in controlled circumstances (e.g. a classroom), and may itself influence the way in which subjects behave. It is not easy to get at either what triggers a dictionary consultation or exactly what happens when it occurs. A further question that deserves investigation is whether users access electronic dictionaries differently from print dictionaries (cf. Nesi 1999).

One dictionary that claims to have consulted its potential users and to have adjusted its content accordingly is the *Encarta Concise English Dictionary* (2001). Kathy Rooney, the Editor-in-Chief, states in her 'Introduction':

> People like you said they wanted answers to the following questions. Am I spelling this word correctly? What does this word mean? Am I using the word correctly? How do I pronounce this word? Where does the word come from? We also established that you set great store by the ease with which you can understand the information in the dictionary, the clarity with which it is presented, and the speed with which you can navigate through long entries. In addition, we asked 41 professors of English from the UK, Australia, the United States, and Canada about the language problems their students faced. This survey revealed surprisingly similar findings across the globe. All expressed concern that students increasingly have difficulties with basic language skills – especially spelling and grammar.
>
> (p. xi)

On this basis, as well as that of personal experience and anecdote, we may conclude that users consult dictionaries for more than just 'meaning' and 'spelling', though for these primarily. Where a dictionary is consulted during word games, it is usually to verify whether a word exists or is a legitimate formation. We may consult a dictionary to determine the pronunciation of a, usually technical, word that we have met only in print. Students of language may need to find out about word histories and origins, or about the range and contexts of meaning that a word may have. Or, as *Chambers* suggests, people may peruse a dictionary for pleasure, or for 'edification' (Hartmann 2001: 88). Occasions of lookup, or reference needs, are diverse and various: how do dictionaries aid the user to access the specific piece of information they are looking for?

7.3 Accessibility

Let us consider first what may be involved in the dictionary lookup process. Scholfield (1999: 13–14), whose focus is on language learners consulting a dictionary to find out about the meaning of a word, suggests that there are 'five main steps':

1   the learner identifies a vocabulary problem – that is a word or phrase whose meaning is unknown or uncertain
2   the learner makes the decision to use a dictionary to solve the problem, rather than, or in addition to, other possible means
3   he or she has to find an entry for the wordform or phrase being sought
4   the right specific entry or part of an entry has to be located
5   the information about meaning that has been obtained has to be exploited.

The points at which accessibility becomes particularly relevant are steps 3 and 4, which relate to the 'macrostructure' and the 'microstructure' of the dictionary respectively.

A dictionary's macrostructure refers to what constitutes an entry in a dictionary and how the entries are arranged. We assume that a dictionary page has two (sometimes three) columns, and that entries follow each other in alphabetical order. Compare the headword list (from *pros*) for the following two dictionaries of similar size and published within three years of each other shown in Table 7.1.

In this brief headword list, *Chambers* has only one item that is not included in LDEL (*prosauropod*), whereas LDEL has thirteen that are not in the *Chambers* headword list. However, apart from the first two – the abbreviation *pros.* and the prefix *pros-* – they are all contained in *Chambers*, though not as headwords. The macrostructure of the two dictionaries differs most obviously in the decisions about which items feature as headwords. *Chambers* nests all derivatives; so *prosaism* and *prosaist* are both within the entry for *prosaic*, *proscription* is under *proscribe*, *prosecution* under *prosecute*, and so on. Similarly, the noun, verb and adjective uses of *prose*, which have separate headwords in LDEL, are all dealt

Table 7.1

Chambers (1988)	LDEL (1991)
	pros.
	pros–
prosaic	prosaic
	prosaism
	prosaist
prosauropod	
proscenium	proscenium
	proscenium arch
prosciutto	prosciutto
proscribe	proscribe
	proscription
prose	[1]prose
	[2]prose
	[3]prose
prosector	prosector
prosecute	prosecute
	prosecuting attorney
	prosecution
	prosecutor
proselyte	proselyte
	proselytism
	proselytize
prosencephalon	prosencephalon

with in the one entry in *Chambers*, as is the more usual practice. LDEL puts its abbreviations, like *pros.* in the headword sequence; *Chambers* collects them together in an appendix. Such macrostructure decisions affect the accessibility of headwords, and so the search in Scholfield's Step 3. All the words beginning with the combining form *neur(o)-*, for example, are under a single headword in *Chambers*, but each has headword status in LDEL; arguably, it is easier to find a word like *neuroleptic* in LDEL, by scanning down the headword list, than in *Chambers*, which requires perusal of a continuous paragraph, even though the lexemes themselves are in bold typeface.

A dictionary's microstructure refers to the layout and organisation of the individual entry. Compare the following entries for *nest* from *Chambers* and COD10:

> **nest** *nest, n.* a structure prepared for egg-laying, brooding, and nursing, or as a shelter: a place of retreat, resort, residence or lodgment: a den: a comfortable residence: a group of machine-guns in a position fortified or screened by sandbags or the like: a place where anything teems, prevails, or is fostered: the occupants of a nest, as a brood, a swarm, a gang: a set of things (as boxes, tables) fitting one within another: a set of buildings, as advance factories, divided into blocks and units: an accumulation: a tangled mass. –

v.i. to build or occupy a nest: to go bird's-nesting. *–v.t.* and *v.i.* to lodge, settle. *–n.* **nest'er** one who builds a farm or homestead on land used for grazing cattle (*U.S. hist.; derog.*): a nest-builder. **–nest'-egg** an egg, real or sham, left or put in a nest to encourage laying: something laid up as the beginning of an accumulation: money saved; **nest'ing-box** a box set up for birds to nest in; **nest'ing-place. –feather one's nest** see **feather.** [O.E. *nest*; Ger. *Nest*, L. *nidus*.]

(*Chambers*)

nest • n. 1 a structure or place made or chosen by a bird for laying eggs and sheltering its young. ▶ a place where an animal or insect breeds or shelters. ▶ a snug or secluded retreat. ▶ a bowl-shaped object likened to a bird's nest. **2** a place filled with undesirable people or things: *a nest of spies.* **3** a set of similar objects of graduated sizes, fitting together for storage. **• v. 1** use or build a nest. **2** fit (an object or objects) inside a larger one. **3** (especially in computing and linguistics) place in a hierarchical arrangement, typically in a lower position.
– DERIVATIVES **nestful** n. (pl.**-fuls**).
– ORIGIN OE *nest*, of Gmc origin.
nest box (also **nesting box**) **• n.** a box provided for a bird to nest in.
nest egg • n. 1 a sum of money saved for the future. **2** a real or artificial egg left in a nest to induce hens to lay there.
nester • n. a bird nesting in a specified manner or place: *a scarce nester in Britain.*

(COD10)

Although the exact typefaces are not reproduced, the entries are replicas in all essential respects. *Chambers* represents an entry style that was reflected in the COD up to the seventh edition (1982), while COD10 represents a double shift from COD7, in the direction of a clearer microstructure and enhanced accessibility. The major differences are the following:

•   word classes marked by '•' and a bold abbreviation (**n, v**) in COD10, compared with an italic *n, v.i.* etc. in *Chambers*
•   COD10 has no pronunciation transcription for 'simple' words like *nest*; *Chambers* has a respelling system (see Chapter 9)
•   senses are numbered in COD10, with subsenses marked by '▶'; whereas *Chambers* divides senses with a colon (:)
•   derivatives requiring their own definition are separate headwords in COD10, while remaining nested under the root word in *Chambers*
•   undefined derivatives are clearly marked in COD10
•   etymology is on a separate line, marked by the word 'ORIGIN', in COD10; while *Chambers* has etymology in the traditional square brackets at the end of the entry.

Scholfield's Step 4 is probably easier to complete in COD10 than in *Chambers*. Even so, the user still has to complete Step 5, the task of 'interpreting the information given in the entry' (Béjoint 2000: 156).

ECED attempts to overcome part of the problem of location of information by including 'quick definitions' in bold capitals at the beginning of each sense of polysemous lexemes, a technique similar to that used by some learners' dictionaries (Chapter 11). For example, the entry for *ladder* reads:

> **1 DEVICE WITH RUNGS TO CLIMB ON** a portable piece of equipment with rungs fixed to sides made of metal, wood, or rope, used for climbing up or down **2 PATH TO ADVANCEMENT** a series of hierarchical levels on which somebody moves up or down within an organization or society o *She joined the firm at a fairly low level but quickly moved up the ladder.* **3 LINE OF MISSING STITCHES IN TIGHTS** a vertical line of stitches that have come undone in tights, a stocking, or a knitted garment, leaving only the horizontal stitches in place **4 LIST OF RANKED PLAYERS** a list of contestants in an ongoing sports or games competition, arranged according to ability

The aim is for the user to run their eye down the entry, reading only the 'quick definitions', in order to locate more easily the specific sense being looked for.

There are, though, conventions of dictionary microstructure that a user must become familiar with: what a headword is, normally a transcription of pronunciation, irregular inflections, division of the entry into word classes if relevant, identification of different senses, the wording of definitions, the placement of derivatives, phrases and idioms, etymology usually in square brackets at the end. Then, it is the rare dictionary that does not utilise a degree of abbreviation, at least for the word classes, and usually for the 'transitive' (*v.t.*) and 'intransitive' (*v.i.*) uses of verbs, as well the languages referred to in the etymology (O.E. for 'Old English', Ger. for 'German', L. for 'Latin', Gmc for 'Germanic'). In the Preface to the first edition of COD (1911), the editors, F.W. and H.G. Fowler, aimed to save space 'by the severest economy of expression – amounting to the adoption of telegraphese – that readers can be expected to put up with'. Ninety years later, dictionary users can be expected to put up with far less abbreviation than their forebears, and in some dictionaries (e.g., NODE) abbreviation is deliberately kept to a minimum.

Even with improvements in the macro- and microstructure of dictionaries in recent years, to make information more readily accessible, the user must expect to develop reference skills in order to become an efficient user of dictionaries. The evidence from studies of dictionary use is that few users read the front matter of their dictionary, which explains how the dictionary is structured, how users may locate various items of information, what the various labels and abbreviations mean, and what special features the dictionary contains. In general terms, users must develop skills in finding the appropriate headwords – the base form of an inflected word, where a compound or derived word is entered, under which headword to look for a phrase or idiom. Also, users must be familiar with entry structure, the division into word classes, the principles of sense division, the wording of definitions, the contribution of examples, and so on. Many have argued for training in dictionary use to be given in schools and universities, rather than leaving it to chance and native wit (Hartmann 2001: 92, Béjoint 2000: 168). But is there perhaps a fault in the dictionaries themselves?

7.4 Record or reference?

When we take the user's perspective, issues of accessibility are naturally to the fore, and the concentration is on the dictionary as a reference manual. But 'dictionaries must be faithful recorders of the language' (*Chambers* Preface). We saw in Chapter 4 how dictionaries grew into the role of being a record of the language, and in Chapter 5 how the OED compilers interpreted that role in historical terms. In Chapter 3, we argued for the dictionary as a linguistic description complementary to the grammar, the latter dealing with the general rules of sentence structure, and the former with the operation of individual lexical items as well as with the overall structure of the vocabulary of a language.

Within its size and scope a dictionary is a lexical description. It specifies the lexical items that the vocabulary contains; it aims to be comprehensive, in the sense discussed in 7.1; it gives for each lexical item that it identifies a complete lexical account – spelling, pronunciation, inflections, derivations, meanings, usage, origin – that describes its idiosyncratic operation (Chapter 3). This is the sense in which a dictionary is expected to be a 'faithful recorder' of the language. The information that should be included is more or less given (Hudson 1988; Ilson 1991); how it should be presented is a matter of convention, tweaked by imaginative development and innovation on the part of dictionary compilers, editors and publishers.

The consequence of dictionaries' recording function is that vast amounts of information in any dictionary remain unconsulted by anyone except, perhaps, the most assiduous dictionary scholar. Conventional native-speaker dictionaries are attempting to perform simultaneously two functions that may be in conflict with each other: to provide a lexical description, and to provide a source of ready reference to satisfy the needs of various types of user. Is there an argument for a range of different types of dictionary, to fulfil the different functions and user needs, just as there is a range of different types of grammar book, from reference to pedagogical?

The most popular dictionary in Germany is the *Duden Rechtschreibung*, now in its twenty-second edition (2000). It is essentially a spelling dictionary, with indications of alternative spellings, syllabification, and inflections; but also, for less familiar words and phrases, it gives brief definitions, synonyms or examples of usage, as well as pronunciation and language of origin for loanwords. So it fulfils the two basic needs of dictionary users: a guide to spelling, and an explanation of 'hard' words. No popular dictionary for English follows this format. English has specialist spelling dictionaries (e.g. West 1964), and it has specialist dictionaries for the terminology of subject disciplines and particular topics, from archaeology to zoology; but it has no regular dictionary of the type represented by the *Duden*.

ECED, on the basis of its user research (7.2) makes some provision for meeting the spelling needs of its target users (mainly students). It includes common misspellings of words in its alphabetical listing of headwords, but in grey type and with a line through; the correct spelling is then given beside it, e.g.

~~preperation~~ incorrect spelling of **preparation**

It also includes notes entitled 'SPELLCHECK' after words that are pronounced the same (i.e. homophones), e.g. *here* and *hear*, as well as 'usage' notes for pairs that are frequently confused, e.g. *complement* and *compliment*.

The dictionary in the electronic medium (see 6.7) offers the possibility of allowing the user to choose which types of information about headwords will be displayed on any lookup occasion. The OED2 on CD-ROM has built in a number of options of this kind. The user can choose whether to have the quotations displayed or not, and there are 'switches' to activate the display of 'pronunciation', 'spellings' (i.e. form history), and 'etymology'. If all the options are turned off, the display offers only the definitions and usage labels for the numbered senses of a lexeme. The *Oxford Talking Dictionary* has a more limited set of switches: the quotations can be excluded, and the thesaurus facility is activated by a switch. Electronic dictionaries generally divide their display into a headword list window and a dictionary entry window, and each can be scrolled separately. The headword list window operates in part like a spelling dictionary, except that derivatives, compounds and so on that are nested in dictionary entries may not be included in the list. The electronic medium does, though, open up possibilities for selective display of dictionary information that have not yet been fully exploited.

7.5 Learners

There are two sets of users whose needs have been carefully considered and for whom dictionaries have been specifically tailored: children, and learners. Children's dictionaries range from the large-format work with pictures and an imaginative use of colour, aimed at those just beginning to learn to read, to school dictionaries that look like the adult version, except with a more selective headword list, the omission of some word senses and of information such as etymology, and definitions written in a simpler language. We could examine more closely the range of children's dictionaries, but our focus here will be on dictionaries aimed at learners of English as a foreign or second language. We discuss these dictionaries in detail in Chapter 11; in the context of the present chapter, we look just at the reference needs of this group.

A learner, or indeed a native speaker, may consult a dictionary when engaged in one of two broad types of language task. On the one hand, a learner may be engaged in the task of reading or listening, and they encounter a word or phrase that makes no sense to them and whose meaning they cannot deduce from the context: the dictionary is used as an aid to 'decoding' the item read or heard. On the other hand, a learner may be engaged in the task of writing or preparing to speak, and they do not necessarily need to find an unknown word, but rather to discover how a known word may be used in the appropriate context: the dictionary is used as an aid to 'encoding' acceptable sentences and texts. For a native speaker, spelling is the main encoding purpose that they might consult a dictionary for; whereas learners may need to find out about spelling, pronunciation, inflections, how a word fits into grammatical structure, what other words can appropriately accompany it (its collocations), and whether there are any social or cultural restrictions on its usage.

Dictionaries for learners, therefore, need to consider not only their decoding needs, which are not vastly different from those of native speakers, but more particularly their encoding needs. This means that learners' dictionaries need to contain more explicit, more comprehensive and more systematic information about the syntactic and lexical operation of words than a dictionary for native speakers. Arguably, this information should be contained in any dictionary that purports to be an accurate and comprehensive lexical description (Hudson 1988), but in practice it is precisely in these areas that in native speaker dictionaries the information is scantiest and least systematic (see Chapter 9). Besides, as we noted earlier, it is not just a matter of containing the information, it is also a matter of presenting the information in such a way that it is readily accessible and takes account of users' prior knowledge and reference skills (Jackson 1995).

The early learners' dictionaries, such as H.E. Palmer's *A Grammar of English Words* (1938) or the precursor to the OALD, A.S. Hornby *et al.*'s *Idiomatic and Syntactic English Dictionary* (1942), concentrated, as their titles suggest, on providing accurate and systematic information about the grammatical operation of words. The subsequent history of learners' dictionaries (Cowie 1999) shows the development and elaboration of that purpose, not only in grammar but also in phraseology and collocation, with an increasing attention more recently on making the information more readily accessible and usable. This has been achieved in a number of ways. For example, the early editions of OALD presented information about the grammatical operation of verbs by means of a set of codes based on a system of 'verb patterns' developed by Hornby. Each sense of a verb was coded (e.g. 'VP6, VP15, VP21'). The regular user of the dictionary would learn which patterns were represented by the commonly occurring codes, and could look the less familiar ones up in the guide to the dictionary in the front matter. The coded information was usually supported by illustrative examples, so that the user could see a typical context for the word in the given sense. It became clear over time that, while language teachers may have made good use of the grammatical codes, many student users of the dictionary did not make the effort to learn the system and relied largely on the examples. In later editions of OALD the coding system has been abandoned; the grammatical information is presented in a more accessible form, e.g. by means of formulae such as '~sth (to sb)'; and more attention is paid to ensuring that the examples provide a suitable model.

As we shall see in Chapter 11, learners' dictionaries have developed in more varied ways than just in the presentation of grammatical information. Entry structure has in some cases been substantially revised, information and advice on usage is incorporated, various types of additional material is included. Much of the innovation has been in response to the perceived needs of this particular user group, so that the learner's dictionary has in many respects moved away from the conventions of the native speaker dictionary (Rundell 1998).

7.6 Further reading

It is useful to read the prefaces and other front matter to a number of dictionaries, as well as the blurb on their dust jackets, to gain an idea of how dictionaries are presenting themselves to their potential users. Chapters 4 and 5 of Henri Béjoint's *Modern Lexicography* (2000) discuss the aims of dictionaries, their functions in society, and the reference needs of their users. A 'user perspective' is also provided by Chapter 6 of Reinhard Hartmann's *Teaching and Researching Lexicography* (2001). Bo Svensén discusses dictionary users in relation to types of dictionary in Chapter 2 of his *Practical Lexicography* (1993).

8 Meaning in dictionaries

In Chapter 7, we identified checking spelling and finding out about meaning as the two principal reasons why someone would consult a dictionary. Because dictionaries are based on the written form of the language and their word lists are arranged in alphabetical order, they coincidentally and inevitably provide information about spelling. It is, thus, in explaining, describing and defining the meaning of words that the major function of dictionaries is considered to lie, and on which they are judged. We discussed some of the components of word meaning in Chapter 2, and in this chapter we explore how and with what success dictionaries describe the various aspects of lexical meaning. First, though, we need to determine exactly what the objects are whose meaning dictionaries are attempting to characterise.

8.1 The objects of definition

Dictionaries present us with a list of headwords as the objects to be defined, though some items within the entry under a headword may also be subject to definition. The headword list may contain a variety of types of item. Consider the two following short lists from CED4:

> hook, hookah, hook and eye, hooked, hooker[1], hooker[2], Hooke's law, hooknose, hook-tip, hook-up, hookworm, hookworm disease;
>
> its, it's, itself, itsy-bitsy, ITU, ITV, -ity, i-type semiconductor, IU, IU(C)D, Iulus, -ium

The headword list in CED4 (personal and geographical names are excluded) contains 'simple' words like *hook* and *hookah*, but it also contains a range of other items:

- derived words – *hooked*, *hooker[2]*
- compound words, including those written solid (*hooknose, hookworm, itself*), those hyphenated (*hook-tip, hook-up, itsy-bitsy*), and open compounds (*Hooke's law*), as well as combinations of these (*hookworm disease, i-type semiconductor*)
- binomials (*hook and eye*)

- abbreviations (*ITU, ITV, IU, IU(C)D*), whose 'definition' consists only in spelling out the words whose initial letters make up the acronym or initialism
- affixes (*-ity, -ium*), which have similar definitions to those for words
- contractions (*it's*), for which only the full forms are given.

Some headwords – abbreviations, contractions – are not included for definition as such, just for explanation; similarly, word forms manifesting irregular inflections are often entered with a cross-reference to the base form (or lemma), e.g.

felt the past tense and past participle of **feel**

Some of the items that CED4 includes in its headword list would feature as nested or run-on items in other dictionaries, including derivatives and some compounds. The practice varies, with, for example, some dictionaries listing solid compounds as headwords, but not hyphenated or open compounds. CED4 itself includes some items within entries that are further defined. Under *hook*, for example, it defines: by hook or (by) crook; get the hook; hook, line, and sinker; off the hook; on the hook; sling one's hook; hook it. These are various kinds of phrase, including idioms (*by hook or crook, sling one's hook*), trinomials (*hook, line, and sinker*), and slang expressions (*get the hook, hook it*).

One item in the list is entered twice: *hooker*, with the same pronunciation, and with the following main meanings:

hooker[1] a commercial fishing boat using hooks and lines instead of nets

hooker[2] a person or thing that hooks

At first glance, you would think that the meaning of *hooker[1]* would be included in the more general meaning of *hooker[2]*. Why then does *hooker* have two homographs (in fact, homonyms), which are entered as separate headwords, especially as the meanings seem so close? The basic criterion that dictionaries use to identify homographs is etymology: if two or more different origins can be identified for the same spelling, then the orthographic word is entered as many times as there are different etymologies. In the case of *hooker*, the first homograph is identified as a loanword from Dutch *hoeker* in the seventeenth century, and the second is the derivation by means of the suffix *-er* from the verb *hook*, which has its origin in the Old English *hoc*.

With *hooker*, the homographs have not too dissimilar meanings. The opposite case can also be found. Consider the following meanings for the word *table* (definitions from CED4):

a flat horizontal slab or board, usually supported by one or more legs, on which objects may be placed

an arrangement of words, numbers, or signs, usually in parallel columns, to display data or relations.

Intuitively, you might think that these meanings must be associated with words of different origin, but that is not the case. There is a single entry for *table* in CED4, since both meanings are associated with the word that came into English from Old French in the twelfth century, with its origin in Latin *tabula*, 'a writing tablet'.

Another criterion that may be used to trigger multiple headwords for the same spelling is word class membership. This criterion operates in LDEL, where *table* has three entries, one each for the noun, adjective (e.g. *table manners*), and verb. The criterion operates alongside the etymological one, so that a homograph identified by etymology may also have multiple entries on the basis of word class membership. For example, *line* is entered four times in LDEL2: [1]*line* (put a lining in, for example, a garment) is distinguished from the others on the basis of etymology: it has its origin in Middle English *linen*, derived from *lin*, the Old English for 'flax', which developed into modern English *linen*. The other entries for *line* also have a Middle English origin, but from Old French *ligne*, though this word, interestingly, goes back to a Latin word meaning 'made of flax'. This *line* has three homographs based on word class membership, one each for the noun, verb and adjective.

Many words are polysemous; they have more than one meaning, as *table* cited earlier. For any spelling (orthographic word), therefore, for which a lexicographer identifies multiple meanings, a decision must be made whether the different meanings arise from polysemy or because there are homographs. The lexicographer applies the criterion of etymology, and, according to dictionary policy, that of word class membership. If the criteria are satisfied, then multiple headwords are entered in the dictionary. If not, then a single headword is entered with multiple meanings or senses. We shall see (Chapter 11) that these criteria do not necessarily apply in learners' dictionaries, because they may be regarded as not serving the reference needs of this user group.

8.2 Lumping and splitting

If polysemy is identified, how does a lexicographer decide how many meanings or senses of a word to recognise? The lexicographer collects the evidence, such as citations and concordance lines (Chapter 13), which indicate the different contexts of use. What is then done with the evidence depends on whether the lexicographer is a 'lumper' or a 'splitter' (Allen 1999: 61):

> The 'lumpers' like to lump meanings together and leave the user to extract the nuance of meaning that corresponds to a particular context, whereas the 'splitters' prefer to enumerate differences of meaning in more detail; the distinction corresponds to that between summarizing and analysing.

Here are the entries for the noun *horse* from NODE and from CED4: one of these is a 'splitting' and the other a 'lumping' dictionary.

horse ▶ **noun 1** a solid-hoofed plant-eating domesticated mammal with a flowing mane and tail, used for riding, racing, and to carry and pull loads.

• *Equus caballus*, family Equidae (the **horse family**), descended from the wild Przewalski's horse. The horse family also includes the asses and zebras.

■ an adult male horse; a stallion or gelding. ■ a wild mammal of the horse family. ■ [treated as *sing.* or *pl.*] cavalry: *forty horse and sixty foot.*

2 a frame or structure on which something is mounted or supported, especially a sawhorse.

v *Nautical* a horizontal bar, rail, or rope in the rigging of a sailing ship for supporting something. v short for **VAULTING HORSE**

3 [mass noun] *informal* heroin.

4 *informal* a unit of horsepower: *the huge 63-horse 701-cc engine.*

5 *Mining* an obstruction in a vein.

(NODE)

horse *n* **1** a domesticated perissodactyl mammal, *Equus caballus*, used for draught work and riding: family *Equidae*. **2** the adult male of this species; stallion. **3 wild horse**. **3a** a horse (*Equus caballus*) that has become feral. **3b** another name for **Przewalski's horse**. **4a** any other member of the family *Equidae*, such as the zebra or ass. **4b** (*as modifier*): *the horse family*. **5** (*functioning as pl*) horsemen, esp. cavalry: *a regiment of horse*. **6** Also called: **buck**. *Gymnastics*. a padded apparatus on legs, used for vaulting, etc. **7** a narrow board supported by a pair of legs at each end, used as a frame for sawing or as a trestle, barrier, etc. **8** a contrivance on which a person may ride and exercise. **9** a slang word for **heroin**. **10** *Mining*. a mass of rock within a vein or ore. **11** *Nautical*. a rod, rope, or cable, fixed at the ends, along which something may slide by means of a thimble, shackle, or other fitting; traveller. **12** *Chess*. an informal name for knight. **13** *Informal*. short for **horse-power**. **14** (*modifier*) drawn by a horse or horses: *a horse cart*.

(CED4)

NODE has five numbered senses, by comparison with CED4's fourteen. The first sense in NODE encompasses the first five senses in CED4; NODE's second sense encompasses senses six, seven and eleven in CED4; NODE's 3 corresponds to CED4's 9, NODE's 4 to CED4's 13, and NODE's 5 to CED4's 10. CED4 has some senses not covered by NODE: 8, 12, 14. Some of CED4's senses are 'subsenses' (introduced by the symbol ■) to the 'core' senses in NODE. The arrangement of NODE suggests that it is essentially a 'lumping' dictionary, whereas CED4 falls more obviously into the 'splitting' category. Most dictionaries tend to be of the 'splitting' type, though different dictionaries do not necessarily agree on where to make the splits between senses. Compare the following entries for the noun *length* in COD9 and CCD4:

length n. 1 measurement or extent from end to end; the greater of two or the greatest of three dimensions of a body. **2** extent in, of, or with regard to, time (*a stay of some length*; *the length of a speech*). **3** the distance a thing extends (*at arm's length*; *ships a cable's length apart*). **4** the length of a swimming pool as a measure of the distance swum. **5** the length of a horse, boat, etc., as a measure of the lead in a race. **6** a long stretch or extent (*a length of hair*). **7** a degree of thoroughness in action (*went to great lengths*; *prepared to go to any length*). **8** a piece of material of a certain length (*a length of cloth*). **9** *Prosody* the quantity of a vowel or syllable. **10** *Cricket* **a** the distance from the batsman at which the ball pitches (*the bowler keeps a good length*). **b** the proper amount of this. **11** the extent of a garment in a vertical direction when worn. **12** the full extent of one's body.

(COD9)

length *n* **1** the linear extent or measurement of something from end to end, usually being the longest dimension. **2** the extent of something from beginning to end, measured in more or less regular units or intervals: *the book was 600 pages in length*. **3** a specified distance, esp. between two positions: *the length of a race*. **4** a period of time, as between specified limits or moments. **5** a piece or section of something narrow and long: *a length of tubing*. **6** the quality, state, or fact of being long rather than short. **7** (*usually pl*) the amount of trouble taken in pursuing or achieving something (esp. in **to great lengths**). **8** (*often pl*) the extreme or limit of action (esp. in to any length (s)). **9** *Prosody, phonetics.* the metrical quantity or temporal duration of a vowel or syllable. **10** the distance from one end of a rectangular swimming bath to the other. **11** *NZ inf.* the general idea; the main purpose.

(CCD4)

Table 8.1 shows how the senses match in these two concise dictionaries.

COD9 has only half of its twelve meanings directly matched in CCD4, while CCD4 has seven of its eleven senses matched in COD9; the disparity arises from the fact that Sense 7 in COD9 is matched to two senses (7 and 8) in CCD4. There is one sense that looks closely related but is not a direct match: Sense 6 in COD9 and Sense 5 in CCD4. The two dictionaries have not carved up the meaning of *length* in the same way, and there are senses in each that do not have counterparts in the other (the gaps in Table 8.1).

Are there any criteria, or rules of thumb, that lexicographers use in deciding what senses to recognise in analysing the meaning of a lexeme? Context, clearly, plays a part, but context can be analysed more or less finely. For example, the first four senses of the noun *interest* in CED4 are given the following definitions:

1 the sense of curiosity about or concern with something or someone
2 the power of stimulating such a sense
3 the quality of such stimulation
4 something in which one is interested; a hobby or pursuit.

Table 8.1

COD9	CCD4	CCD4	COD9
1	1	1	1
2	4	2	
3	3	3	3
4	10	4	2
5		5	
6		6	
7	7, 8	7	7
8		8	7
9	9	9	9
10		10	4
11		11	
12			

LDEL2 encapsulates these meanings under one numbered sense with two parts:

> **5a** readiness to be concerned with, moved by, or have one's attention attracted by something; curiosity **5b** the quality in a thing that arouses interest . . . *also* something one finds interesting

Clearly, in the end, it comes down to the lexicographer exercising their informed judgement in the face of the evidence that they have to work with.

There are, however, two factors that a lexicographer can take into account when distinguishing the senses of words: grammar, and collocation (Clear 1996). It is possible that the use of *length* 'usually plural' as against 'often plural' led the CCD4 lexicographer to distinguish senses 7 and 8 (see above). The fact that *reply* can be used intransitively, as against transitively with a clause as object, distinguishes the first two senses in CED4:

> **1** to make an answer (to) in words or writing or by an action; respond: *he replied with an unexpected move.* **2** (*tr; takes a clause as object*) to say (something) in answer: *he replied that he didn't want to come.*

Some senses have a specialised or restricted use, and are labelled as such, e.g. the Gymnastics, Mining, Nautical, Chess and Informal uses of *horse* in the CED4 entry given earlier. Some senses enter into particular collocations; as indicated by the words in brackets in these senses for *isometric* from CED4:

> (of a crystal or system of crystallization) having three mutually perpendicular equal axes

> (of a method of projecting a drawing in three dimensions) having the three axes equally inclined and all lines drawn to scale.

However, collocation has not been exploited as much as it could be by lexico-graphers for this purpose (Clear 1996).

   Having decided what senses to recognise for a polysemous lexeme, the lexi-cographer must then decide how to order them in the dictionary entry. In an historical dictionary – OED or SOED – the order is given: from earliest sense to latest sense, according to the citational evidence. However, even in historical dictionaries, things are not always as simple: some words have a complicated 'sense history', with more than one 'branch' (see Berg 1993 for a description of the entry structure in OED2). In general-purpose dictionaries, the practice varies. *Chambers* follows the historical order:

> There are at least two possible ways of ordering . . . definitions. One way is to give the most modern meaning first and the oldest last. The other is the way selected for this dictionary, historical order. In this method the original or oldest meaning of the word is given first and the most modern or up-to-date last. Both methods are equally easy to use but historical order is per-haps more logical since it shows at a glance the historical development of the word, each entry providing a potted history of the word.
>
> (p. vi)

This is a matter of opinion, and whether anyone would consult a general-purpose dictionary for a 'potted history' of a word is debatable. The alternative argument would focus on likely user needs, which would privilege the more modern senses. In fact, dictionaries that follow the 'modern meaning first' prin-ciple are usually rather more subtle in their arrangement of senses, e.g. CED4:

> As a general rule, where a headword has more than one sense, the first sense given is the one most common in current usage. Where the editors con-sider that a current sense is the 'core meaning' in that it illuminates the meaning of other senses, the core meaning may be placed first. Subsequent senses are arranged so as to give a coherent account of the meaning of a headword . . . closely related senses are grouped together; technical senses usually follow general senses; archaic and obsolete senses follow technical senses; idioms and fixed phrases are usually placed last.
>
> (p. xxi)

LDEL2 attempts a synthesis of the historical and contemporary approaches:

> Meanings are ordered according to a system which aims both to show the main historical development of the word and to give a coherent overview of the relationship between its meanings. Meanings that are current through-out the English-speaking world are shown first; they appear in the order in which they are first recorded in English, except that closely related senses may be grouped together regardless of strict historical order. They are fol-lowed by words [sic – presumably for 'meanings'] whose usage is restricted,

such as those current only in informal use or in American English. Senses which have become archaic or obsolete are shown last.

(p. xvi)

Compare the order of senses in the entries for the noun *mate* from CED4 and LDEL2:

> **mate 1** the sexual partner of an animal. **2** a marriage partner. **3a** *Informal, chiefly Brit., Austral., and N.Z.* a friend, usually of the same sex: often used between males in direct address. **3b** (*in combination*) an associate, colleague, fellow sharer, etc.: *a classmate, a flatmate*. **4** one of a pair of matching items. **5** *Nautical*. **5a** short for **first mate**. **5b** any officer below the master on a commercial ship. **5c** a warrant officer's assistant on a ship. **6** (in some trades) an assistant: *a plumber's mate*. **7** *Archaic*. a suitable associate.
>
> (CED4)

> **mate 1a** an associate, companion – often in combination <*flatmate*> <*play-mate*> **1b** an assistant to a more skilled workman <*plumber's* ~> **1c** *chiefly Br & Austr* a friend, chum – used esp as a familiar form of address between men **2** an officer on a merchant ship ranking below the captain **3** either member of a breeding pair of animals <*a sparrow and his* ~> **3c** either of two matched objects <*a* ~ *to this glove*> **4** *archaic* a match, peer
>
> (LDEL2)

Mate entered the language during the Middle English period, with the general 'companion' meaning. The LDEL2 entry reflects the later (sixteenth-century) addition of the 'sexual partner' meaning, though this comes first in CED4 because it is considered the more common and central meaning in modern English.

8.3 Definitions

Once identified, each sense needs a definition. The definition is a characterisa-tion of the meaning of the (sense of the) lexeme; it is not an exhaustive expla-nation of the possible referents (Zgusta 1971: 252ff.). Like other linguistic statements, definitions in monolingual dictionaries consist of 'language turned back on itself', using the same language to describe as is being described. Much of the art of lexicography (compare the title of Landau 1989, 2001) consists in finding apt wording for constructing telling definitions. A number of general principles can be identified:

- a word should be defined in terms simpler than itself (Zgusta 1971: 257), which is not always possible with the 'simple' words
- circularity of definition should be avoided, i.e. defining two or more lexemes in terms of each other (Svensén 1993: 126)

- a definition should be substitutable for the item being defined; so the head of the definition phrase should belong to the same word class as the defined lexeme (Zgusta 1971: 258; Svensén 1993: 127)
- different forms of definition are appropriate to different types of word (Zgusta 1971: 258).

The most common form of definition is the 'endocentric phrase' (Zgusta 1971: 258), the 'completely analytical one-phrase definition' (Preface to W3), which consists of 'stating the superordinate concept next to the definiendum (*genus proximum*) together with at least one distinctive feature typical of the definiendum (*differentia specifica*)' (Svensén 1993: 122). A good example of such a definition is that given for the first sense of *horse* in NODE, cited earlier:

> a solid-hoofed plant-eating domesticated mammal with a flowing mane and tail, used for riding, racing, and to carry and pull loads.

The 'definiendum' (*horse*) is related to its 'genus' (*mammal*), i.e. its 'superordinate concept', and given a number of 'differentiae' (*solid-hoofed, plant-eating, domest-icated, with a flowing mane and tail, used for riding*, etc.), which are 'typical features' serving to distinguish this mammal from other mammals.

The 'genus + differentiae' style of definition, as it is sometimes called, is used for a great many words from most of the word classes, with 'differentiae' appro-priate to whether the meaning is concrete or abstract, referring to a thing, event, quality, and so on. Here are some further examples from a range of types of word, taken from a number of dictionaries (the 'genus' is in each case in italics):

> **beat** (verb) to *strike* with or as if with a series of violent blows [CED4]
>
> **clean** (adjective) *free* from dirt, stain, or whatever defiles [Chambers]
>
> **glamour** (noun) a romantic, exciting, and often illusory *attractiveness* [LDEL2]
>
> **humble** (adjective) *of* low social or political *rank* [COD9]
>
> **somewhat** (adverb) *to a* moderate *extent* or *by a* moderate *amount* [NODE]
>
> **see** (verb) *perceive* with the eyes [COD10]
>
> **variety** (noun) the *quality* or *condition* of being diversified or various [CED4]

A second major type of definition consists of a synonym, a collection of synonyms, or a synonymous phrase. Many, especially abstract, words are not easily defined analytically by the 'genus + differentiae' style; and lexicographers resort to the use of synonyms. It is this type of definition that is most likely to create circu-larity, where a set of synonyms is used to define each other. Smaller dictionaries, where space is more limited, use synonymy as a defining method more exten-sively. Compare these entries from the *Collins Pocket English Dictionary* (2000):

miserable **1** very unhappy, wretched. **2** causing misery. **3** squalid. **4** mean

unhappy **1** sad or depressed. **2** unfortunate or wretched

wretched **1** miserable or unhappy. **2** worthless

The larger *Collins Concise* (1999) is already an improvement; although it still relies largely on synonymy for defining, its more extensive treatment creates less circularity:

miserable **1** unhappy or depressed; wretched. **2** causing misery, discomfort, etc. **3** contemptible. **4** sordid or squalid. **5** mean; stingy.

unhappy **1** not joyful; sad or depressed. **2** unfortunate or wretched. **3** tactless or inappropriate.

wretched **1** in poor or pitiful circumstances. **2** characterised by or causing misery. **3** despicable; base. **4** poor, inferior, or paltry.

Interestingly, the parent, desk-size CED4 adds almost nothing to the definitions of the *Concise* for these words.

A third style of definition specifies what is 'typical' of the referent. This style is normally used in combination with one of the others, usually the analytical style, and is introduced by the adverb *typically*. Here are some examples from COD10:

day of rest a day set aside from normal activity, typically Sunday on religious grounds

gingham lightweight plain-woven cotton cloth, typically checked

measles an infectious viral disease causing fever and a red rash, typically occurring in childhood

scramble move or make one's way quickly and awkwardly, typically by using one's hands as well as one's feet

ululate howl or wail, typically to express grief

The last example adds a typifying definition to a synonym one, while the others add it to an analytical definition.

A fourth type of definition explains the 'use' to which a word or sense of word is put, usually in the grammar of the language. This type is typically employed for defining 'grammatical' or 'function' words (determiners, pronouns, conjunctions, prepositions, auxiliary verbs – see Chapter 1), especially where these have no reference outside of language. Here are some examples from COD10:

and (conjunction) used to connect words of the same part of speech, clauses, or sentences

> **do** (auxiliary verb) used before a verb in questions and negative statements
>
> **ever** (adverb) used for emphasis in questions expressing astonishment or outrage
>
> **herself** (pronoun) used as the object of a verb or preposition to refer to a female person or animal previously mentioned as the subject of the clause
>
> **that** (pronoun/determiner) used to identify a specific person or thing observed or heard by the speaker
>
> **us** (pronoun) used by a speaker to refer to himself or herself and one or more others as the object of a verb or preposition

All these definitions are introduced by *used*, and they are mostly framed in terms of how the word operates in the grammatical structure of the language. In the case of the adverb *ever*, though, the 'use' relates to its function in discourse, i.e. for emphasis.

   Definitions aim to describe the reference relations (Chapter 2) of a lexeme, specifically their denotations. They do not usually comment on the connotative or associative meaning of a lexeme, though this may occasionally find mention, as in the definitions of *champagne* and *youth* in NODE:

> **champagne** a white sparkling wine from Champagne, regarded as a symbol of luxury and associated with celebration
>
> **youth** the state or quality of being young, especially as associated with vigour, freshness, or immaturity.

More often, connotation is indicated by appropriate labelling (see Chapter 9), as for the following words in COD9:

> **crony** (often *derog[atory]*) a close friend or companion
>
> **ethnic cleansing** (*euphem[istic]*) the mass expulsion or extermination of people from opposing ethnic or religious groups within a certain area
>
> **ladyship** (*iron[ical]*) a form of reference or address to a woman thought to be giving herself airs
>
> **missive** (*joc[ular]*) a letter, esp. a long and serious one
>
> **wrinkly** (*slang offens[ive]*) an old or middle-aged person.

8.4 Sense relations

In Chapter 2, we identified the 'sense relations' that may hold between lexemes within the vocabulary as: synonymy, antonymy, hyponymy, and meronymy. In this section, we shall explore how these meaning relations are represented in dictionaries. We have noted already (8.3) that (loose) synonymy is used as a defining style for some words. A somewhat tighter synonymy is sometimes indicated by the phrase 'also called', when an alternative term is given for the headword under consideration. For example, both CED4 and NODE give 'also called: **viper**' under *adder*, and 'also called: **hydrophobia**' under *rabies*. But there is no consistency of treatment. For example, in CED4 *hookah* is given the following alternatives: *hubble-bubble, kalian, narghile, water pipe*; and their definitions all contain the phrase 'another name for **hookah**'. NODE, however, does not give these alternatives in its entry for *hookah*, though *hubble-bubble* is defined simply as 'a hookah', *narghile* has 'a hookah' included in its definition, and *water pipe* has a similar definition to that for *hookah* but without making the connection. *Kalian* is not entered in NODE. CED4 is perhaps particularly commendable for making these synonym connections, as the following examples from a single column in the dictionary show:

love apple an archaic name for **tomato**

lovebird another name for **budgerigar**

love feast Also called: **agape**

love-in-a-mist See also **fennelflower**

love-in-idleness another name for the **wild pansy**

love knot Also called: **lover's knot**

lovemaking an archaic word for **courtship**

lovey *Brit. informal.* another word for **love** (sense 11).

Another way of treating synonyms in dictionaries is to draw together near-synonyms under one of the items and discuss them. This procedure is used by LDEL2 and by ECED. The latter has the following account of 'generous' words:

SYNONYMS *generous, magnanimous, munificent, bountiful, liberal*

CORE MEANING: giving readily to others

generous willing to give money, help, or time freely; **magnanimous** very generous, kind, or forgiving; **munificent** very generous, especially on a grand scale; **bountiful** (*literary*) generous, particularly to less fortunate people; **liberal** free with money, time, or other assets.

The sense relation of antonymy is sometimes used in definitions, when the opposite of the (sense of the) lexeme being defined is preceded by *not*, e.g. (from COD9)

artificial not real

conventional not spontaneous or sincere or original

long-standing not recent

vacant not filled or occupied

Sometimes, an antonym may be indicated more explicitly. NODE, for example, introduces antonyms with the phrase 'the opposite of', but this is for a limited number of mostly quite technical terms, e.g. anode – cathode, holism – atomism, sinistral – dextral, zenith – nadir. CED4 uses the phrase 'compare' to fulfil a similar function, but again with a small number of fairly technical terms. Antonymy is not a well-represented sense relation in the text of dictionaries.

Hyponymy is better represented, largely because the analytical definition (8.3) is formed using the hyponymy relation. The 'genus' term is, or should be, the superordinate of the lexeme being defined, the 'definiendum'. Consider the following definition from CED4:

serge   a twill-weave woollen or worsted fabric used for clothing

Serge is a hyponym of *fabric*, the 'genus' term in this definition, and it can be related as a co-hyponym to other words that have *fabric* as their 'genus', such as *corduroy*, *lace*, *velvet*, *worsted* and so on. What you cannot find out from a conventional dictionary is the set of all the co-hyponyms of a particular superordinate term (see Chapter 12). If a dictionary is consistent, though, co-hyponyms should be related to the same genus term. But dictionaries are not noted for their consistency in such matters. For example, NODE relates *fork* and *spoon* to the genus term *implement*, but *knife* is related to *instrument*. NODE defines *handwritten* as 'written with a pen, pencil, or other hand-held implement', but *pen* and *pencil* both have *instrument* as their genus term.

Meronymy, the 'part-of' relation, is a less well recognised as well as a less pervasive sense relation. It is, though, used in the definitions of some lexemes, e.g. (from COD10):

algebra   the part of mathematics in which . . .

coast   the part of the land adjoining or near the sea

loin   the part of the body on both sides of the spine between the lowest ribs and the hip bones

vamp   the upper front part of a boot or shoe

Again, we should not look for consistency in conventional dictionaries. While *upper* is defined in COD10 as 'the part of a boot or shoe above the sole', *sole* has a quite different type of definition: 'the section forming the underside of a piece of footwear'.

The dictionary that has most consistently treated sense relations is the learners' dictionary COBUILD1, where synonyms, antonyms and superordinate terms are indicated in the dictionary's 'extra column' (further in Chapter 11).

8.5 Phraseology

The other major component of meaning that we identified in Chapter 2 was collocation, the regular or particular company that a word keeps. We noted in 8.2 that collocation may offer a method for distinguishing the senses of a lexeme (cf. Clear 1996). Collocation is, in the end, a matter of statistical frequency of co-occurrence, and lexicologists have not yet collected full data on the collocational behaviour of words. Where dictionaries note collocation, it is in cases either of a known restriction to the range of a word or where a collocation appears in a particular context. The possible collocates or the restrictions are usually contained within brackets before the definition and introduced by 'of' or 'especially of'. Here are some examples from NODE:

> **bijou** (especially of a house or flat) small and elegant
>
> **bifacial** *Botany* (of a leaf) having upper and lower surfaces that are structurally different. *Archaeology* (of a flint or other artefact) worked on both surfaces
>
> **convoluted** (especially of an argument, story, or sentence) extremely complex and difficult to follow
>
> **meander** (of a river or road) follow a winding course. (of a person) wander at random. (of a speaker or text) proceed aimlessly or with little purpose
>
> **teem** (of water, especially rain) pour down; fall heavily
>
> **terrigenous** *Geology* (of a marine deposit) made of material eroded from the land.

Most of the lexemes for which collocates are indicated belong to the adjective word class: the collocates specify the nouns or types of noun they typically accompany. Some verbs (e.g. *meander*, *teem*) may have their typical Subject or Object noun collocates specified. Collocation is the subject of considerable research currently, especially following the development of extensive computer corpora that promise to yield interesting and reliable data on this topic. Lexicographers of learners' dictionaries have begun to include some of this information in their works, since it is an area of particular interest and difficulty for learners of English as a second or foreign language (see Chapter 11).

Another area of interest to learners is that of idioms and other fixed expressions, especially where the meaning of the expression cannot be deduced from the meanings of its individual words. Some dictionaries, as we saw in 8.1, list binomials, and perhaps trinomials, as headwords. COD9, for example, has some

120 such items as headwords, e.g. *bells and whistles, flotsam and jetsam, sweet and sour, waifs and strays*. More difficult to locate are idioms proper, which are normally entered under one of the 'main' words of the idiom. Many dictionaries are not very explicit about the rules for finding an idiom, though the rule of thumb is that it will be under the first 'main' word. For example, *a storm in a teacup* will be under *storm*, *shoot one's mouth off* will be under *shoot*, but *take a bull by the horns* will be under *bull*, because *take* does not count as a 'main' word. Sometimes the rules are more complicated; LDEL2, for example, follows an older tradition:

> An idiom is entered at the first noun it contains; hence **on the ball** appears at **ball** and **in spite of** at **spite**. If it contains no noun, it is entered at the first adjective; hence **give as good as one gets** is shown at **good**. If it contains no adjective, it is entered under the first adverb; if no adverb, under the first verb; if no verb, under the first word. In any case, cross-references to the entry where the idiom appears are given at the entries for other major words in it: **hand** ... – see also **take the** LAW **into one's own hands**. The entry where the idiom appears is shown in SMALL CAPITAL letters.
>
> (p. xiv)

Not all dictionaries are as good about cross-referencing, and locating an idiom can turn into something of a hunt at times, especially as they are usually nested towards the end of an entry. Some of the more modern layouts do make the hunt easier, e.g. in COD10, which has a separate paragraph marked 'PHRASES' where this is relevant in an entry. Under *shoot*, for example, the following phrases are listed:

> shoot the breeze (or the bull), shoot one's cuffs, shoot oneself in the foot, shoot a line, shoot one's mouth off, the whole shooting match, shoot through.

Each phrase is then given a definition, and any appropriate restrictive label.

Summarising, the treatment of meaning in dictionaries goes beyond simply the definition; it includes the distinction of homographs, the identification of senses and their ordering, the contribution of the sense relations, the incorporation of collocational information, and the consideration of idioms and other phrasal expressions.

8.6 Further reading

Sidney Landau deals with 'definition' in Chapter 4 of *Dictionaries: The Art and Craft of Lexicography* (1989), as does Bo Svensén in Chapter 10 of his *Practical Lexicography* (1993). The section on defining styles owes something to Barbara Kipfer's treatment in Chapter 6 of *Workbook on Lexicography* (1984), where she also discusses the ordering of senses.

9   Beyond definition

In the previous chapter we discussed the treatment of what is often considered the main function of dictionaries: the description of word meaning. In this chapter, we investigate some of the other information about words that dictionaries may contain, some of the 'facts about words' that we outlined in Chapter 2. While we shall look at topics such as spelling, pronunciation, inflections, word classes, and usage, we shall leave etymology until the next chapter.

9.1 Spelling

As we have noted before, dictionaries cannot help but give information about spelling, since as alphabetically organised word books they are founded on the written form of words. Consulting the dictionary to check the spelling of words we also found to be one of the major occasions of their use (Chapter 7). While headwords, or nested derivatives, supply information about the usual spellings of words, there is additional information, about variations in spelling, that dictionaries also give. The variation can be of various kinds.

Some words simply have alternative spellings, where the choice of one rather than the other is purely a matter of personal preference. Both spellings are equally acceptable. Here are some examples (from COD9):

> absorption – absorbtion, baptistery – baptistry, caddie – caddy, diffuser – diffusor, extrovert – extravert, filigree – filagree, gizmo – gismo, horsy – horsey, judgement – judgment, movable – moveable, neurone – neuron, pendent – pendant, regime – régime, smidgen – smidgeon – smidgin, tranquillity – tranquility, yogurt – yoghurt.

A surprisingly large number of words have alternative spellings, and from this list we can observe some possible patterns: final -ie or -y, suffix -er or -or, z or s, possible loss of e after dg or v plus suffix, loss of accent from vowels of words borrowed from French, and so on.

Many British dictionaries take account of the differences between British and American spelling. CED4, for example, enters the American spelling of words like *center* and *pediatrics* at the appropriate place in the headword list, and then gives a cross-reference to the British spelling. For words like *savior* and *theater*, which would occur close to the British spelling, the American alternative is simply given under the British spelling. There are two further spelling variations that are often seen as differences between British and American English: the *ae – e* alternation in *aesthetics – esthetics*, and the *s – z* alternation in *-ise/-ize* (e.g. *marginalise/-ize*). The *-ise/-ize* alternation is no longer regarded as a British/American difference; British dictionaries merely note these as alternative spellings. The *ae – e* alternation is not yet fully accepted in British spelling. In most dictionaries, with the exception of *Chambers*, *encyclopedia* is entered as the main spelling, with *encyclopaedia* as the alternative; similarly with *medieval* and *mediaeval*. However, *archaeology* is the main spelling (or sole spelling – *Chambers*, *LDEL*); *archeology* is given as an alternative in CED4, and is marked as American in NODE and other Oxford dictionaries. And in the case of *aesthetics*, *paediatrics*, etc. the alternative is usually marked as American.

One other area where dictionaries pay attention to spelling is where alterations occur as a consequence of adding an inflectional suffix, such as *cry – cried*, *big – bigger*. We will consider this in 9.3, where we discuss dictionary information about inflections.

9.2 Pronunciation

How a word is pronounced is one of its idiosyncractic facts; it is the phonological counterpart of spelling (orthography), its shape in the medium of sound as against its shape in the medium of writing. We would expect, therefore, that dictionaries would indicate at least the sounds that constitute the pronunciation of the word, and for words of more than one syllable the stress pattern. There are two issues in relation to pronunciation in dictionaries: first, how pronunciation is represented in the written medium that the dictionary uses, i.e. the transcription system; and second, the model that is used for pronunciation, and how much variation is indicated.

In most modern British dictionaries, the transcription system used to represent pronunciation is the International Phonetic Alphabet (IPA), developed in the late nineteenth century as a system, based on the Roman alphabet, that could be used for transcribing the speech of any language, and as an aid in learning the pronunciation of a foreign language. The alternative transcription to the IPA is a 'respelling' system. When James Murray was devising a transcription system for the OED in the mid-nineteenth century, the IPA had not yet been invented, and he developed a respelling system. However, when the second edition of the OED was put together, the only wholesale revision was to replace Murray's respellings with IPA transcriptions. Other Oxford dictionaries followed suit: COD7 (1982) had respelling, COD8 (1990) changed to the IPA. LDEL uses respelling; so does ECED and *Chambers*, but *Chambers 21st Century Dictionary* uses IPA, as do the Collins dictionaries. American dictionaries, however, usually use a respelling system.

Both transcription systems have the aim of a one-to-one correspondence between sound and symbol, and unique representation of each sound. In the

Table 9.1

	Chambers	LDEL2	CED4	COD9
binary	bī'nər-i	'bienəri	'baɪnərɪ	'bʌɪnərɪ
creation	krē-a'-shən	kri'aysh(ə)n	krɪː'eɪʃən	kriː'eɪʃ(ə)n
genuflect	jen'ū–flekt	'jenyoo,flekt	'ʤɛnjʊ,flɛkt	'ʤɛnjʊflɛkt
orphan	ör'fən	'awf(ə)n	'ɔːfən	'ɔːf(ə)n
Thursday	thûrz'di	'thuhzdi	'θəːzdɪ	'θəːzdɪ

case of the IPA, because it uses symbols additional to those in the Roman alphabet, it mostly uses a single symbol to represent each sound. A respelling system, restricting itself to the symbols of the Roman alphabet, perhaps with the addition of the 'schwa' symbol /ə/, needs to use digraphs and even trigraphs in order to achieve a unique one-to-one correspondence. Table 9.1 shows some examples of transcription from a variety of dictionaries.

The argument used in favour of respelling is that it uses mostly familiar symbols (Paikeday 1993), whereas the IPA employs a considerable number of symbols that are not contained in the Roman alphabet. On the other hand, a respelling system either has to use diacritics, as in the *Chambers* version, or a large number of digraphs, as in the LDEL system (e.g. oo, aw, uh). Arguably, any transcription system will constitute a learning task for the user who needs to consult it, or at least the ability to interpret the table where the transcription is described and illustrated. Some dictionaries provide reminders of the symbols at the bottom of each page, e.g. COD9, with vowels on one double-page and consonants on the next. Some CD-ROM versions of dictionaries provide a recorded pronunciation of each transcription contained in the dictionary (e.g. COD9).

Pronunciation is not information that native speakers regularly consult a dictionary for. If they do, it is likely to be in order to check the pronunciation of a word that they have met only in writing. Perhaps in recognition of this, NODE and subsequently COD10 do not give a transcription of the pronunciation of 'ordinary, everyday words', rather:

> In the *New Oxford Dictionary of English*, the principle followed is that pronunciations are given where they are likely to cause problems for the native speaker of English, in particular for foreign words, foreign names, scientific and other specialist terms, rare words, words with unusual stress patterns, and words where there are alternative pronunciations or where there is a dispute about the standard pronunciation.
>
> (Introduction, p. xvii)

What counts as an ordinary word must be a matter of judgement. By way of comparison, here are lists of words from one page of COD10 distinguishing those that have been provided with a transcription and those that have not:

With transcription: traipse, trait, trajectory, Trakehner, Traminer, trammel, tramontana, tramontane, trampoline, trance, tranche, trans-

Without transcription: training college, training shoe, train mile, train oil, train shed, trainspotter, traitor, tra la, tram, tramlines, tramp, trample, tram road, tram silk, tramway, trank, tranny, tranquil, tranquillize, transaction, transactional analysis.

The exclusion of pronunciation information for many words in NODE and COD10 represents a move, albeit small, away from subservience to the 'recording' function of general-purpose dictionaries towards consideration of what the user might or might not need.

The second issue concerns the model of pronunciation that is offered, and the degree of variation that is recorded. COD9 says that its IPA transcriptions are 'based on the pronunciation associated especially with southern England (sometimes called "Received Pronunciation")'. In CED4, the 'pronunciations of words . . . represent those that are common in educated speech'. In LDEL2,

> the pronunciation represented . . . is what may be called a 'standard' or 'neutral' British–English accent: the type of speech characteristic of those people often described as having 'no accent', or, more accurately, having an accent that betrays little or nothing of the region to which the speaker belongs.

NODE represents 'the standard accent of English as spoken in the south of England (sometimes called Received Pronunciation or RP)'. Some of these dictionaries acknowledge the existence of other accents, both in other English-speaking countries and regionally within Britain, but argue that it is impossible to do them all justice. *Chambers*, which describes some of the ways in which pronunciation differs in other national varieties of English, claims that its respelling system of transcription 'allows for more than one interpretation so that each user of the dictionary may choose a pronunciation in keeping with his speech'.

However it is described, it is the 'educated' accent of southern England, with its /bʌt/ rather than /bʊt/ pronunciation of *but*, and /grɑːs/ rather than /græs/ for *grass*, that is the model represented in British dictionaries. At one time, it was argued that this accent was the one most widely understood, the one used predominantly in public discourse, the one taught to foreign learners of English, and so on. This is presumably the sense in which it might be considered a 'standard accent' (NODE), though NODE acknowledges that it is not a static accent:

> The transcriptions reflect pronunciation as it actually is in modern English, unlike some longer-established systems, which reflect the standard pronunciation of broadcasters and public schools in the 1930s.

(p. xvii)

The status of this accent as the prestige accent for British English has been constantly challenged by phoneticians of English, and there is a much greater diversity of accents heard now in public life. It is perhaps becoming an anachronism to continue to record this accent in modern dictionaries, but the debate on which pronunciation should be recorded has hardly begun.

Dictionaries do record some variation in pronunciation. Learners' dictionaries, which have a worldwide market, now routinely include American pronunciation as well as British (Chapter 11). Native speaker dictionaries, on the other hand, record variation within the chosen accent, for example the /i:k../ and /ɛk../ beginnings to *economics*. Here are some further examples, drawn from COD9:

- coastguard /ˈkəʊs(t)gɑːd/
- distribute /dɪˈstrɪbjuːt/ – /ˈdɪstrɪbjuːt/
- February /ˈfebrʊəri/ – /ˈfebjʊəri/
- oceanic /əʊʃɪˈanɪk/ – /əʊsɪˈanɪk/
- sedentary /ˈsɛd(ə)nt(ə)ri/
- vin rosé /van rəʊˈzeɪ/ – /vɛ̃roze/

They show a number of types of variation in pronunciation, even in the chosen accent: omission of sounds in more rapid or 'less careful' enunciation (the sounds in brackets in *coastguard* and *sedentary*); variation in stress placement, as in *distribute*; one or more alternative sounds, as in *February* and *oceanic*; and for loanwords, the anglicised and the original, 'foreign', pronunciation, as for *vin rosé*.

9.3 Inflection

For most words that can be inflected in English – nouns, verbs, adjectives (see Chapter 1) – the inflection follows from the general rules of morphology, is not idiosyncratic to the individual lexeme, and is therefore not appropriate to the lexical information contained in dictionaries. However, there are some exceptions to this generalisation, which dictionaries do record. A small number of adjectives, some nouns, and a larger number of verbs inflect 'irregularly', not according to the general pattern, and these are given for each lexeme concerned, e.g.

- *adjective* bad – worse – worst
- *noun* foot – feet, mouse – mice, ox – oxen, sheep – sheep
- *verb* bring – brought – brought, feel – felt – felt, give – gave – given, hit – hit – hit, see – saw – seen, wear – wore – worn, etc.

These basic irregularities do not exhaust the possible idiosyncracies, and dictionaries tend to give any inflection that is likely to cause a difficulty for writers, including predictable spelling variations.

For the plural inflection of nouns, the following may well be noted:

- loanwords that retain their original, 'foreign' plural, e.g. *cactus – cacti, criterion – criteria, kibbutz – kibbutzim, phylum – phyla, vertex – vertices*. More and more of these plurals are becoming regularised, including *cactuses* and *vertexes*.
- nouns that end in *-o* or *-i*, where there is often confusion about whether the inflection is *-s* or *-es*, e.g. *curio-s, domino-es, etui-s, halo-es* or *-s, piccallili-es* or *-s*.
- nouns ending in *-y*, which may change the *y* to *i* and add *-es*, or may simply add *-s*, e.g. *abbey-s, academy – academies, monkey -s, mystery – mysteries, odyssey-s, symmetry – symmetries*.
- nouns that change either the spelling or pronunciation of their final sound (voicing of /θ/, /f/ or /s/) when the plural suffix is added, e.g. *bath-s, hoof – hooves, house-s, mouth-s, shelf – shelves, truth-s, wolf – wolves*.

For the inflections of verbs, the following may well be noted:

- where the final consonant of the root is doubled in spelling with the addition of a suffix: *flip – flipping – flipped, lag – lagging – lagged, prod – prodding – prodded, refer – referring – referred, shovel – shovelling – shovelled, sin – sinning – sinned*.
- where the final consonant might be expected to double, but does not, e.g. *benefit – benefiting – benefited, galop – galoping – galoped, gossip – gossiping – gossiped, market – marketing – marketed, pilgrim – pilgriming – pilgrimed*.
- where the final consonant is *-c* and a *k* is added before the inflectional suffix, e.g. *bivouac – bivouacking – bivouacked, magic – magicking – magicked, picnic – picnicking – picnicked*.
- where the final consonant is *-y*, which may change to *i* before an inflectional suffix, e.g. *cry – cries – cried* (but *crying*), *shy – shies – shied, supply – supplies – supplied, weary – wearies – wearied*.

For adjective inflections, the following usually apply:

- the consonant doubling rule, as for verbs, e.g. *big – bigger – biggest, hip – hipper – hippest, sad – sadder – saddest*.
- the *y* to *i* rule, as for verbs, e.g. *dry – drier – driest, fluffy – fluffier – fluffiest, lively – livelier – liveliest, rosy – rosier – rosiest, wacky – wackier – wackiest* (but not *sly -er, -est*).

Additionally, two-syllable adjectives that form their comparative and superlative by means of inflectional suffixes, rather than the periphrastic *more/most* construction, may be marked as such in the dictionary (e.g. NODE), such as *common -er/-est, narrow -er/-est, thirsty -er/-est*. However, while NODE notes the

-er/-est suffixes for *narrow* – and *sallow* – it does not indicate them for *mellow* or *shallow*.

One other point is worth mentioning here, though strictly speaking it belongs to derivational morphology rather than to inflectional. English has a number of nouns that survive from Old English which have a related adjective that has been borrowed into English usually from Latin, e.g. *church* – *ecclesiastical*. Some dictionaries usefully indicate these connections, e.g. CED4. Further examples are: *lung* – *pneumonic, pulmonary, pulmonic; mind* – *mental, noetic, phrenic; wall* – *mural*.

9.4 Word class

It is one of the traditions of lexicography to identify the word class(es) or part(s) of speech that each lexeme in a dictionary belongs to. The traditional terms, usually abbreviated, are: noun (n), verb (v, vb), adjective (adj), adverb (adv), pronoun (pron), preposition (prep), conjunction (conj), and interjection (interj). Under the influence of modern descriptive linguistics the adjective class in some dictionaries (e.g. CED, NODE) is divided into adjectives proper and 'determiners' (see Chapter 1). CED in addition recognises a class of 'sentence connectors' (e.g. *however, therefore*) and a class of 'sentence substitutes' (e.g. *no, maybe*), both of which are traditionally assigned to the adverb class. In COD10, the interjection class is renamed 'exclamation' (exclam) and it includes *yes* and *no*.

So far, most dictionaries follow the tradition. Practice begins to vary in the information provided over and above the basic word class label. COD10 provides none. Its predecessor, the COD9, followed another tradition in respect of verbs and marked verbs or senses of verbs as 'transitive' (tr) or 'intransitive' (intr), or indeed 'reflexive' (refl). For example, *kick* is marked 'tr' for the 'strike or propel forcibly with the foot or hoof etc.' sense, 'intr' for the 'strike out with the foot' sense, and 'refl' for the 'kick oneself' sense. COD10 perhaps excludes these terms in recognition of the fact that they are not familiar to most modern dictionary users; its larger parent, NODE, also eschews them, using 'with obj', i.e. 'object', and 'no obj' instead.

Indeed, NODE goes further than most general-purpose native speaker dictionaries in the ways in which it subclassifies words. For nouns, it indicates when a noun is used as a 'mass noun', e.g. *legislation*, which cannot be made plural or be preceded by the indefinite article (*a/an*). It also uses the term 'count noun' for a sense of a mass noun that can be made plural and countable, e.g. *observance* in the sense of 'religious or ceremonial observances'. Otherwise nouns are assumed to be countable. NODE recognises a subclass of 'sentence adverb', with 159 adverbs or senses of adverbs so marked, including *coincidentally, fortunately, paradoxically, regrettably, thankfully*. It also marks a subclass of 'submodifier' adverbs, which are used to modify adjectives and other adverbs, some 277 of them, including *altogether, decidedly, hideously, predictably, simply, utterly*.

The word class label, and any subclassification, represents grammatical information about words, where they can operate in the syntax of sentences, what their combinatorial possibilities are. Some dictionaries provide grammatical information over and above word class labelling, though it is difficult to draw a clear distinction between word (sub-)class information proper and other syntactic labelling. Indeed, NODE in its discussion of these matters in the 'Guide to the Use of the Dictionary' makes no such distinction.

9.5 Other grammatical information

The distinction between 'mass' and 'count' noun, for example, is not simply a word class subdivision; it is also an indication of the determiners that may combine with a noun, e.g. numerals with count nouns, but not with mass nouns. Similarly, the 'transitive'/'intransitive' subclassification of verbs relates to whether, in the specified sense, the verb takes an object or not, and additionally whether the sentence in which the verb occurs can be made passive.

For nouns, NODE also specifies when they can be used 'as modifier', before another noun, with an adjectival function, e.g. *keynote* as in *keynote address* or *shadow* as in *shadow minister of* . . . CED likewise notes such uses of some nouns, but dictionaries may differ in their categorisations. One way of treating such uses of nouns would be to recognise the derivation of an adjective by the word formation process of 'conversion' (see Chapter 2): CED4 marks *key*, as in *a key person*, as 'modifier', while NODE recognises an adjective *key* to cover this usage. The other peculiarity of nouns that dictionaries often mark is when there may be a mismatch between the form of a noun (singular or plural) and its use syntactically. For example, *darts* and *economics* have a plural form but are usually 'treated as sing(ular)'. On the other hand, singular so-called 'collective' nouns, such as *government* or *team* may be 'treated as sing or pl(ural)'. In NODE also, 'in sing' is used to mark (the sense of) a count noun that can only be used in the singular (e.g. *riot* as in *the garden was a riot of colour*) or the sense of a mass noun where an indefinite article may be used (e.g. *wealth* in *a wealth of information*).

For adjectives, NODE specifies three possible syntactic positions that they may be restricted to: before the noun ('attrib(utive)'), after a verb like *be*, *become* or *seem* ('predic(ative)'), and immediately after the noun ('postpositive'). CED4's equivalent terms are: 'prenominal', 'postpositive' and 'immediately postpositive'. Here are some examples:

- attributive *bridal, custom, geriatric, innermost, mere, opening, teenage, zero-sum*
- predicative *aglow* (and many others with prefix *a*-), *catching, disinclined, legion, privy, tantamount, well* (i.e. 'not ill')
- postpositive *aplenty, designate, enough, galore, incarnate, par excellence,* as well as a number of adjectives connected with cooking and heraldry.

The case of verb syntax is more complicated. If a dictionary is to record the peculiarities of each lexical item, then the crude transitive/intransitive distinction does not do justice to the syntactic operation of many verbs. Nor does the threefold distinction of NODE: 'with obj', 'no obj', and 'with adverbial' (e.g. *behave, clamber*). Unlike learners' dictionaries (Chapter 11), native speaker dictionaries generally do not systematically and comprehensively record the possible syntactic patterning of verbs. Few go beyond 'transitive' and 'intransitive'. However, compare the following entries for *argue* from CED4 and NODE:

> **argue 1** (*intr*) to quarrel; wrangle: *they were always arguing until I arrived*. **2** (*intr;* often foll. by *for* or *against*) to present supporting or opposing reasons or cases in a dispute; reason. **3** (*tr; may take a clause as object*) to try to prove by presenting reasons; maintain. **4** (*tr; often passive*) to debate or discuss: *the case was fully argued before agreement was reached*. **5** (*tr*) to persuade: *he argued me into going*. **6** (*tr*) to give evidence of; suggest: *her looks argue despair*.
>
> [CED4]

> **argue 1** (*reporting verb*) give reasons or cite evidence in support of an idea, action, or theory; typically with the aim of persuading others to share one's view: [*with clause*] *sociologists* **argue that** *inequalities in industrial societies are being reduced* | [*with direct speech*] *'It stands to reason,' she argued*.
> • [*with obj.*] (**argue someone into/out of**) persuade someone to do or not to do (something) by giving reasons: *I tried to argue him out of it*.
> **2** [*no obj.*] exchange or express diverging or opposite views, typically in a heated or angry way: *don't* **argue with** *me* | *figurative I wasn't going to* **argue with** *a gun* | [*with obj.*] *she was too tired to* **argue the point**.
>
> [NODE]

These two dictionaries give considerably more syntactic information for verbs, both by way of labels and in examples, than has been customary in general-purpose dictionaries, even of desk size, until recently. NODE justifies this approach both by pointing to the role of grammar in distinguishing the meanings or senses of lexemes and with the following argument:

> the aim is to present information in such a way that it helps to explain the structure of the language itself, not just the meanings of the individual senses. For this reason, special attention has been paid to the grammar of each word, and grammatical structures are given explicitly.
>
> (p. xi)

9.6 Usage

All dictionaries have a set of labels to mark words or senses of words that are restricted in some way in the contexts in which they may occur. The contextual restrictions may be geographical (i.e. dialectal), historical (e.g. archaic), stylistic (e.g. informal), according to topic (e.g. Botany), and so on. In this section, we review the types and range of usage labels used in general-purpose dictionaries.

9.6.1 *Dialect*

Dialect labels refer to geographical restriction, and we can take this to include both national varieties and regional dialects within a national variety. Most British dictionaries nowadays claim an international perspective and include words peculiar to the vocabulary of other English-speaking countries, but still largely confined to North America, Australia and New Zealand, and South Africa. The newer Englishes of, say, the Indian subcontinent, or West Africa, or the Caribbean, or Singapore tend to receive lesser attention. However, COD10, for example, contains around fifty words marked 'W. Indian', and a rather larger number labelled 'Indian', e.g.

- West Indian *braata, dotish, fingle, higgler, mamguy, nancy story, spraddle, tafia*
- Indian *babu, charpoy, durzi, haveli, lakh, nullah, sadhu, zamindar.*

NODE claims around 14,000 geographical labels spread through the dictionary, but these are mainly 'regionalisms encountered in standard contexts in the different English-speaking areas of the world' (p. xvi). The largest number, inevitably, belong to the vocabularies of English spoken in North America, for which NODE has three labels: 'N. Amer.' (i.e. North American), 'US' (i.e. United States), and 'Canadian'. The last two are presumably for cases where the restriction is more limited, e.g. in the case of *blue box*:

1. chiefly *US* an electronic device used to access long-distance telephone lines illegally.

2. chiefly *Canadian* a blue plastic box for the collection of recyclable household materials.

A similar labelling is used for words specific to Australian and New Zealand Englishes, where the majority are marked 'Austral./NZ' (e.g. *mullock* 'rubbish, nonsense'), because they are shared by both varieties, and some are marked separately, rather more 'Austral' (e.g. *gunyah* 'bush hut') than 'NZ' (e.g. *kumara*, 'sweet potato'). There is no such confusion about South African English words (e.g. *koppie* 'small hill'), though some are shared with other varieties, e.g. *dingus* (shared with 'N. Amer') 'a thing one cannot or does not wish to name specifically', *dropper* (shared with 'Austral./NZ') 'a light vertical stave in a fence'. Words or senses that are exclusive to the British English variety are also appropriately marked (over 4,000 in NODE), e.g. *fly-past, gobstopper, knacker, linctus, nearside, peckish, scrapyard.*

When it comes to dialects within Britain, NODE/COD10 are less specific. While they have a label 'Scottish' and 'N(orthern) English' (often occurring together for a word), all other dialect words are marked simply as 'dialect', except that one word (*scally*) is noted as N(orth) W(est) English, and a handful are labelled 'black English'. LDEL and, more especially, CED have both a greater

representation of British English dialect words and a more differentiated labelling. CED4 notes in its Guide:

> Regional dialects (*Scot. and northern English dialect, Midland dialect, etc.*) have
> been specified as precisely as possible, even at the risk of overrestriction, in
> order to give the reader an indication of the appropriate regional flavour.
>
> (CED4, p. xxi)

So, *chine*, in the sense of 'a deep fissure in the wall of a cliff', is labelled 'Southern
English dialect'; *flash* meaning 'a pond, esp. as produced as a consequence of
subsidence' is marked 'Yorkshire and Lancashire dialect'; *maungy* '(esp. of a
child) sulky, bad-tempered or peevish' is labelled 'West Yorkshire dialect'; *snicket*
'a passageway between walls or fences' has the label 'Northern English dialect';
and *tump* 'a small mound or clump' is marked 'Western English dialect'.

9.6.2 Formality

A number of words or senses are marked as 'formal' or 'informal', though the
latter label usually greatly outnumbers the former: in COD10, for example, the
'informal' label occurs over seven times more frequently than the 'formal' label.
These terms relate to the formality of the context in which a word is deemed to
be appropriate. They are defined in the LDEL2 Guide as follows:

> The label *informal* is used for words or meanings characteristic of conversa-
> tion and casual writing (e.g. between friends and contemporaries) rather
> than of official or formal speech or writing.
>
> The label *formal* is used for words or meanings which are characteristic
> of writing rather than speech (except for formal speech situations, such as
> a lecture), and particularly of official, academic, literary, or self-important
> writing. In other contexts, such words may seem over-elaborate or
> pompous.
>
> (LDEL2, p. xviii)

The term 'colloquial' is sometimes used instead of 'informal' (e.g. in *Chambers*).
Many dictionaries identify 'slang' as a point further down the formality scale,
but we shall deal with slang under 9.6.3.

Here are some examples of words marked as 'formal' and 'informal' in COD10
(you may need to look them up, if they are new to you):

- formal *abnegate, circumambulate, emolument, gustation, jocose, lucubration, nor-
  mative, pinguid, sapient, theretofore, wheresoever*
- informal *baby boom, beanfeast, dekko, expat, gasbag, haywire, junkie, lashings,
  manky, nitty-gritty, once-over, prang, rozzer, shambolic, townie, vapourware,
  wannabe, yonks, zilch.*

Informal terms, since they are the staple of ordinary conversation, have a tendency to date; and you may consider that some of the terms listed might belong to your parents' or grandparents' speech, but not to yours.

9.6.3 Status

By 'status' we mean the propriety of the use of a word, even in ordinary conversation. Under 'status' we would include the term 'taboo'. A taboo is defined in COD10 as 'a social or religious custom placing prohibition or restriction on a particular thing or person', while COD9 also includes as a second sense 'a prohibition or restriction imposed on certain behaviour, word usage, etc., by social custom'. A taboo word, therefore, is one that you would not use in ordinary conversation, unless you wanted to shock. Such taboo words would include: those connected with sexual and excretory functions, blasphemies, and other 'swear' words. However, there is little left in our society that is taboo, and so modern dictionaries no longer use the label; CED4 is an exception. Not even COD9, which mentions the connection with 'word usage' in its definition of *taboo* uses it as a label, preferring 'coarse slang' instead. In NODE and COD10, this has become 'vulgar slang'; LDEL2 and *Chambers* use simply 'vulgar'.

In the Oxford dictionaries, then, the connection is made with 'slang', the other term under this heading, and glossed by CED4 as follows:

> **Slang** This refers to words or senses that are racy or extremely informal. The appropriate contexts in which slang is used are restricted, for example, to members of a particular social group or those engaged in a particular activity. Slang words are inappropriate informal speech or writing.

'Slang' is, therefore, not just 'very informal'; it implies a restriction beyond simply the formality of the context of use, to defined social groups, and it includes a consideration of appropriacy. It belongs with 'taboo'. Even more so than with informal words, the slang status of words may change over a relatively short period of time and quickly become dated. Not only that, but people's tolerance of slang varies considerably, and it is no surprise that dictionaries differ in their labelling of such words. In fact, COD10 does not use the label 'slang' on its own, unlike COD9, but only in conjunction with a preceding defining adjective, such as 'nautical', 'military', 'theatrical', 'black', as well as 'vulgar'. A number of the words marked as 'slang' in COD9 have become 'informal' in COD10, e.g. *acid* (= LSD), *aggro*, *awesome* (= excellent), *banger* (= sausage, old car), *dough* (= money). However, those that are marked 'coarse slang' in COD9 generally have the label 'vulgar slang' in COD10, e.g. *arse*, *crap*, *piss*, *turd*, not to mention the many words for the male and female genitalia. Incidentally, though, *fart* is labelled 'coarse slang' in COD9, but only 'informal' in COD10.

9.6.4 *Effect*

There is a set of usage labels used in dictionaries that relate to the effect that a word or sense is intended by the speaker or writer to produce in the hearer or reader. Any dictionary usually makes a selection from these labels. One set reflects the attitude of the speaker and includes: 'derogatory' (intending to be disrespectful), 'pejorative' (intending to show contempt), 'appreciative' (intending to show a positive attitude), 'humorous' or 'jocular' (conveying a light-hearted attitude). Closely related is the term 'offensive', which may have intent on the part of the speaker or may be unconscious, but which could be taken by a hearer as offensive, either racially or in some other way. Other kinds of 'effect' label include: 'euphemistic', i.e. using an oblique word to refer to an unpleasant topic; 'literary' and 'poetic', i.e. words that tend to be confined to literary texts or poetry and have a 'literary' effect when they are used elsewhere. Here are some examples:

- derogatory *banana republic, bimbo, cronyism, fat cat, lowbrow, newfangled, psychobabble, slaphead, woodentop* (from COD10)
- jocular *argy-bargy, bounder, doughty, funniosity, industrial-strength, leaderene, osculate, purloin, square-eyed, walkies* (from COD9)
- offensive *bogtrotter* (= Irish person), *cripple* (= disabled person), *mongrel* (= person of mixed parentage), *wog* (= foreigner, especially non-white) (from COD10)
- euphemistic *cloakroom* (for 'toilet'), *ethnic cleansing* (for 'forced mass expulsion of a group of people from an area'), *interfere with* (for 'sexually molest'), *passing* (for 'death') (from COD9)
- literary *apace, bestrew, connubial, fulgent, incarnadine, nevermore, plenteous, slumber, vainglory, wonted* (from COD10).

Even more than with formality and status labels, we would expect effect labels to vary between dictionaries, since they require a greater exercise of judgement on the part of the lexicographer and are more likely to be variously perceived.

9.6.5 *History*

Most dictionaries include labels for words or senses that are either no longer in current use or whose currency is questionable or suspect. The term 'obsolete' refers to words or senses that have definitely ceased to be used. It is, of course, an important term in the OED, but in dictionaries that purport to contain current vocabulary, it is not often used. LDEL2 includes it, however, with the gloss:

> The label *obs* (obsolete) means there is no evidence of use of a word or meaning since 1755 (the date of publication of Samuel Johnson's *A Dictionary of the English Language*). This label is a comment on the word being defined, not on the thing it designates.

> (p. xvii)

For example, *fay*, meaning 'faith' is marked 'obs' in LDEL2; in SOED4 it is marked as 'long archaic, rare'. CED4 also claims to use the 'obsolete' label and notes that 'in specialist or technical fields the label often implies that the term has been superseded' (p. xx); it also uses the label 'old fashioned' (e.g. of the 'illegitimate' sense of *bastard*), which it does not discuss in the 'Guide'.

NODE and COD10 use the labels 'dated', 'archaic', and 'historical' to mark words or senses no longer current; and to these we might add the label 'rare'. These labels are defined as follows:

> 'dated': no longer used by the majority of English speakers, but still encountered, especially among the older generation.

> 'archaic': old-fashioned language, not in ordinary use today, though sometimes used to give a deliberately old-fashioned effect and also encountered in the literature of the past.

> 'historical': still used today, but in reference to some practice or artefact that is no longer part of the modern world.

> 'rare': not in normal use.

The 'historical' label marks not words as such but the things that they denote as being no longer current. It is not clear how 'rare' might differ from 'archaic'. Perhaps some examples (from COD10) will help to distinguish them:

- dated *aeronaut, cobble* (= repair, e.g. shoes), *gamp* (= umbrella), *jerry* (= chamber pot), *necktie, picture palace* (= cinema), *spiffing, wireless* (= radio)
- archaic *asunder, chapman, fandangle, guidepost, mayhap, poltroon, therewithal, vizard*
- historical *approved school, dolly tub, footpad, jongleur, margrave, pocket borough, safety lamp, tumbril, velocipede*
- rare *argute* (= shrewd), *comminatory* (= threatening, vengeful), *lustrate* (= purify, e.g. by sacrifice), *toxophilite* (= archer), *vaticinate* (= foretell future).

9.6.6 Topic or field

Where a word or sense is restricted to a, usually specialised or technical, field of study or activity, dictionaries generally add an appropriate label. Topics may range from the sciences, technologies and medicine, through the professions such as law or business, to sports and leisure pursuits. The label marks a word or sense as belonging to the technical vocabulary of the topic. Here are a few examples to illustrate the point, taken from NODE:

- *handshaking* computing
- *periventricular* anatomy and medicine
- *quiddity* philosophy
- *sopranino* music
- *top edge* cricket

- *weather helm* nautical
- *white hole* astronomy.

9.6.7 Disputed usage

Dictionaries regard one of their functions as being to draw attention to words whose usage is a matter of controversy, and perhaps to offer an opinion for the linguistically insecure. The word or sense that is the subject of dispute may be labelled as such, e.g. 'disp' in COD9, as for *decimate* in the sense of 'kill or remove a large proportion of'. More often, a dictionary will append a 'usage note' to explain the nature of the dispute and proffer advice, e.g. in NODE, for *disinterested*:

> Nowhere are the battle lines more deeply drawn in usage questions than over the difference between **disinterested** and **uninterested**. According to traditional guidelines, **disinterested** should never be used to mean 'not interested' (i.e. it is not a synonym for **uninterested**) but only to mean 'impartial', as in *the judgements of **disinterested** outsiders are likely to be more useful*. Ironically, the earliest recorded sense of **disinterested** is for the disputed sense. Today, the 'incorrect' use of **disinterested** is widespread: around 20 per cent of citations on the British National Corpus for **disinterested** are for this sense.

Besides usage notes, CED4 also has a label 'not standard' to apply to appropriate items, such as *ain't* or *worser*. LDEL2 has the labels 'nonstandard' and 'substandard' and distinguishes them as follows:

> The label *nonstandard* is used for words or meanings that are quite commonly used but considered incorrect by most educated users of the language:
>
> **lay** . . . *vi* . . . **5** *nonstandard* LIE
>
> The label *substandard* is used for words or meanings used by some speakers but not generally considered to be part of standard English:
>
> **learn** . . . *vb* . . . **2** *substandard* to teach. (p. xviii)

This is about as prescriptive as it gets. CED4 labels this sense of *learn* as 'not standard', and it provides a usage note to discuss the differences between *lay* and *lie*. By comparison, we might note that *Chambers* labels *ain't* as 'coll(oquial)' and the disputed usages of *learn* and *lay* as 'illit(erate)'.

9.7 Further reading

For information on how an individual dictionary or edition deals with the topics discussed in this chapter the 'Guide to the Dictionary' is the place to start.

Dick Hudson's article on 'The linguistic foundations for lexical research and dictionary design' in the *International Journal of Lexicography* (1988) surveys the lexical information that dictionaries should take account of. Bo Svensén's *Practical Lexicography* (1993) has chapters on most of the concerns of this chapter.

Sidney Landau has a chapter on usage (Chapter 5) in *Dictionaries: the Art and Craft of Lexicography* (1989, 2001). Juhani Norri has two articles in *IJL* on labelling: 'Regional labels in some British and American dictionaries' (vol. 9, 1996), and 'Labelling of derogatory words in dictionaries' (vol. 13, 2000).

10 Etymology

Since the late seventeenth century general-purpose native speaker dictionaries have included information about the etymology of words (see 4.3). Indeed, common words were included in dictionaries initially merely for the sake of recording their etymologies. The etymology section of a dictionary entry aims to trace the history of a word (see 2.1) to its ultimate source. Where a word has come into existence as the result of a word formation process, e.g. derivation or compounding, then it is not usually given an etymology, unless it is unclear what the elements of the new word are and how they have been combined. In general, therefore, it is base (root) forms that are given etymologies.

The 'Introduction' to NODE likens the tracing of etymologies to archaeology:

> the evidence is often partial or not there at all, and etymologists must make informed decisions using the evidence available, however inadequate it may be. From time to time new evidence becomes available, and the known history of a word may need to be reconsidered.
>
> (p. xiv)

We now consider many of the etymologies proposed by eighteenth-century dictionaries to be rather fanciful, particularly in the light of nineteenth- and twentieth-century scholarship. Most larger dictionaries have an etymology consultant, and the OED continues to add to etymological scholarship by its ongoing research into the histories of words. It is to the OED that most dictionaries look as the primary source for their etymological information.

To understand the discussion in this chapter, it will be useful to keep in mind the outline history of English, as expressed in the basic periods of the language (Jackson and Zé Amvela 2000: 23ff.):

- *Old English* 450 (settlement by Angles, Saxons and Jutes) to 1066 (Norman conquest)
- *Middle English* 1066 to between 1450 (beginning of the Renaissance) and 1500 (including the beginning of printing in Britain – Caxton 1476)
- *Early Modern English* 1500 to 1800 (growth of technology, and beginnings of empire)
- *Modern English* 1800 to the present.

The dates are, of course, to an extent, arbitrary; but they serve to mark approximate transition points in the development of the language in the light of changes in society and culture.

10.1 Interpreting etymologies

In historical dictionaries (OED, SOED), the etymology is given at the beginning of the entry, in keeping with their historical orientation. *Webster's Third* also puts etymology in this position in its entries, but the more usual position is towards or at the end of an entry. In either position, it is conventional to present etymological information within square brackets [ ], though NODE and COD10 present the information in a separate paragraph of the entry, introduced by 'ORIGIN' in small capital letters.

The amount of detail contained in an etymology depends in large part on the size of the dictionary, with smaller (e.g. Pocket) dictionaries containing perhaps only the immediate source of a word. Larger dictionaries contain that, and often much more. The immediate origin of a word is the obligatory part of an etymology, whether it is an Old English or Anglo-Saxon word, or whether it has been 'borrowed' into the language either during or subsequent to the Old English period. In addition to the immediate origin, some dictionaries will include an approximate date at which, according to the evidence (from written sources), the word came into English. This may consist of just a number for the century (CED, COD10), or it may divide each century into three – early, mid, late (NODE).

Besides the immediate source and possibly a date, etymologies in larger dictionaries trace the origin of a word back to its earliest known source language. For words borrowed from French, for example, this may involve indicating a Latin source of some kind. Some of the words taken directly from Latin can be traced back to a Greek original. Words of Old English or Old Norse origin can often be assigned an earlier Germanic source. Here is an example with an interesting etymology (from NODE):

> **abacus** late Middle English (denoting a board strewn with sand on which to draw figures): from Latin, from Greek *abax*, *abak-* 'slab, drawing board', of Semitic origin; probably related to Hebrew '*ābāq* 'dust'.

Some etymologies, as in this one for *abacus*, give the meanings of these original forms, and this has led to the so-called 'etymological fallacy', according to which the 'real meaning' of a word is its original meaning. So, it is argued, the real meaning of *decimate* is 'kill or remove every tenth person', because it derives from the Latin *decimus* 'tenth', and indeed the verb *decimare* referred to the Roman practice of killing every tenth soldier in a mutinous legion. But it is a fallacy to argue in this way, because words undergo semantic as well as phonological and orthographic changes. The meaning of *decimate* has changed to denote any large-scale killing or destruction, and, in any case, for English users the connection with *decimus* has been all but lost (though compare *decimal*).

In the case of words having an Old English origin, the etymology may additionally record 'cognate' words in other Germanic languages. The languages concerned are the Scandinavian languages (Old Norse, Swedish, Danish), Dutch, and German. All these languages are thought to derive from a common ancestor language, which has been termed 'Germanic', but for which no records survive. The cognates, therefore, demonstrate the Germanic origin of the Old English words concerned. For example, NODE gives the etymology of *speak* as: 'Old English *sprecan*, later *specan*, of West Germanic origin; related to Dutch *spreken* and German *sprechen*'. CED4 gives the etymology of *through* as: 'Old English *thurh*; related to Old Frisian *thruch*, Old Saxon *thuru*, Old High German *duruh*'.

The etymology of some words can be traced to particular cultural beliefs and practices, sometimes known as 'folk etymology'. For example, the NODE etymology for *bigwig* reads: 'early 18th cent.: so named from the large wigs formerly worn by distinguished men'; and the CED4 etymology for *crocodile tears* reads: 'from the belief that crocodiles wept over their prey to allure further victims'.

To interpret etymologies, not only do you need to understand what the various parts of the entry might signify, e.g. immediate origin, ultimate source, cognates, folk etymology, but you also need to be able to make sense of the language names used, e.g. Old High German, Middle Dutch, Late Latin, which in many dictionaries, especially those of concise size or smaller, will be in the form of abbreviations (OHG, MDu, LL). For the Germanic languages and French, the terms 'Old', 'Middle' and 'Modern' correspond approximately to their use for English, i.e. pre-medieval, medieval, and post-medieval. In the case of Latin, the plain term relates to the classical period, and 'Late Latin' to the period from approximately 200 AD to 400 AD. A label 'New Latin' (NL) is used to refer to words coined in Latin since the Renaissance, especially scientific terms. Where these are common to a number of (European) languages, the label ISV, for 'International Scientific Vocabulary', is used by W3 and some other dictionaries. The following discussion and illustration of etymologies will serve to illuminate some of these points.

10.2 Original English

Words labelled 'Old English' (OE) in etymologies have their origin in the Germanic dialects spoken by the Anglo-Saxon tribal people, invited in the early fifth century by the Celtic peoples then inhabiting most of these islands to help them defend their country against the marauding Picts and Scots from the north, after the departure of the Roman legions as a consequence of the beginning of disintegration of the empire. The guests from northern Europe became invaders, and the Celtic peoples fled to the west, finding habitation in Wales and Cornwall. The proportion of words in modern English with an OE origin is very small: COD10 has only 2,515 of its 64,679 headwords marked as of OE origin, less than 4 per cent. But they are the common words of everyday speech, and any informal text or discourse will be made up of a great majority of OE words.

A very small number of words marked as OE are further noted as being of Celtic origin. They are the few survivors, borrowed by the Anglo-Saxon invaders. Examples include: *ass, bin, brock* (i.e. 'badger'), *combe, hog, rich, tor*. A number of other loanwords survive from OE, taken largely from Latin as a consequence of the introduction of the Roman form of Christianity into Britain from the late sixth century; they are mostly religious words, e.g. *anthem, candle, charity, disciple, martyr, noon, psalm, verse*.

Old English also took some words from its sister Germanic language Old Norse, the language spoken by the Viking invaders from across the North Sea, who during the eighth and ninth centuries came first on raiding expeditions and then to stay, eventually ruling half the country in the territory known as 'Danelaw'. Old Norse (ON) has had a significant effect on place names in the north and east of the country: any place whose name ends in *-by, -thorpe*, or *-thwaite*, for example, had a Viking origin or settlement. Although many words are cognate in OE and ON, there were borrowings from ON into OE, such as: *arrow, baulk, fang, glove, knife, plough, skin, tidings, wrong*. They are labelled in dictionary etymologies as 'OE from ON'. Other ON words were borrowed into English later, during the Middle English period, such as: *anger, birth, dirt, ferry, ill, keg, odd, raise, sky, tether, ugly, want*. These are labelled as 'ME from ON'.

10.3 Latinate loans

We noted in 2.1 that English vocabulary consists of a substratum of Germanic words, its Old English base, and superstrata of words taken either directly or indirectly from Latin. The first such superstratum was laid in the centuries following the Norman conquest in 1066, the second during and following the sixteenth-century Renaissance period. NODE labels 8322 words as having their immediate origin in Middle English (see 10.1); of these 3234 are borrowed either directly (most of them) or indirectly from Old French, e.g.

> **lavish** late Middle English (as a noun denoting profusion): from Old French *lavasse* 'deluge of rain', from *laver* 'to wash', from Latin *lavare*.

Some of the indirect borrowings are via Anglo-Norman (387 in NODE), the language that developed among the French-speaking ruling elite in Britain, e.g.

> **astray** Middle English (in the sense 'distant from the correct path'): from an Anglo-Norman French variant of Old French *estraie*, past participle of *estraier*, based on Latin *extra* 'out of bounds' + *vagari* 'wander'.

Some of the Latinate words borrowed into Middle English come not from Old French but directly from Latin (1885 in NODE). This is mostly in the latter part of the period, as the transition to the Renaissance begins, e.g.

interrupt late Middle English: from Latin *interrupt-* 'broken, interrupted', from the verb *interrumpere*, from *inter-* 'between' + *rumpere* 'to break'.

In each of the sixteenth and seventeenth centuries, in excess of 2000 loanwords from Latin are noted in NODE, of which between a quarter and a third came into English via French, e.g.

exterior early 16th cent.: from Latin, comparative of *exter* 'outer'.

loyal mid 16th cent.: from French, via Old French *loial* from Latin *legalis*.

precarious mid 17th cent.: from Latin *precarius* 'obtained by entreaty' (from *prex, prec-* 'prayer') + -OUS

fatigue mid 17th cent. (in the sense 'task or duty that causes weariness'): from French *fatigue* (noun), *fatiguer* (verb), from Latin *fatigare* 'tire out', from *ad fatim, affatim* 'to satiety or surfeit, to bursting'.

'Latin' is a label that occurs with high frequency in etymologies, nearly 12,000 times in COD10 (18 per cent of the headwords), and over 15,000 times in NODE.

Romance languages, i.e. those descended from Latin, that also feature in etymologies include: French (10,500 in NODE), Italian (1,500), Spanish (1,100), and Portuguese (300). Direct borrowings from French include: *abattoir* (nineteenth century), *democrat* (late eighteenth century), *lacquer* (late sixteenth century, ultimately from Portuguese), *tirade* (early nineteenth century), *voyeur* (early twentieth century) – as well as numerous food and culinary terms. Italian has also given a number of food words, as well as much of English musical terminology, e.g. *adagio, al dente, finale, lasagne, pergola, saltimbocca, vibrato*. While Spanish and Portuguese have added words from themselves, they have also been vehicles for words from more exotic languages, from days of colonisation and empire, e.g. *amok* (via Portuguese from Malay), *embargo* (early seventeenth–century Spanish), *guanaco* (via Spanish from Quechuan), *marmalade* (late fifteenth-century Portuguese).

The other, more recent source of Latin borrowings are the neo-Latin 'classical compounds' (see 1.6), mostly technical terms of the sciences, technology and medicine. Classical compounds are also formed with elements taken from Greek. In fact, more of the 'combining forms' that make up classical compounds are derived from Greek than from Latin. The etymology of the combining form is usually given, but not necessarily of the classical compound, unless its formation has some peculiarity, e.g. (from NODE):

hetero- from Greek *heteros* 'other'

heteromorphic (a term of Biology, meaning 'occurring in two or more different forms, especially at different stages in the life cycle') – no origin given, since it is made up of the combining forms *hetero-* and *-morph(ic)*, both entered in the dictionary.

heterodyne   early 20th cent.: from HETERO- 'other' + -*dyne*, suffix formed irregularly from Greek *dunamis* 'power' (here the second part is not a regular combining form).

10.4 Other loans

English has taken words from a large variety of languages from around the world, for a number of reasons: to fill a gap in the English vocabulary, to have a term to refer to a phenomenon not found in English culture, to provide a 'foreign' flavour, and so on. Etymologies indicate at least the language from which the loanword comes; larger dictionaries may give the meaning in the original language, as an explanation of the motivation for the loanword. If the donor language itself borrowed it earlier, then this may also be given. Here, first, are some examples from European languages to illustrate these points.

Gastarbeiter   German, from *Gast* 'guest' + *Arbeiter* 'worker' (NODE)

plankton   C19: via German from Greek *planktos* wandering, from *plazesthai* to roam (CED)

csardas   Hungarian *csárdás* from *csárda* 'inn' (COD9)

coach   mid 16th cent. (in sense 3): from French *coche*, from Hungarian *kocsi (szekér)* '(wagon) from *Kocs*', a town in Hungary (NODE)

babushka   Russian: grandmother, from *baba* old woman (CED)

cosmonaut   C20: from Russian *kosmonaut*, from COSMO- + Greek *nautes* sailor; compare ARGONAUT (CED)

bamboo   Dutch *bamboes* via Portuguese *mambu* from Malay (COD9)

intelligentsia   early 20th cent.: from Russian *intelligentsiya*, from Polish *inteligencja*, from Latin *intelligentia* (NODE)

To illustrate the variable treatment of etymology, depending on the nature of the loanword, we now give some examples of etymologies of Chinese loanwords, as recorded in COD9:

cheongsam   Chinese (the Chinese word denotes 'a woman's garment with a high neck and slit skirt, worn in China')

gung-ho   Chinese *gonghe* 'work together', slogan adopted by US Marines in 1942

kowtow   Chinese *ketou*, from *ke* 'knock' + *tou* 'head'

lychee   Chinese *lizhi*

yin   Chinese *yin* 'shade, feminine, the moon'

The etymology provides enough information for the reader to understand something of the motivation for the borrowing into English. The other point to note here is that the Chinese writing system has been transliterated into Roman characters.

Transliteration is usually provided for words from any language with a non-Roman script, including Greek, Russian and other Slavic languages with the Cyrillic script, Arabic, Hebrew, South Asian languages (including Urdu, Punjabi), and so on. There are usually conventions for such transliterations, and they may involve the use of diacritics to indicate particular features, e.g.

sepoy   Urdu and Persian *sipāhi* 'soldier' from *sipāh* 'army'

kosher   Hebrew *kāšēr* 'proper'

mango   Portuguese *manga* via Malay *mangā* from Tamil *mānkāy*, from *mān* 'mango tree' + *kāy* 'fruit'

sherbet   Turkish *şerbet*, Persian *šerbet* from Arabic *šarba* 'drink', from *šariba* 'to drink'

Finally under this heading, there follows a selection of etymologies for words borrowed into English from around the world:

aardvark   Afrikaans from *aarde* 'earth' + *vark* 'pig' (South Africa)

batik   Javanese (South Asia)

cassava   Taino (Caribbean)

gong   Malay (South Asia)

impala   Zulu (South Africa)

karaoke   Japanese

kiwi   Maori (New Zealand)

kayak   Inuit *qayaq* (North America)

pariah   Tamil (South India)

pampas   Quechua, via Spanish (South America)

safari   Swahili from Arabic *safara* 'to travel' (East Africa)

shampoo   Hindi (North India)

skunk   Abnaki *segankw* (North America)

wombat   Dharuk (Australia)

yak   Tibetan *gyag* (South Asia)

yogurt   Turkish

zombie   Kongo (West Africa)

10.5 Historical dictionaries and some comparisons

As we might expect, an historical dictionary – in the case of English the *Oxford English Dictionary* and the abbreviated *Shorter OED* – is more detailed in its etymology. Examine the following entry for *zenith* from OED2:

> a. OF. *cenith* (F. *zénith*) or med.L. *cenit* (cf. It. *zenit*, Sp. *cenit*, Pg. *zenith*, G. *zenith*, etc.), obscurely ad. Arab. *samt*, in *samt ar-rās* lit. way or path over the head (*samt* way, *al* the, *rās* head); cf. AZIMUTH (*al* the, *sumūt* pl. of *samt*).

This needs some interpretation, if you are not familiar with reading OED etymologies. The initial 'a. OF . . . or med.L.' means 'adopted from Old French . . . or medieval Latin'; the modern French (F.) is given in brackets; then cognates are given ('cf.' = *confer* 'compare') in Italian (It.), Spanish (Sp.), Portuguese (Pg.) and German (G.). The word is said to be 'obscurely adapted (ad.) from Arabic (Arab.), and the supposed Arabic origin is explained (lit. = 'literally', pl. = 'plural'). The OED makes a distinction in borrowing between 'adoption' (with little or no alteration to the form of the borrowed word) and 'adaptation' (where the spelling/pronunciation is conformed to the conventions of English).

The SOED, as might be expected, given its smaller compass, presents a truncated version of this etymology:

> OFr. *cenit* (mod. *zenith*) or med.L *cenit* (also *zenith*), ult. f. Arab. *samt* in *samt-ar-ra's* 'path over the head': cf. AZIMUTH.

Here, mod. = 'modern', ult. = 'ultimately', f. = 'from'. Interestingly, CED4 has an etymology that is as detailed, along with some variations:

> C17: from French *cenith*, from Medieval Latin, from Old Spanish *zenit*, based on Arabic *samt*, as in *samt arrās* path over one's head, from *samt* way, path + *al* the + *rās* head

CED has a policy of avoiding abbreviations where possible, especially in etymologies, in the interests of user accessibility, a policy also followed by NODE:

> late Middle English: from Old French or medieval Latin *cenit*, based on Arabic *samt (ar-ra's)* 'path (over the head)'.

NODE and CED disagree on the entry of the word into English; the first quotation in OED2 is dated 1387, followed by a 1391 quotation from Chaucer, which would seem to support the NODE date of 'late Middle English'. However, the Spanish part of the derivation noted in CED is supported by Skeat's (1961) *Concise Etymological Dictionary*:

Zenith (F. – Span. – Arab.) M.E. *senyth.* – O.F. *cenith*; F. *zénith.* – Span. *zenit*, O.Span. *zenith.* – Arab. *samt*, a way, road, path, tract, quarter; whence *samt-ur-ras*, the zenith, vertical point of the heavens; also as *as-samt*, an azimuth. *Samt* was pronounced *semt*, of which Span. *zenit* is a corruption; again, *samt* is here short for *samt-ur-ras* or *semt-er-ras* (as above), lit. the way overhead, from *ras*, the head. See Azimuth.

The specialist etymological dictionary goes into a more detailed explanation of how the word was supposedly adapted from Arabic into English via Spanish and French.

By way of comparison, here is the quite different etymology of *car*, first of all as given in the historical dictionaries, then in the general-purpose dictionaries, and finally in the specialist etymological dictionary:

OED: ME. *carre*, a. ONF. *carre*:–late L. *carra*, a parallel form to *carrus, carrum* (whence It., Sp. *carro*, Pr. *car, char*, ONF. *car*, F. *char*, ME. *CHAR*), a kind of 2-wheeled wagon for transporting burdens. The L. was a. OCelt. **karr-os, *karr-om*, whence OIr. (also mod.Ir. and Gael.) *carr* masc. 'wagon, chariot,' OWelsh *carr*, Welsh *càr*, Manx *carr*, Bret. *kar*. (Late L. *carra* also gave WGer. *carra fem.*, in OHG. *charra*, Ger. *karre*, MDu. *carre*, Du. *kar* fem., Sw. *karra*, Da. *karre*.)

(Note: ME = 'Middle English', ONF = 'Old Northern French', late L = 'late Latin', Pr = 'Provençal', OCelt = 'Old Celtic', OIr = 'Old Irish', mod.Ir = 'modern Irish', Gael = 'Gaelic', Bret = 'Breton', WGer = 'West Germanic', OHG = 'Old High German', MDu = 'Middle Dutch', Sw = 'Swedish', Da = 'Danish'.)

SOED: LME. [AN, ONFr. *carre* f. Proto-Romance var. of L *carrum* neut., *carrus* masc., f. Celt. base repr. by (O)Ir. *carr*, Welsh *car*]

(Note: LME = 'Late Middle English', AN = 'Anglo-Norman', f. = 'from', var. = 'variant', repr. = 'represented'.)

CED: C14: from Anglo-French *carre*, ultimately related to Latin *carra, carrum* two-wheeled wagon, probably of Celtic origin; compare Old Irish *carr*

NODE: late Middle English (in the general sense 'wheeled vehicle'): from Old Northern French *carre*, based on Latin *carrum, carrus*, of Celtic origin

SKEAT: (F. – C.) M.E. *carre.* – O.NorthF. *carre*, a car (Ducange, s.v. *Marcellum*). – Late L. *carra*, f.; allied to L. *carrus*, a car; of Gaulish origin. – Bret. *karr*, a chariot; W. *car*, O.Gael. *cár*, Irish *carr*. Allied to L. *currus*, a chariot; Brugm. i. § 516.

(Note: F = 'French', C = 'Celtic', s.v. = *sub verbo* 'under the word' (Ducange refers to 'Ducange Anglicus', *Vulgar Tongue*, 1857), W = 'Welsh', Brugm = 'Brugmann, *Grundriss der vergleichenden Grammatik* (Outline of Comparative Grammar), 1897.)

From these examples, you can see how the etymology varies according to the type of dictionary and its intended user group. By and large, the historical dictionaries are aimed at scholars and students of the language, as indeed is the specialist etymological dictionary (Skeat). The assumption of the general-purpose dictionaries is that, within their compass, a basic set of information about etymology is of interest to the ordinary dictionary user. It is this assumption that we will now examine.

10.6 Why etymology?

It could be argued that etymology has no place in a general-purpose dictionary, and it should be left to historical or specialist dictionaries. Learners' dictionaries (Chapter 11) do not contain etymological information, though its exclusion from these dictionaries has been challenged (Ellegård 1978; Ilson 1983). Of the three Collins dictionaries we looked at in Chapter 3 (3.2), the smallest, the *Pocket*, does not contain etymologies, but the two larger ones do. It was only half a century or so after the first monolingual English dictionary that etymologies began to be included in dictionaries (see Chapter 4); so they have a long pedigree. Hudson (1988) – see Chapter 2 (2.4) – includes etymology among the 'lexical facts' about words that dictionaries should pay attention to. But there is little evidence (Chapter 7) that users routinely resort to a dictionary for this information. So, is there any justification for the inclusion of etymological information in general-purpose dictionaries aimed at the ordinary user?

We have noted before (7.4) that dictionaries have a double function: as a record of the vocabulary of the language, i.e. a lexical description, and as a reference work to meet the needs of users for information about words and their usage. On neither count is the inclusion of etymology uncontroversially obvious. As a record, a dictionary describes the contemporary vocabulary; it omits obsolete words and meanings and marks as 'archaic' those whose currency is beginning to wane. As a reference work, a dictionary does not have the space to give a full account of the etymology of words, such as might be found in an historical dictionary, as we have seen in 10.5. Moreover, the etymological information is probably the hardest of all the parts of a dictionary entry to decode, needing as it does some background knowledge in history, and specifically in the history of languages. Otherwise, what sense can anyone make of terms like 'Old High German'?

Sidney Landau expresses the opinion that 'of all the elements included in modern dictionaries, etymology has the least to do with the essential purpose of a synchronic dictionary' (2001: 127). Etymology does not make a contribution to the description of the contemporary meaning and usage of words; it may help to illuminate how things have got to where they are now, but it is as likely to be misleading as helpful (as with the 'etymological fallacy'). Etymology offers no advice to one who consults a dictionary on the appropriate use of a word in the context of a written text or spoken discourse. It merely provides some passing insight for the interested dictionary browser with the requisite background knowledge and interpretative skills. On this perspective, Landau is right: etymology does not have the same status as other elements of lexical description in a dictionary.

Etymology could be said to be part of dictionary information by historical accident. The 'hard words' tradition (4.2), which started monolingual dictionaries in English, included only words that had been borrowed, mostly from the classical languages. It was only a short step to indicate systematically their language of origin, as indeed dictionaries had done to an extent from the beginning. Combined with the increasing interest in cultural and linguistic history that flourished during the eighteenth century, etymology became firmly established in the tradition of monolingual dictionaries. Dictionary making does have its own tradition, its own set of principles and conventions, which are to a large extent independent of those associated with other branches of linguistic scholarship. It is only recently, in the last quarter of the twentieth century, that the discipline of linguistics has exercised any major influence on the processes of dictionary making. On this perspective, it is not surprising that etymology continues to be an element of the information given for words, at least in the larger general-purpose dictionaries. Radical departures from the expected content and format of dictionaries are undertaken reluctantly by publishers: purchaser expectations have to be met.

There is, perhaps, one further and sounder reason for the inclusion of etymological information in monolingual dictionaries of English at least. It arises from the nature of the English vocabulary, which we have commented on in Chapter 2 and explored in the earlier part of the present chapter. The sources of English words are so diverse, with such a small proportion being 'original' Anglo-Saxon, and so many being 'borrowed' from a range of other languages, that there would seem to be some justification for providing information at least about the immediate origin of a word. In this way, the users of the language can see how their vocabulary has been constituted. It is a means of celebrating the diversity of the English lexicon, and it should guard against any temptation to linguistic xenophobia or notions of linguistic purity.

10.7 Further reading

The 'Guide to Using the Dictionary' in a dictionary's front matter will contain brief information on how to interpret the etymology in the work concerned. Donna Lee Berg's *A Guide to the Oxford English Dictionary* (1993) contains a section (pp. 22ff) on the OED's etymology.

Barbara Kipfer's *Workbook on Lexicography* (1984) contains a chapter (12) on etymology, as does David Crystal's *The Cambridge Encyclopedia of the English Language* (1995), though much of it is about place and personal names. Landau

(2001) offers a perspective on etymology in dictionaries (pp. 127–34), as does Svensén (1993), Chapter 15.

A specialist etymological dictionary is a further source for following up on the topic of this chapter.

11 Dictionaries for learners

We introduced the four major British learners' dictionaries in 6.6 and noted in 3.2 that such dictionaries have been at the forefront of lexicographical innovation in the last half-century. In this chapter, we examine this dictionary type in some detail and show how they have been developed to meet the perceived needs of learners of English as a second or foreign language. Such dictionaries are aimed at the intermediate to advanced learner. They are based on the observation that, as learners become more proficient, they need to move from a bilingual dictionary as their lexical reference source to a monolingual dictionary. Monolingual learners' dictionaries (MLDs) have therefore attempted to fulfil this need by providing information about the meaning and use of English words that in many respects goes well beyond that offered in bilingual dictionaries.

11.1 Rise of the monolingual learners' dictionaries

The genesis of the learner's dictionary lies in the endeavours, during the interwar years, of three teachers of English as a foreign language, two of whom worked in Japan (H.E. Palmer and A.S. Hornby) and the other in India (Michael West). Not only did they attempt to improve the standard of language teaching in their respective areas, they also became involved in research projects that had a bearing on the task of teaching English. Michael West became a leading contributor to the 'vocabulary control' movement (McArthur 1998, Ch. 5), which sought to identify the essential vocabulary that would lead to a more rapid competence in the language (West 1953; West and Endicott 1935). Harold Palmer worked on the grammatical patterning of words, especially verbs (Palmer 1938), as later did Hornby (1954). Palmer and Hornby also investigated collocations and idioms, which fed into the first general-purpose learner's dictionary, the *Idiomatic and Syntactic Dictionary of English* (Hornby et al. 1942).

The *Idiomatic and Syntactic Dictionary* was published in Japan, from where Hornby was repatriated in 1941. After the war, Oxford University Press became interested in the dictionary and they republished it in 1948 with the title *A Learner's Dictionary of Current English*, changed in 1952 to *The Advanced Learner's Dictionary of Current English*. *Oxford* replaced *The* in the title from the third (1974) edition onwards, and it is now known by the initialism 'OALD'. Until its third edition, the OALD had the advanced learners' dictionary market to itself. It sold prolifically, the first two editions alone had sales of 7 million copies (Hebert 1974). To illustrate the aims of the OALD, peruse the following entries for the verb *confide* and the noun *confidence*:

> **con·fide**/kənˈfaɪd/*vt, vi* **1** [VP14] **~ sth/sb to sb,** tell secrets to sb; give (sth or sb to sb) to be looked after; give (a task or duty to sb): *He ~d his troubles to a friend. The children were ~d to the care of the ship's captain. She ~d to me that . . . .* **2** [VP3A] **~ in,** have trust or faith in: *Can I ~ in his honesty? There's no one here I can ~ in.* **con·fid·ing** *adj* truthful; trusting: *The girl is of a confiding nature,* ready to trust others, unsuspicious. **con·fid·ing·ly** *adv*
>
> **con·fi·dence**/ˈkɑnfidəns/ *n* **1** [U] (act of) confiding in or to. **in strict ~,** expecting sth to be kept secret: *I'm telling you this in strict ~.* **take a person into one's ~,** tell him one's secrets, etc. '**~ man/trickster**, one who swindles people in this way. **2** [C] secret which is confided to sb: *The two girls sat in a corner exchanging ~s about the young men they knew.* **3** [U] belief in oneself or others or in what is said, reported, etc.; belief that one is right or that one is able to do sth: *to have/lose ~ in sb; to put little/complete/no ~ in sb/ sth; Don't put too much ~ in what the newspapers say. There is a lack of ~ in the government,* People do not feel that its policies are wise. *I hope he will justify my ~ in him/my ~ that he will do well. The prisoner answered the questions with ~.*

You will notice: information about grammatical patterning, both in formulae (~ sth/sb to sb – i.e. 'confide something/somebody to somebody') and in coding (VP = 'verb pattern', U = 'uncountable', C = 'countable'); extensive use of examples, both to illustrate grammatical patterning and to indicate typical collocation (*to put little/complete/no ~ in . . .*); inclusion of set phrases (*in strict ~*); fairly brief definitions, but explanation of examples where needed (*The girl is of a confiding nature,* ready to trust others . . .). The examples are mostly invented for the purpose and some of them have a rather dated ring. The verb patterns are explained and exemplified in the front matter of the dictionary. Note also the dots in the middle of the headwords and derivatives, to indicate 'word division', i.e. where a word could be split at the end of a line of writing.

The first rival to the OALD was published by Longman in 1978, the *Longman Dictionary of Contemporary English*, edited by Paul Proctor. LDOCE introduced a number of improvements or innovations. The most significant was the use of a restricted 'defining vocabulary'; the lexicographers attempted to define every sense in the dictionary using only 2000 of the more common words of English, which were listed in an appendix. Where it proved impossible to define a sense without using a word not from the defining vocabulary, the item appeared in small capitals, to imply a cross-reference to its entry in the dictionary. In fact, many of the items in the defining vocabulary had multiple meanings, and the list also contained derivational affixes that could be added to the words in the list.

At a late stage in compilation, the dictionary text was subjected to a computer program that checked each definition to ensure that no word outside the defining vocabulary had been used, or at least that it had been written in small capitals.

LDOCE also tried to improve on the coding of grammatical information, especially in respect of verb syntax. While a significant innovation in OALD, Hornby's verb patterns – twenty-five in all, but amounting to over fifty when sub-patterns are included – had to be constantly looked up with the aim of being memorised. No doubt a regular user of the dictionary would get to recognise at least the more common patterns, but the pattern numbers were not suggestive of the pattern itself. LDOCE introduced a coding that was uniform for verbs, adjectives and nouns, consisting of a letter plus a figure. The letter was mnemonic where this was possible: 'T' stood for 'transitive', 'I' for 'intransitive'. The figure stood for different types of complement and the like: 'Ø' stood for 'zero' (so, 'IØ' indicated a genuinely intransitive pattern; '1' stood for 'noun (phrase) or pronoun', '6' for '*that*-clause', and so on. A table of codes was included in the inside back cover for easy reference. The aim was to help the learner understand the coding by making it more suggestive and accessible. Research on user behaviour (e.g. Béjoint 1981) indicated, however, that few students made use of, or even understood, the coding schemes in their dictionaries, preferring to glean grammatical information from the examples.

As the second edition of LDOCE was published nine years later, in 1987, a third MLD appeared on the market, with many significant innovations: *Collins COBUILD English Dictionary*. The COBUILD project was instigated by John Sinclair, the Professor of English Language at the University of Birmingham, with the sponsorship of the Glasgow-based publisher William Collins and Sons Ltd. The aim was to compile a learners' dictionary on the basis of a computer corpus of texts – the Collins (CO)/Birmingham University (BU) International Language Database (ILD). The corpus available to the lexicographers of the first edition of COBUILD amounted to 7.3 million words of text, with an additional 13 million words in a 'reserve' corpus. Since renamed 'The Bank of English', the corpus now runs to over 400 million words. The use of a large corpus not only allowed the lexicographers to ascertain reliable information about the relative frequency of occurrence of words and senses, but more importantly to obtain data, in the form of concordances, for deciding on the senses and meanings of words. The use of a corpus was not only new, it was revolutionary: all MLDs and most NSDs now claim to make use of corpus techniques in the compilation of their dictionaries.

COBUILD was not just the first dictionary to be based on a computer corpus; it innovated in a number of other ways as well. First, all the definitions are complete sentences; they are intended to sound like the teacher explaining the meaning in the classroom, and they give some idea of typical contexts, e.g.

> *joyride* If someone goes on a *joyride*, they steal a car and drive around in it at high speed.

jukebox A *jukebox* is a record player in a place such as a pub or a bar. You put a coin in and choose the record you want to hear.

junk You can use *junk* to refer to old and second-hand goods that people buy and collect.

Second, all the examples are from the corpus – 'real English' – sometimes with minor adaptation or truncation. Third, the grammatical information is not included in the main entry, but provided in an 'extra column', to the right of the main column; this column also includes information about synonyms and antonyms. Fourth, there is only one entry per spelling, and senses are listed in frequency order; all inflections are given, whether regular or irregular. Each sense begins a new paragraph, and nearly all senses have at least one example.

The last MLD to enter the market did so in 1995, the 'year of the dictionaries', in which OALD published its fifth edition, LDOCE its third and COBUILD its second. The new dictionary was the *Cambridge International Dictionary of English*, edited by Paul Proctor, who had been responsible for the first edition of LDOCE. CIDE took the opposite decision on headwords to COBUILD: each major sense has a separate entry, followed where appropriate by a 'guide word' to the meaning; for example *job* has six entries: **job** employment, **job** piece of work, **job** duty, **job** problem, **job** example, **job** crime. Every grammatical pattern is illustrated by an example, and examples also show typical collocations. Indeed the dictionary pays a lot of attention to the phraseological potential of words, and it includes an extensive 'Phrase Index', in which phrases are entered under all of their constituents, each of which has a reference to the page, column and line number where it is treated in the dictionary. The 'International' in the title is justified on the one hand by its treatment of American and Australian, as well as British English, and on the other by its tables of 'false friends' for some sixteen languages, including Japanese, Korean and Thai. The latter derive from an analysis of the Cambridge Learner Corpus, a corpus of learners' English; the main dictionary is based on the 100 million-word Cambridge Language Survey corpus.

The EFL market is a lucrative one for publishers, and an advanced MLD is only one publication among many, including course books, grammars, readers and so on, which serve the needs of learners and their teachers. The competition has been an incentive to improve and innovate, and as successive editions have appeared, a clear development can be perceived. Moreover, MLD lexicography has been extensively debated both by practising lexicographers (e.g. Rundell 1998) and by academics (e.g. Herbst and Popp 1999), with increasing attention being paid to the needs of learners and the reference skills that they can be expected to possess.

11.2 Learners' decoding needs

One of the major differences between NSDs and MLDs is that the latter take into account users' encoding needs (in writing and speaking) to an extent that

NSDs do not (see 11.3). Users of MLDs have the same decoding needs that NSD users have – looking up the meaning of unfamiliar words or senses – and may experience more difficulty in locating the information, as well as in understanding the definitions once the appropriate one has been found. We will discuss solutions to these two potential problems.

A dictionary look-up for decoding usually involves finding the appropriate sense of a word that has been encountered in writing and that cannot be interpreted from its context. In this case, the user knows the spelling of the word; but if a word has been heard but not seen, there may be a difficulty in relating sound to spelling and so locating the word in the dictionary. To address this particular need, LDOCE2 (1987) included a laminated card with a list of sound-spelling correspondences on one side (the other side contained a table of the grammar codes). In most cases, however, the user will have the orthographic form for looking up. The difficulty that is then likely to arise relates to identifying the appropriate sense of words with multiple senses; the more common the word, the larger the number of senses it may have. To facilitate the learner's look-up in such cases, a number of the MLDs have attempted to provide easier access to sense differentiation. We have noted already the CIDE innovation of multiple headwords for a lexeme, accompanied by a 'guideword'. LDOCE3 and OALD6 also offer similar solutions under the one headword, e.g. for the lexeme *stamp*:

CIDE: **stamp** letter, **stamp** foot, **stamp** mark, **stamp** quality.

LDOCE3: **stamp**[1] *n* 1 MAIL, 2 TOOL, 3 the stamp of sth, 4 PAYMENT, 5 TAX, 6 IN A SHOP, 7 a man/woman of his/her stamp; **stamp**[2] *v* 1 FOOT, 2 stamp your foot, 3 stamp your feet, 4 MAKE A MARK, 5 stamp on sb/sth, 6 AFFECT SB/STH, 7 stamp sb as sth, 8 MAIL.

OALD6 : **stamp** *noun* ON LETTER/PACKAGE 1, PRINTING TOOL 2, PRINTED DESIGN/WORDS 3, PROOF OF PAYMENT 4, CHARACTER/QUALITY 5, 6, OF FOOT 7; *verb* FOOT 1, WALK 2, PRINT DESIGN/WORDS 3, SHOW FEELING/QUALITY 4, 5, ON LETTER/PACKAGE 6, CUT OUT OBJECT 7.

The aim is that the user should be able to glance down the entry and quickly find the sense relevant to their look-up by relating the guideword to the context in which the word being looked up is situated.

The other problem identified in relation to decoding concerns understanding the definition that is encountered. We noted earlier that LDOCE innovated with a specified restricted defining vocabulary, though it must be said that the original OALD compilers were also aware of the need to define within the supposed vocabulary of the users. The current editions of LDOCE, OALD and CIDE all have a specified defining vocabulary, which is listed in an appendix to the dictionary. COBUILD's solution is to define using full sentences, a practice that is used in some instances by the other MLDs. Compare the definitions for the noun *knuckle*:

OALD6: any of the joints in the fingers, especially those connecting the fingers with the rest of the hand – picture at BODY

LDOCE3: the joints in your fingers including the ones where your fingers join your hands

COBUILD3: Your **knuckles** are the rounded pieces of bone that form lumps on your hands where your fingers join your hands, and where your fingers bend.

CIDE: one of the joints of the fingers, esp. between the hand and the fingers . . . PIC **Body**.

You will notice that two of the dictionaries refer the user to an illustration (picture); LDOCE also contains pictures, though COBUILD does not. The pictures are usually line drawings dispersed throughout the text, though LDOCE3 and OALD6 also contain full-page colour plates. Pictures supplement the verbal definitions, especially for nouns with a concrete reference, and they are often grouped (e.g. under 'body') so that the terms for a lexical field are displayed together.

Now consider the definitions for the verb *smear*.

OALD6: to spread an OILY or soft substance over a surface in a rough or careless way

LDOCE3: to spread a liquid or soft substance over a surface, especially carelessly or untidily

COBUILD3: If you **smear** a surface with an oily or sticky substance or **smear** the substance onto the surface, you spread a layer of the substance over the surface.

CIDE: to spread (a thick liquid or a soft sticky substance) over a surface.

All the definitions have the essential components of 'spread', 'liquid/soft substance' 'over surface'; OALD6 and LDOCE3 also include a component of 'carelessly'. Note the capital letters for *oily* in the OALD6 definition, because it is not in its defining vocabulary; COBUILD has no such restriction on using it. Note, too, the use of brackets in the CIDE definition, in the conventional manner, for indicating typical collocations, in this case as object of the verb. The COBUILD3 definition is rather cumbersome because it is also indicating the typical patterns for the verb (*smear* a surface *with* a substance/*smear* a substance *on* a surface), which are indicated separately in the other dictionaries, either in formulae (~ sth on/over sth | ~ sth with sth – OALD6) or in examples (. . . *smeared the walls of their cells* **with** *excrement* – CIDE).

Let us now examine the definitions for the abstract adjective *versatile*:

OALD6: (*approving*) **1** (of a person) able to do many different things. **2** (of food, a building, etc.) having many different uses

LDOCE3: *approving* **1** good at doing a lot of different things and able to learn new skills quickly and easily. **2** having many different uses

COBUILD3: **1** If you say that a person is **versatile**, you approve of them because they have many different skills. **2** A tool, machine, or material that is **versatile** can be used for many different purposes.

CIDE: able to change easily from one activity to another or able to be used for many different purposes.

All apart from CIDE separate out the use of *versatile* to refer to people as against things, though LDOCE is not as explicit as OALD and COBUILD. However, all four dictionaries contain examples that make the distinction clear, though the range of 'things' to which *versatile* may be applied is not clearly stated: OALD suggests 'food' and 'buildings', while COBUILD specifically mentions 'tool', 'machine' and 'material'. OALD and LDOCE have the attitudinal label 'approving', which is incorporated into the definition in COBUILD and not mentioned in CIDE. This, together with the preceding sets of definitions, gives some impression of how successful MLDs have been in making definitions understandable to their learner-users.

11.3 Learners' encoding needs

For decoding a learner is as likely to consult a bilingual dictionary, but for encoding the MLD will prove to be a more comprehensive and reliable source of information. MLDs have made it their business to provide extensively for their users' encoding requirements, especially in writing. There are two main ways in which they have done this, together with some more minor additional information.

The first way has been to provide comprehensive grammatical information (cf. Bogaards and van der Kloot 2001), so that users can construct syntactically natural sentences in English. For nouns, this essentially means recording the distinction between 'countable' and 'uncountable' uses; the abbreviations 'C' and 'U', used by Hornby *et al.* in OALD1, have become common symbols for this distinction. For adjectives, the inflectional possibilities need to be indicated (i.e. whether an adjective is gradable or not), as well as any restrictions on the syntactic positioning of adjectives (e.g. attributive only or predicative only). Compare the entries for *mere*:

OALD6: [only before noun] (*superlative* **merest**, no *comparative*)

LDOCE3: [only before noun, no comparative]

COBUILD3: **merest Mere** does not have a comparative form. The superlative form **merest** is used to emphasize how small something is, rather than in comparisons. ADJn

CIDE: [not gradable]

COBUILD has the most extensive and explicit explanation; 'ADJn' (in the Extra Column) indicates that *mere* is restricted to attributive position, signalled by 'only before noun' in OALD and LDOCE. CIDE is the least informative; it does, however, have a separate entry for *merest*, and all its examples show attributive use only.

The most important grammatical information for encoding is given for verbs, since they are the pivotal element of sentences and to a large extent determine the syntax of the clause or sentence in which they occur (Jackson 2002). This is the area that Hornby and his colleagues paid particular attention to from the beginning of the development of the learner's dictionary. The crucial question is how to display this information. The initial solution (OALD1, OALD2) was by means of coding, supported by examples; these were in turn supplemented by formulae (OALD3) – compare the entries for *propose* from OALD2 and OALD3:

> **OALD2**: *v.t. & i.* **1.** (VP 1, 2, 11, 17B) offer or put forward for consideration, as a suggestion, plan, or purpose: *I ~ an early start (to start early, that we should start early, starting early). We ~ leaving at noon. The motion was ~d by Mr X and seconded by Mr Y.* **~ a toast (sb.'s health)**, ask persons to drink sb.'s health or happiness. **2.** (VP 1, 21) offer marriage (*to* sb.): *Did he ~ (marriage) to you?* **3.** put forward (sb.'s name) (*for* an office, *for* membership of a club, etc.): *I ~ Mr Smith for chairman. Will you please ~ me for your club?*

> **OALD3**: *vt, vi* **1** [VP6A,D,7A,9] offer or put forward for consideration, as a suggestion, plan or purpose: *I ~ starting early/an early start/to start early/ that we should start early. We ~ leaving at noon. The motion was ~d by Mr X and seconded by Mr Y.* **~ a toast/sb's health**, ask persons to drink sb's health or happiness. **2** [VP6A,2A] **~ (marriage) (to sb)**, offer marriage. **3** [VP14] **~ sb (for sth)**, put forward (sb's name) for an office/for membership of a club/etc: *I ~ Mr Smith for chairman. Will you please ~ me for your club?*

The Verb Patterns were dropped from OALD after the third edition. In the latest (sixth) edition, the formulae are linked to examples, so that coding and exemplification work together:

> **OALD6**: *verb*

> SUGGEST PLAN **1** (*formal*) to suggest a plan, an idea, etc. for people to think about and decide on: [VN] *The government proposed changes to the voting system.* ◇ *What would you propose?* ◇ [Vthat] *She proposed that the book be banned.* ◇ (*BrE* also) *She proposed that the book should be banned.* ◇ [VNthat] *It was proposed that the president be elected for a period of two years.* ◇ [V-ing] *He proposed changing the name of the company.* ◇ [VNtoinf] *It was proposed to pay the money from public funds.* HELP This pattern is only used in the passive.

INTEND **2** to intend to do sth: [**Vto**inf] *What do you propose to do now?* ◇ [**V–ing**] *How do you propose getting home?*

MARRIAGE **3** ~ **(sth) (to sb)** to ask sb to marry you: [V] *He was afraid that if he proposed she might refuse.* ◇ *She proposed to me!* ◇ [VN] *to propose marriage.*

AT FORMAL MEETING **4** [VN] ~ **sth** | ~ **sb (for/as sth)** to suggest sth at a formal meeting and ask people to vote on it: *I propose Tom Ellis for chairman.* ◇ *to propose a motion* (= to be the main speaker in support of an idea at a formal debate) – compare OPPOSE, SECOND

SUGGEST EXPLANATION **5** [VN] (*formal*) to suggest an explanation of sth for people to consider **SYN** PROPOUND: *She proposed a possible solution to the mystery.*

IDM propose a toast (to sb) | **propose sb's health** to ask people to wish sb health, happiness and success by raising their glasses and drinking: *I'd like to propose a toast to the bride and groom.*

You can see the whole variety of means in this entry by which grammatical and other pattern information is being communicated: formulae ([**Vthat**], ~ **sb (for/as sth)**), examples (*She proposed that the book be banned*), and phrases (**propose a motion**). Coding and examples work together in an even more integrated manner in CIDE:

propose (obj) SUGGEST v to offer or state (a possible plan or action) for other people to consider • *I propose **that** we wait until the budget has been announced before committing ourselves to any expenditure.* [+ *that* clause] *He proposed deal**ing** directly with the suppliers.* [+ v-ing] *She proposed a boycott of the meeting.* [T] • *He proposed a **motion** that the chairman resign.* [T] • To propose someone is to suggest them for a position or for membership of an organization: *To be nominated for union president you need one person to propose you and another to second you.* [T] • If you propose (**to** a person) you ask someone to marry you: *I remember the night your father proposed to me.* [I] ○ *She felt sure he was going to propose.* [I]

The coding formulae are contained in square brackets at the end of the examples, and the example sentences contain bold items that also indicate grammatical patterning. In COBUILD, as indicated earlier, the whole-sentence definitions contribute towards identifying the grammatical patterns in which the word typically occurs with the sense being defined. Additionally, the Extra Column contains more explicit coding for the syntactic operation of words, e.g. for *propose*, V n/-ing, V that, V to-inf, V *to* n, V, V n *to* n.

The second main way in which MLDs provide encoding information for learners is in respect of lexical patterning, specifically collocations, idioms, and other types of phraseology. In COBUILD, the definitions again have the task of indicating typical collocational patterns. Consider the following definitions for *propose* and *proposition*:

> If you **propose** a theory or explanation, you state that it is possibly or probably true, because it fits in with the evidence that you have considered.

> If you describe something such as a task or an activity as, for example, a difficult **proposition** or an attractive **proposition**, you mean that it is difficult or pleasant to do.

In the case of the *propose* definition, it indicates that the subject of *propose* is a person (by the use of *you*), and that the object is either the words *theory* or *explanation*, or something that counts as either of these. In the case of the *proposition* definition, the adjectives *difficult* and *attractive* are indicated as typical collocates for this sense of the noun. In CIDE, collocations can be indicated in the conventional way by means of brackets (see the entry for *propose* above), but more usually by using bold type in the examples, e.g. for *malaise*:

> They claim it is **a symptom of** a **deeper** and more **general** malaise in society. • They spoke of the feeling of moral and **spiritual** malaise, the lack of will to do anything. • They were discussing the roots of the current **economic** malaise.

These examples show that typical adjectives accompanying *malaise* include *deep*, *general*, *spiritual* and *economic*, and that it enters into the phrase *a symptom of . . . malaise*. OALD6 has a 'study page' on collocations; it, too, relies on the examples to indicate typical collocations. For *malaise* it has:

> economic/financial/social malaise, a serious malaise among the staff

For *sample*, the examples are:

> The interviews were given to a **random sample** of students. The survey covers a **representative sample** of schools. a sample survey. a blood sample. Samples of the water contained pesticide. 'I'd like to see a sample of your work,' said the manager. a **free sample** of shampoo. sample exam papers.

The items in bold type represent 'important collocations'. LDOCE shows collocations (and fixed phrases) in bold type within an entry, followed by an explanation or example, or both. In the entry for *door*, for example, the following are given:

> open/close/shut/slam the door, knock on/at the door, kitchen/bathroom/bedroom etc door, front/back/side door, revolving/sliding/swing doors,

at the door, answer the door, show/see sb to the door, two/three doors down etc, (from) door to door, out of doors, behind closed doors, show sb the door, lay sth at sb's door, be on the door, an open door policy, open doors for sb, open the door to, shut/close the door on, at death's door.

MLDs take both grammatical and lexical patterning seriously and they have come a long way in their treatment of these areas since Hornby and his colleagues identified them as the major encoding needs of learners of English.

Learners' encoding needs are taken account of by two further types of information provided by MLDs. The first of these is the explicit indication of sense relations (2.3.3) such as synonymy and antonymy. COBUILD has been especially prolific with this kind of information, though more so in the first edition than in the later ones; the first included information on hyponymy, not subsequently included. In COBUILD the information on sense relations is given in the Extra Column by means of the symbols '=' (for synonyms) and '≠' (for antonyms). For example, *heavy* as in *a heavy meal* is marked in COBUILD3 with '= filling', '≠ light'; and as in *the air is heavy*, it is marked with '= oppressive', '≠ cool, fresh'. OALD6 marks synonyms with **SYN** and antonyms with **OPP**, e.g. *impute* has **SYN** ATTRIBUTE, and *left-winger* has **OPP** RIGHT-WINGER; but OALD6 is more sparing with this information than COBUILD.

The second additional type of encoding information comes in the form of usage notes of various kinds. Some of this is in the form of labelling, as in NSDs, though sometimes with a little variation, e.g. OALD6 has the symbol of an exclamation mark in a triangle to warn users that the word or sense is slang or taboo. COBUILD2 has the term PRAGMATICS in the Extra Column to show that usage information is shown within the definition; in COBUILD3 the definition no longer contains this information and a specific label such as 'disapproval' or 'informal' has been substituted for PRAGMATICS in the Extra Column. The other dictionaries have 'usage notes' (LDOCE) of various kinds, as well as more extensive discussion on 'study pages' (OALD6) or in 'language portraits' (CIDE). OALD6, for example, has scattered through the dictionary boxed items entitled 'Vocabulary Building' (e.g. ways of saying *approximately*), 'Which Word?' (e.g. as/like), 'British/American' (e.g. already/just/yet), 'Grammar Point' (e.g. avenge/revenge), 'Word Family' (e.g. clear – clarity – clarify), 'More About' (e.g. of course). There is a recognition that learners need a range of information about words – grammatical, semantic and pragmatic – in order to be able to construct accurate and appropriate sentences in the target language.

11.4 Additional information

Some of the information mentioned in the previous paragraph goes beyond that strictly required for encoding. It is serving to enhance the learner's knowledge and understanding of the vocabulary of English in a wider sense, not just for the specific task that may have occasioned the look-up. Some of the information of this kind is cultural, putting words into a context that enhances understanding of them. In CIDE, for example, there is a boxed article entitled 'WORK' in the appropriate part of the dictionary, which discusses 'some common words and expressions we use in everyday conversation to talk about the work we do, leaving work, being out of work and looking for a job' (p. 1681), including differences between British and American English.

Some of the additional information is dispersed through the dictionary, near to relevant words. Other types are collected together, either in appendices or in groups of pages inserted at some point in the dictionary. OALD6 has a set of eight colour plates (between pages 372 and 373) of sets of objects (bread, cakes and desserts; fruit and vegetables; clothes and fabrics; the animal kingdom; games and toys); a set of sixteen 'study pages' (between 756 and 757), dealing in part with grammatical and lexical matters and in part with letter and CV writing; and an eight-page set of colour maps (between 1140 and 1141). Additionally, OALD6 contains appendices dealing with: irregular verbs; geographical names; numbers; punctuation; the language of literary criticism; an index to the usage notes; and the defining vocabulary.

The use of computer corpora has enabled lexicographers to obtain fairly reliable data on the frequency of occurrence of words and senses. This information has informed the design of MLDs since COBUILD1. From the beginning, COBUILD has included this information in the dictionary itself by marking words with a set of five diamonds. If all five diamonds are black, this indicates that the word belongs to the most frequent 700 in the language (e.g. *main*, *paper*); if four are filled in, the word belongs to the next 1200 most frequent (e.g. *maker*, *management*); if three are black, then it belongs to the next 1500 most frequent words (e.g. *panel*, *panic*); if two are black, then the word belongs to the next 3200 most frequent (e.g. *loyalty*, *lounge*); and if only one is black, then the word belongs to the next 8100 most frequent (e.g. *malt*, *mandatory*). So the diamond markings account for the 14,700 most frequent words according to the Bank of English corpus. The top two bands (1900 words), it is claimed, 'account for 75% of all English usage' (COBUILD2, p. xiii).

LDOCE3 also gives frequency information, but differentiates between occurrence in spoken English and in written English; and it accounts for only the 3000 most frequent words in each mode. The frequencies are indicated by the letters 'W' (for written) and 'S' (for spoken), followed by a numeral between '1' and '3': '1' indicates within the 1000 most frequent, '2' within the next 1000 most frequent, and '3' within the next 1000 most frequent. For example, *common* is marked S1, W1; *commitment* S2, W2; *compete* S3, W3; *committee* S3, W1; *comment* S1, W2; *comparison* S3, W2; *compensation* W3 only; *complicated* S2 only. This information is of interest to an advanced learner, and of particular use to teachers and course designers when considering how to sequence the introduction of vocabulary items. MLDs have developed far beyond their original conception in the 1930s and 1940s, not only in the range of information that they offer the learner, but also in the attention to the learner's needs and reference skills. The next development offers yet more.

11.5 MLDs on CD-ROM

All the four MLDs discussed in this chapter are available in CD-ROM format. In general, the MLDs have exploited the possibilities of the electronic medium rather more extensively than the NSDs (see 6.7), with additional features, cross-referencing and searching. For all except COBUILD the CD-ROM is available packaged together with the print dictionary, at a slightly higher price for the package than for the print version alone, though in the case of OALD it is a severely cutdown version of a separately available CD-ROM ('Text and Sound' only). Each CD-ROM offers a different set of features, and where applicable they have been developed from earlier versions: Heuberger (2000), for example, reviews electronic MLDs published in the late 1990s, whereas those reviewed here came out in 2000 or 2001.

LDOCE on CD-ROM, published in 2000 and based on LDOCE3, contains four sets of data, each with its own index: the dictionary, verb conjugations, pictures, tables (e.g. of numbers, word formation, geographical names). The dictionary index contains the A–Z headword list, and the picture index contains all the words that are illustrated by or within a picture. The dictionary entries and the words in the pictures are interlinked, by a camera icon in the dictionary entries, and by clicking on the words in the pictures. Similarly, the dictionary entries and verb conjugations are interlinked, so that if a user is unsure about the appropriate inflectional form of a verb, they can click on the 'V' icon in the dictionary entry for the verb.

Typing in a word in the 'choice' box takes you automatically to the appropriate part of the list. When a dictionary entry is selected, the pronunciation of the headword is given; it may also be selected by clicking on the speaker icon; however, only British pronunciation is given. Clicking on a further icon, a white cross in a white circle, gives a list of 'related words', i.e. headwords that contain the item concerned; for example, the related words given for *support* include *supporting, child support, life support system, price support, support group*. LDOCE on CD-ROM offers two further types of search, by activating the 'Search' item hidden in the 'Book' menu. One is a 'text' search, which allows searching for up to three words, joined by Boolean operators (*and, not, or*); you can search for a word (or words) in definitions (e.g. *insect*, to find all the 'insect' words) or for a label (e.g. 'determiner' or 'slang'). The other search is a 'headword' search, which allows the use of wildcards ('?' for any letter, '*' for any number of letters, including zero): '*gry' would find all the words ending in *gry* (only *angry* and *hungry*!), '?oo?' would find all the four-letter words with double 'o' in the middle (289 in LDOCE).

OALD on CD-ROM, published in 2001 and based on OALD6, contains a number of additional features. However, few of these are operational in the 'Text and Sound' version packaged with the print dictionary, though they are demonstrated. Like most CD-ROM dictionaries, the headword list is on the left of the screen, including a box in which a desired headword can be typed, with a larger window for the dictionary text on the right-hand side. Selection of a headword gives, in the headword list, the compounds that contain the word, followed by words whose definitions include it. Clicking on the appropriate speaker icon in the dictionary entry gives either British or American pronunciation of the headword. An 'Advanced Search' facility allows the selection of up to three words, joined by Boolean operators. Additionally, the search may be narrowed by selecting one of the 'Types' and/or one of the 'Filters'. A 'type' narrows the search to a particular type of information in the dictionary, e.g. headwords, idioms, collocates, definitions, examples. The 'filters' largely relate to labelling in the dictionary, e.g. for part-of-speech, register, and geography (British vs. American).

Additional features on the CD-ROM are accessed by clicking on a tab at the top of the screen. The tabs are labelled: 3-D Search, Pictures, Maps, Exercises, Games, Extras. All of these, apart from the first and the last, are self-explanatory. The 'Extras' section contains a lot of the extra material that is distributed through the print dictionary, such as the Guide to Using the Dictionary, the Topics pages, the Language Study pages, and so on. The really interesting and innovative feature is the '3-D Search facility'. This gives access to a set of 'spider' diagrams representing lexical fields (words that share the same 'area of meaning' – see Chapter 12), so that a user can locate the word they are looking up in relation to other closely related words in the vocabulary. At the least, this is useful vocabulary building information.

COBUILD on CD-ROM was published in 2001 and is based on COBUILD3, replacing an earlier version (1995) based on COBUILD2. However, the CD-ROM contains more than just the dictionary; it is an integrated resource with dictionary, thesaurus, grammar book, usage manual, and a 5-million 'Wordbank' drawn from the Bank of English to supply examples. When a word is typed in for look-up, the index points to all the sections of the CD-ROM in which it features, so that a range of information can be accessed from a single index. Indeed the index has two forms: 'Entries' and 'Full Text'. 'Entries' simply has the sections in which the word concerned occurs, i.e. dictionary, thesaurus, grammar, usage. 'Full Text' indexes are: 'Headings', i.e. headwords, including compounds, in which the item occurs; 'Explanations', i.e. headwords whose definitions contain the item; 'Sample Lists' from the grammar that contain the item; 'Examples', i.e. entries from the dictionary, usage, grammar and wordbank that contain the item; 'Synonyms', in the dictionary and thesaurus; and 'Antonyms' in the dictionary. Here is a wealth of interlinked information for exploring the meaning and use of a word and for finding guidance on employing it appropriately in writing.

Within the dictionary entries, each form (inflection) of a word has a speaker icon for activating its (British only) pronunciation. There are also buttons allowing both browsing through the dictionary entries, either forwards or backwards, as well as retracing the search history that a user has undertaken. As with other CD-ROM dictionaries, double-clicking on any word in the definitions or examples links to the entry for that word. The major feature of COBUILD on CD-ROM is the integration of the various lexical and grammatical information sources.

CIDE on CD-ROM was published in 2000 and is based on the first (1995) edition of the print dictionary. However, in many ways it is the most sophisticated of the CD-ROM dictionaries in the extent to which it goes beyond the print version in the exploitation of the electronic medium. It has two separate windows, which can be individually manipulated for size and position on the screen: one is the 'Search Panel', containing the indexes and various options for searching; the other is the 'Content Window', containing the dictionary entries, as well as sets of Exercises, Pictures, and Study Sections (e.g. on grammar, cultural information, word building, letter writing, and so on). Entering a word in the 'Find' box on the Search Panel automatically creates an index of related words, e.g. for *support*: **support**, *supportable*, *supported*, *support group*, **supporting**, *supportive*, *supportively*, *supportiveness*, *support system* (those in bold are main entries, the others sub-sentries within a main one). Clicking on any of these activates a more extensive index, which includes all the headwords for the item, followed by open compounds containing it, followed by headwords whose definitions contain it. Clicking on any of these brings the appropriate dictionary entry into the Content Window. Both British and American pronunciation can be activated.

Every entry in CIDE on CD-ROM is supplied with a link labelled 'Related words'. Clicking on this link activates the highly innovative feature of this CD-ROM dictionary, a differentiated and categorised lexical field analysis of the vocabulary. For example, clicking on the 'Related words' link for *support* (BEAR) offers three lexical fields: 'Psychology, Psychiatry and Psychoanalysis', 'Allowing and permitting', and 'Tolerating and enduring'. Selecting the last of these activates in the Search Panel a list of other verbs with a similar meaning, followed by words from other parts of speech, as well as phrases and expressions (e.g. *take it on the chin*). The lexical field analysis can be viewed in the Search Panel, which allows for a field to be selected and all the words and expressions in the field to be listed. The vocabulary is analysed at the most general level into 17 broad categories:

1 art and entertainment
2 building and civil engineering
3 clothes, belongings and personal care
4 communication
5 education
6 finance and business
7 general/abstract
8 history
9 life, death and the living world
10 light and colour
11 movement and location
12 religion
13 science
14 society
15 sports, games and pastimes

16   thinking and understanding
17   war and the military.

Each of these has further sub-divisions and sub-divisions of sub-divisions. With this facility, CIDE on CD-ROM not only provides an aid for a learner's vocabulary building, but, lexicographically, bridges the gap between alphabetical dictionary and thematic thesaurus (see Chapter 12).

CIDE on CD-ROM's Search Panel allows other differentiated searches to be undertaken: by 'Part of Speech', by 'Label' (including geographical and register), by 'Grammar', by 'Category' (i.e. of text – Headword, Idiom, Definition text, Example text, Usage notes, etc.), and by 'Frequency'. The 'Grammar' search allows specification of grammatical features or structures indicated in the dictionary; for example, '+ object + that clause' finds all the verbs (42 in CIDE) that are followed by an Object and a *that*-clause, '+ two objects' all the ditransitive verbs (152 in CIDE), 'after verb' all the predicative only adjectives (322 in CIDE), and 'not gradable' all the non-gradable adjectives (3202 in CIDE). The 'Frequency' search has categories from 'Rare' to 'Very Common', along with 'Defining Vocabulary'; selecting 'Very Common' lists the 611 words so designated, and 'Common' the 3181 words with this frequency. Information of this kind is invaluable to the teacher and course writer, and certainly of interest to the advanced student.

All the MLDs on CD-ROM have in different ways begun to exploit the electronic medium for extending what they can offer to users of learners' dictionaries, CIDE more so than the others. But the medium has yet to be exploited to the full (Jehle 1999).

11.6 Further reading

The development of learners' dictionaries, up to the 'third generation' (OALD4, LDOCE2 and COBUILD1), is told in Tony Cowie's *English Dictionaries for Foreign Learners: A History* (1999). The process of compiling COBUILD1 is reported by some of those involved in *Looking Up: An Account of the COBUILD Project* (1987), edited by John Sinclair.

Articles on the 1995 generation of MLDs are contained in *The Perfect Learners' Dictionary(?)* (1999) edited by Thomas Herbst and Kerstin Popp. Reinhard Heuberger reviews both print and CD-ROM versions of MLDs in his doctoral thesis, published as *Monolingual Dictionaries for Foreign Learners of English* (2000).

The Hausmann *et al.* (1989–91) *International Encyclopedia of Lexicography* contains a number of articles on learners' dictionaries. A seminal contribution is Michael Rundell's (1998) article, 'Recent Trends in English Pedagogical Lexicography', in the *International Journal of Lexicography*.

12 Abandoning the alphabet

If you look up the word *dictionary* in a dictionary, you will find a definition along the lines of:

> a book that consists of an alphabetical list of words, with their meanings, parts of speech, pronunciations, etymologies, etc.

> (CCD4)

'Dictionary order' is synonymous with 'alphabetical order'. We expect dictionaries to use alphabetical ordering of their headwords, just as we expect other reference works to do so as well, such as telephone directories, encyclopedias, and indexes of all kinds. Because we have learnt the order of the letters in the alphabet, it is the most convenient system for locating an item in a written list. Our skill in using the alphabet for this purpose can be generalised to all manner of written lists.

As a reference manual, therefore, a dictionary's headword list is ideally arranged alphabetically, so that users can readily access the item that they are seeking. And it is usually a single item that is being looked up. However, we must ask, first, whether an alphabetical ordering is best for presenting a description of the vocabulary as a whole, and second, whether there are some users' needs that would be better served by an alternative arrangement of words in a dictionary.

12.1 Disadvantages of A–Z

One of the drawbacks of an alphabetical listing is that some words that belong together morphologically become separated. This applies, in particular, to two kinds of relation. First, words that are derived by prefixation (see 2.2.2) are entered separately from their root, and there is usually no indication at the entry for the root that it has a prefixed derivative. Derivatives by suffixation are entered either as separate headwords, but close to the root in the alphabetical sequence, or as run-ons under the root; so that the relation between root and derivative is clear. For example, *courage* and its derivative *courageous* come in close proximity in the alphabetical list, but *discourage* and *encourage* are distant and the connection is not made. The second kind of morphological link relates to words – mostly nouns of OE origin – that have a matching word – mostly adjectives of Latinate origin – in another word class. For example, *lung* (noun) has matching *pulmonary* (adjective), *church* has *ecclesiastical*, *mind* has *mental*, *earthquake* has *seismic*, *horse* has *equine*, and so on. CED notes at the noun the 'Related adj.', but dictionaries do not as a rule make the connection.

A more serious disadvantage of alphabetical ordering is the perspective that it presents on the vocabulary as a whole. It presents an atomistic view of the vocabulary, treating each word in isolation, the headword with its entry, and making few of the connections that exist between words. Just like other areas of language – phonology, grammar – the lexicon is a system, with paradigmatic (synonymy, antonymy, hyponymy, meronymy) and syntagmatic (collocation) relations (Jackson and Zé Amvela 2000, Ch. 5). In lexicology, an attempt is made to capture some of these relations in the notion of 'semantic/lexical fields' (Lehrer 1974; Jackson 1988: 210–16). A lexical field is a set of lexemes that are used to talk about a defined area of experience; Lehrer (1974), for example, has an extensive discussion of the field of 'cooking' terms. A lexical field analysis will attempt to establish the lexemes that are available in the vocabulary for talking about the area under investigation and then propose how they differ from each other in meaning and use. Such an analysis begins to show how the vocabulary as a whole is structured, and more so when individual lexical fields are brought into relationship with each other. There is no prescribed or agreed method for determining what constitutes a lexical field; each scholar must draw their own boundaries and establish their own criteria. Much work still needs to be undertaken in researching this approach to vocabulary. Lexical field analysis is reflected in dictionaries that take a 'topical' or 'thematic' approach to presenting and describing words.

The distinction is often drawn in terms of the dichotomy between a 'semasiological' and an 'onomasiological' approach to the description of vocabulary. The semasiological (from Greek *semasia* 'meaning') approach proceeds from forms (terms, words) to meanings or concepts, and it results in traditional, alphabetically ordered dictionaries. The onomasiological (from Greek *onomasia* 'term') approach (Kipfer 1986) proceeds from concepts to terms, and it results in works of the thesaurus type, organised by theme or topic. Some attempts have been made to combine the two approaches, most notably by dictionaries of French published by Dictionnaires Le Robert, where extensive cross-referencing to synonyms and antonyms is made within most entries, e.g.

> **IMMENSE** adj. **1** vx Illimité, infini. **2** Dont l'étendu, les dimensions sont considérables. → **grand, illimité, vaste**. *Perdu dans l'immense océan.* **3** Qui est très considérable en son genre (par la force, l'importance, la quantité). → **colossal, énorme**. *Une foule immense. Une immense fortune.* contr. **Infime, minuscule**.
>
> (*Le Robert Collège* 1997)

The arrow points to synonyms, and the abbreviation 'contr.' (contraire) introduces antonyms. A similar, but less systematic attempt is reflected in the synonym essays provided by LDEL2 and ECED, e.g.

> **synonyms Huge, vast, immense, enormous, mammoth, elephantine, giant, gigantic, colossal, gargantuan, titanic**: **huge** is a general term, expressing great size, bulk, or capacity *<a huge man> <huge piles of wheat>*. **Vast** stresses extent or range *<vast distances>*. **Immense** and **enormous** suggest size or degree far in excess of what is usual, with **immense** sometimes implying almost infinite *<immense vistas of blue sky> <enormous strength>*. **Mammoth** and **elephantine** suggest the large size and unwieldy nature of the animals they recall. Used figuratively, **mammoth** can mean 'excessive' or 'extravagant' *<a mammoth darts tournament>*. **Giant** and **gigantic** suggest something abnormally large; **gigantic** is preferred for figurative use *<a giant doll> <a gigantic bill for repairs>*. **Colossal** suggests something of awesomely large proportions, while **titanic** implies the colossal size and primitive strength of the Titans. The hugeness of **gargantuan** is like that of Rabelais' hero: larger than life, especially with regard to food and appetites. **antonyms** tiny, minute, minuscule.
>
> (LDEL2)

But that is about as far as it goes in conventional general-purpose dictionaries for native speakers. Learners' dictionaries often provide more information, at least about synonyms and antonyms, e.g. COBUILD in its 'Extra Column' (Chapter 11).

12.2 The thematic tradition in lexicography

The alphabetisation of word lists goes back to the Latin–English glossaries compiled by scholar monks during the Old English period, but so does the arrangement of vocabulary by topic (see 4.1). The most famous of the latter is Ælfric's *Glossary*, published as an appendix to his *Grammar* of Latin. Ælfric, who lived from around 955 to 1020, became Abbot of Eynsham, near Oxford, in 1005; his tasks included the teaching of Latin to English-speaking novices. The *Glossary* groups Latin words with their English glosses into sets, and Werner Hüllen, in his account of Ælfric's work (1999: 62ff), suggests that the sets might have the following titles and structure:

1   God, heaven, earth, mankind
2.1 Parts of the human body
2.2 church offices
2.3 family relationships
2.4 state offices, including crafts and instruments as well as tools
2.5 negative features of human character
2.6 intellectual work

2.7 diseases, afflictions, merits
2.8 weather, universe
3   Birds
4   Fish
5   Wild animals
6   Herbs
7   Trees
8.1 Buildings (churches, monasteries), materials and objects used there
8.2 war, castles, arms, valuable materials
8.3 various
8.4 human vices.

Ælfric's hope was to encompass the whole vocabulary in his scheme, though he recognised that he had not done so. The topical organisation certainly betrays the concerns of an early medieval churchman.

As dictionary making, both bilingual and monolingual, developed, the alphabetical tradition dominated, but, especially under the influence of the Renaissance, thematic wordbooks were also compiled, most famously that by the Moravian Comenius (Johann Amos Komensky, 1592–1670) under the title *Ianua linguarum reserata* (*The Gate of Tongues Unlocked*), of which a Latin and a German version were published in 1631. In English, the most famous work of the time is that of John Wilkins, as part of his proposal for a 'universal language', with the title *An Essay Towards a Real Character, And a Philosophical Language*, published in 1668. As part of his proposal, Wilkins put forward a scheme for classifying the vocabulary of any language; at its most general level, it is described in eleven chapters in the *Essay* (Hüllen 1999: 253):

I   the *transcendentals*, the general notions which determine all the subsequent principles of order. They include 'discourse', that is 'words' as opposed to 'things'
II   God, the creator, and the creation, that is the world observed collectively
III   together with all the following chapters is devoted to the world observed distributively . . . the inanimate elements under the 'predicament', that is, the category of substance
IV   the vegetative species
V   the sensitive species
VI   the significant parts of vegetative and sensitive species
VII   various phenomena belonging to 'quantity', a category which is subsumed under the category 'accident'. So are the following four chapters.
VIII   various phenomena belonging to 'quality'
IX   various phenomena belonging to 'action'
X   various phenomena belonging to 'private relation'
XI   various phenomena belonging to 'public relation'.

Each of these broad categories is further divided and subdivided, following a logical, philosophical scheme.

The work by Wilkins was familiar to the author of the best-known thematic wordbook, Peter Mark Roget's *Thesaurus of English Words and Phrases*, first published in 1852 and still in print in a number of editions, the most genuine of which is Kirkpatrick (1995). Roget was by profession a medical physician, but with wide-ranging interests; he contributed to the *Encyclopaedia Britannica* and wrote treatises on electricity and magnetism (McArthur 1992: 871). In 1849, at the age of 70, having retired after 22 years as Secretary of the Royal Society, Roget returned to an undertaking that had interested him for over forty years: to create a reference work containing words 'arranged . . . according to the *ideas* which they express':

> The object aimed at in the present undertaking is . . . the idea being given, to find the word, or words, by which that idea may be most fitly and aptly expressed.
>
> (Introduction)

While motivated by considerations of 'practical utility', Roget's classification scheme reaches back to the notions behind Wilkins' 'philosophical tables'. Roget has six broad 'Classes', which are initially subdivided into 'Sections' (see Table 12.1).

Table 12.1

Class		Section	
I	ABSTRACT RELATIONS	I	Existence
		II	Relation
		III	Quantity
		IV	Order
		V	Number
		VI	Time
		VII	Change
		VIII	Causation
II	SPACE	I	Generally
		II	Dimensions
		III	Form
		IV	Motion
III	MATTER	I	Generally
		II	Inorganic
		III	Organic
IV	INTELLECT	I	Formation of Ideas
		II	Communication of Ideas
V	VOLITION	I	Individual
		II	Intersocial
VI	AFFECTIONS	I	Generally
		II	Personal
		III	Sympathetic
		IV	Moral
		V	Religious

Table 12.2

IV. ORDER				
1. GENERAL	58	Order	59	Disorder
	60	Arrangement	61	Derangement
2. CONSECUTIVE	62	Precedence	63	Sequence
	64	Precursor	65	Sequel
	66	Beginning	67	End
		68 Middle		
	69	Continuity	70	Discontinuity
	71	Term		
3. COLLECTIVE	72	Assemblage	73	Non-assemblage. Dispersion
	74	Focus		
4. DISTRIBUTIVE	75	Class		
	76	Inclusion	77	Exclusion
	78	Generality	79	Speciality
5. CATEGORICAL	80	Rule	81	Multiformity
	82	Conformity	83	Unconformity

Each of the 'Sections' is further subdivided into the lowest level of sets of words arranged where applicable in pairs of opposites, e.g. under Class I, Section IV (see Table 12.2).

The sets of words and phrases are listed in the main body of the *Thesaurus*, on two-column pages, under word classes, with nouns first, followed by verbs, then adjectives and adverbs. No other information is given – no definitions, pronunciation, or etymology; it is intended as a 'storehouse' or 'treasure' (= Greek *thesauros*) of words, which a writer will plunder for the one that is apt for their purpose.

If you are familiar with *Roget's Thesaurus*, you will know that about the last third of the work is taken up with an alphabetical 'Index', and many users find this to be the most convenient route into the thesaurus. During his lifetime – he died in 1869 at the age of 90 – Peter Mark Roget did not include an index in any of the editions that he compiled and edited; that defeated the purpose of the work. It was his son, John Lewis Roget, who added the Index; he also undertook a major revision of the work in 1879 and continued to edit it until his death in 1908. The editorship then passed to his son, Samuel Romilly Roget, who undertook a major revision in 1936, and then sold the rights to Longman in 1952, the year before he died (McArthur 1992: 871). *Roget's Thesaurus* remains as an institution among reference works for the English language and as a monument to the thematic tradition of wordbooks.

12.3 Specialist thesauruses/thesauri

A number of compilers of modern reference books about words have chosen to present their material in a thematic, rather than alphabetic, format. They believe that it serves their purposes to greater effect and gives an enhanced insight into the set of vocabulary that they are describing. We review here four such reference works. The first is *A Thesaurus of Old English* (Roberts *et al.* 1995), which is a presentation of the vocabulary of Old English, as far as it can be gleaned from the extant manuscripts of the period. The vocabulary is arranged in 18 broad classes:

1 the physical world
2 life and death
3 matter and measurement
4 material needs
5 existence
6 mental faculties
7 opinion
8 emotion
9 language and communication
10 possession
11 action and utility
12 social interaction
13 peace and war
14 law and order
15 property
16 religion
17 work
18 leisure.

Each of these classes is further subdivided. For example, '9. Language and Communication' has a general class and seven subclasses:

09   Speech, vocal utterance
09.01   To speak, exercise faculty of speech
09.02   Silence, refraining from speech
09.03   A language
09.04   Sense, purport, meaning
09.05   Curiosity
09.06   To take matter for discourse
09.07   Dispute, debate.

Under each of these is listed the modern English word or paraphrase, followed by the OE term, e.g.

09.01.01 A speech, what is said, words: (ge)spræc, word, wordlac
A dictum, remark, observation: spell
A saying, words: cwide, word, wordcwide
A phrase: foreset(ted)nes
A formula: formala, hiw

An idiom: wise
A verse, sentence (of Bible): fers
A discourse: mæþelcwide, mæþelword, spræce, tospræc
A set speech: getynges
An instructive talk: spell
A thesis, proposition: betynung.

The Thesaurus provides a most insightful analysis of the vocabulary available at this early period in the history of the English language, as well as a sober reminder of the words that disappeared from English as a consequence of the Norman conquest.

The second example is a presentation of the vocabulary of a regional variety of the language, *The Scots Thesaurus* (McLeod 1990). The *Thesaurus* presents some 20,000 Scots words, with the focus on rural Scotland, under fifteen broad categories:

1   birds, wild animals, invertebrates
2   domestic animals
3   water life
4   plants
5   environment
6   water, sea, ships
7   farming
8   life cycle, family
9   physical states
10 food and drink
11 law
12 war, fighting, violence
13 architecture, building, trades
14 religion, superstition, education, festivals
15 emotions, character, social behaviour.

Each category is further subdivided, e.g. 10.6 gives words for 'Bread, Oatcakes, etc.' and 10.7 for 'Cakes, Pastry, Biscuits'. Within the subdivisions, the items are listed in alphabetical order; 10.6 contains almost 90 lexemes, some of which are regionally restricted – the relevant areas or counties of Scotland are indicated, e.g.

* *luifie* a kind of flat bread roll *Ags* [i.e. *Angus*]
* *nickie* an oatcake or bun with an indented edge *chf Fif* [i.e. *chiefly Fife*]
* *rumpie* a small crusty loaf or roll *now Per WC* [i.e. now *Perthshire West Central*]
* *skair scone* a kind of oatmeal-and-flour scone made with beaten egg and milk.

The third example is still under construction in the Department of English Language at the University of Glasgow under the direction of Professor Christian Kay: the *Historical Thesaurus of English*. Begun in 1964 by Kay's predecessor, Professor M.L. Samuels, the *Historical Thesaurus* is based on the materials of the OED, supplemented by further research. It aims to present the vocabulary of English from the earliest written records onwards in a semantic and chronological arrangement, so that a user can see how the vocabulary of English has developed in any particular area of meaning. As with all thematic dictionaries, its effectiveness depends in large part on its classification system:

> The classification which has resulted from examination of the data is based on a modified folk taxonomy. There are three major divisions: (I) The World, including the physical universe, plants and animals; (II) The Mind, covering man's mental activities; and (III) Society, which deals with social structures and artefacts. Within these major divisions the material is arranged in numbered hierarchical categories, each consisting of a defining heading followed by chronological lists of all the words, with their dates of currency, ever used as synonyms or near synonyms for the definition.
>
> (HTE website)

The database of the HTE will be constructed in such a way that sophisticated searches will be possible, e.g. to find all the words meaning 'laugh' that came into the language between 1300 and 1500, or to find all the words current in Renaissance English for a particular area of meaning. The *Thesaurus of Old English*, considered earlier, is an offshoot of this project, but while the OE thesaurus presents, in lexical field arrangement, a snapshot of the vocabulary at a particular time period, the HTE will show how the vocabulary has developed from OE over time, lexical field by lexical field. Further information on the HTE project, together with examples, can be viewed on the *Historical Thesaurus of English* website (see References).The final example of a specialist thematic dictionary is specialist in two ways: it is restricted to a particular area of vocabulary, that of science, and it is directed specifically at learners of English: the *Longman Dictionary of Scientific Usage* (Godman and Payne 1979). This dictionary is aimed at those who are studying science through the medium of English and for whom English is not their first language. The vocabulary of science is presented under 19 broad divisions, numbered 'A' to 'U' ('I' and 'O' are not used). Division A contains 'Basic Terms', and like the other divisions it is subdivided into 'Sets':

AA   Space
AB   Matter
AC   Shape
AD   Existence
AE   Constitution
AF   Movement

AG Change
AH Time
AJ Process
AK Knowledge
AL Word analysis
AM Statement
AN Measurement
AP Relationship
AQ Experiment.

The remaining divisions contain the 'Scientific Terms'; each division contains sets that are semantically related, e.g. H has the following sets:

HA Irritability
HB Nervous System
HC Sight
HD Hearing
HE Sense Organs.

Within each set, the individual terms are arranged, not alphabetically, but in order to form a coherent account of the area of science, proceeding from those terms that have a more general reference to those that are more specific. Each term is provided with a word class label, a definition and explanation, occasionally an example sentence, and extensive cross-references, both to earlier and later within the set and to other sets. For example, from Set HD 'Hearing':

HD001 hearing (*n.*) One of the senses of animals, concerned with the stimulus of sound. Hearing is well developed in tetrapod vertebrates, but poorly developed in fishes; it is well developed in insects but not in most other invertebrates. – **hear** (*v.*) ↓ AUDIBILITY • SCOLOPHORE • STATOCYST • LATERAL LINE SYSTEM • AUDIBLE • EAR • MIDDLE EAR • INNER EAR • MEMBRANOUS LABYRINTH • COCHLEA → IRRITABILITY

HD005 statocyst (*n.*) (In some invertebrates) an organ of balance, consisting of a vesicle containing statoliths with sensory cells on the vesicle walls, Hair-like processes on the sensory cells are stimulated by the statoliths when the animal moves. ↓ OTIDIUM • OTOCYST • STATOLITH ↑ HEARING

The downward-pointing arrow indicates a cross-reference to an item or items later in the set, an upward pointing arrow to those earlier in the set, and an arrow pointing to the right cross-refers to another set. The dictionary is supplied with an alphabetical index, which gives the code for the set in which the term is described, together with its number within the set. The authors envisage that the dictionary will be used in four ways:

1. 'Finding the meaning of a term when reading' – using the index in order to locate the term. This is a conventional dictionary use.

2. 'Using a term when writing' – again the index is used to locate the term, but the focus is on what can be gleaned from the entry about using the term. This is a conventional use for learners' dictionaries.

3. 'Searching for an unknown term when writing' – either with the index using a known term, or with the contents to identify the set that represents the area of meaning being written about. This is the genuine thesaurus use, as envisaged by Roget for his *Thesaurus*.

4. 'Revising the terms of a particular topic' – because each set of terms is logically structured and internally cross-referenced, it gives a good over-view of the topic for revision purposes.

What these four examples show is that the thematic tradition in lexicography can be exploited imaginatively to present information about words for specific purposes, where an alphabetical arrangement would be incapable of yielding the desired insights for the intended uses and users.

12.4 Thematic dictionaries for learners

A thematic presentation can help learners of English as a second or foreign language in at least two ways. First, much language teaching tends to be by topic, and a thematic dictionary would, therefore, be an obvious reference work to accompany such an approach. Second, one of a learner's difficulties in writing, besides ascertaining the appropriate grammatical and collocational pat-terns that a word may enter, is making the appropriate choice of word in the first place. This presupposes knowledge of the vocabulary items that could be used to express the idea or concept, from among which the item may be cho-sen. Moreover, learners benefit from some more explicit help in enabling them to perceive the often subtle semantic and pragmatic distinctions between words with similar meaning.

The first thematic dictionary for learners was Tom McArthur's *Longman Lexicon of Contemporary English* (1981), whose genesis and career he describes in Chapter 14 of McArthur (1998). McArthur consciously places his work in the thematic tradition, which he subsequently reviewed in *Worlds of Reference* (1986):

> The alphabetical dictionary has a logic, but it is not the logic of everyday life. In principle, one feels, words should be defined in the company they usually keep. Two famous moves in this direction have been the *Janua Linguarum Reserata* in 1631, the work of the Bohemian educator Comenius, and Roget's *Thesaurus*, first published by Longman in 1852. The *Longman Lexicon of Contemporary English* belongs in this tradition.
>
> Comenius had a hundred chapters and a religious bias, while Roget used a scheme of universal concepts as a framework for his prodigious lists. The

Lexicon, however, has only fourteen 'semantic fields' of a pragmatic, every-day nature.

(Preface, p. vi)

As McArthur indicates, the vocabulary selection that he takes – 15,000 words from the 'central vocabulary of the English language' – is arranged in fourteen broad categories, numbered 'A' to 'N':

A   Life and Living Things
B   The Body: its Functions and Welfare
C   People and the Family
D   Buildings, Houses, the Home, Clothes, Belongings, and Personal Care
E   Food, Drink, and Farming
F   Feelings, Emotions, Attitudes, and Sensations
G   Thought and Communication, Language and Grammar
H   Substances, Materials, Objects, and Equipment
I   Arts and Crafts, Science and Technology, Industry and Education
J   Numbers, Measurement, Money, and Commerce
K   Entertainment, Sports, and Games
L   Space and Time
M   Movement, Location, Travel, and Transport
N   General and Abstract Terms.

Each broad 'semantic field' is subdivided, and within the subdivisions the lexical items are arranged in related sets, often belonging to the same word class. Each item is provided with definitions and examples. Although its compilation preceded it, McArthur had access to the LDOCE1 (1978) materials, so that the entries in the *Lexicon* match those in the *Dictionary*. The careful arrangement of items in sets and the provision of definitions and examples enable a learner to understand the differences between related words and to choose the one appropriate to the particular context of use. By way of illustration, here are the subdivisions of Field F, followed by the entries for the set F173:

F1   Feeling and Behaviour Generally
F20   Liking and Not Liking
F50   Good and Evil
F70   Happiness and Sadness
F100   Anger, Violence, Stress, Calm, and Quietness
F120   Fear and Courage
F140   Admiration, Pride, Contempt, and Abuse
F170   Kindness and Unkindness
F190   Honesty, Loyalty, Trickery, and Deceit
F220   Relaxation, Excitement, Interest, and Surprise
F240   Actions of the Face Related to Feelings
F260   Senses and Sensations.

F173 *adjectives* : **humanitarian and charitable** [B]

humanitarian concerned with trying to improve life for human beings by giving them better conditions to live in and changing laws, esp those which punish too severely

generous showing readiness to give money, help, kindness, etc: *She's not very generous with the food; she gives very small amounts. You are far too generous with your money.* **–ly** [adv]

liberal generous, esp in giving or being given quickly and easily or in large amounts: *He is very liberal with his money. She gave us liberal helpings of food.* **–lly** [adv]

magnanimous having or showing unusually generous qualities towards others: *A country should be magnanimous towards its defeated enemies.* **–ly** [adv]

charitable showing kindness and charity [→ F175]: *Be charitable; try to help them.* **–bly** [adv Wa3]

The codes (B, Wa3) are those from LDOCE1. The *Lexicon* contains line drawings and it is provided with an alphabetical index, where the pronunciation is indicated (in IPA transcription). Where an item has more than one sense, or belongs to more than one word class, which would assign it to different semantic fields or sets, this is given briefly in the Index, e.g.

long   wish *v* F6
measurement *adj* J63
distance or time *adj* L139, N307

The index thus enables a learner to quickly review the semantic range that a word has, as well as to locate the item in the appropriate semantic set.

Unlike Roget's *Thesaurus*, McArthur's *Lexicon* provides in the thematic format the range of information that would be expected in a dictionary, at least for learners. In that sense it is a true 'thematic dictionary'. It is to be regretted that it has never been updated or expanded, or, indeed, that no publisher has dared to produce such a work as a complement to a general-purpose native speaker dictionary. The semantic classification of the words in CIDE on the CD-ROM (see 11.5) proceeds along the same lines and encompasses all the 50,000 headwords of CIDE, but the electronic format does not allow the overview of the structure of the vocabulary that the printed *Lexicon* does. After all, the basic arrangement of the entries in CIDE on CD-ROM is still the alphabetical format of the print version.

There is one further reference work for learners that incorporates some of the insights from the thematic tradition: the *Longman Language Activator* (1993), which advertises itself as 'the world's first production dictionary'. It addresses specifically the needs of learners in writing and speaking to be able to choose the appropriate word and to use it correctly. The *Activator* is constructed around 1052 'concepts' or 'key words':

These concepts express the meanings at the heart of the English language. It should be pointed out straight away, however, that the *Activator* does not address itself to words for 'real world' items, some of which, of course, also belong to the core of English. We believe that concrete nouns, and content words in general, present fewer, less serious problems of correct use for students, so you will not find different types of transport, dogs, machinery or buildings here. That is left to the *Longman Lexicon*, which deals effectively with semantic fields, including real world items.

The concepts . . . have clear, direct names such as FAR, SAD/UNHAPPY, HOPE, INTEND, EASY, FAULT/STH WRONG, and BUT.

(Introduction, p. F8)

The key word entry is structured in the following way. If the word has more than one broad meaning, these are identified first and a reference given to the keyword under which each meaning is explained. For example, the key word *modern* has two meanings identified:

*   *modern places, methods, etc.* → MODERN
*   *using the newest equipment, technology, etc.* → ADVANCED.

Then, under each key word, lexical items are grouped together in related sets, with a summary of the sets at the beginning of the entry, e.g. for *modern*:

1   words for describing machines, systems, processes etc that have been developed using the most recent ideas and equipment
2   using, or willing to use, the most recent ideas and ways of thinking
3   words for describing modern art, literature, music, etc
4   to change something in order to make it modern.

The items in each of these sets are listed, together with the description (as above) at the beginning of the set. For Set 2 of *modern*, the items are: *modern, progressive, innovative, forward-looking, move with the times, go-ahead.* Each of the lexical items is provided with an entry including pronunciation, word class, definition and examples.

The key words are arranged alphabetically in the dictionary, and the alphabetical list contains all the lexemes treated in the dictionary. Those that are not key words are cross-referenced to the key word under which they are treated. The *Activator* has its headwords ordered alphabetically, but under 1052 of them – the 'key words' – a thematic approach is taken and lexical items are organised into lexical sets.

12.5 Continuing the tradition

A thematic dictionary provides an insight into the structure of the vocabulary that an alphabetical dictionary cannot possibly afford. Nevertheless, even with works like *Roget's Thesaurus*, for most people the entry point to any wordbook is through an alphabetical list. Thematic dictionaries such as *Roget* and the *Longman Lexicon* have needed to provide an index in order to facilitate their use, provide an entry point, and enhance their usefulness. This, along with the fact that many words will be entered several times, in different places, in a thematic dictionary, has tended to make such dictionaries either limited in scope – the *Longman Lexicon* has only 15,000 items – or potentially rather unwieldy. Perhaps it is not surprising that no publisher has ventured a general-purpose thematic dictionary. The other potential disadvantage of a thematic dictionary is that, because a word with multiple meanings may be entered partially in several places, no overall view of the word's lexical description is offered.

The electronic medium, however, opens up new possibilities (McArthur 1998, Ch. 15). So far, most, if not all, publishers that have brought out a CD-ROM version of their dictionaries have simply transferred the alphabetically arranged print version to the electronic medium. Any enhancement has, for the most part, been in the search facilities provided for the electronic version, though learners' dictionaries on CD-ROM have gone further. Most notable is CIDE on CD-ROM's semantic field analysis (see 11.5 and above), which assigns each headword/meaning to a set within an elaborately structured hierarchy of fields. It has, thus, bolted a thematic framework onto an alphabetical one, but it is the alphabetical one that is transparent, since you can browse/scroll through the entries in the alphabetical list, but not through those in the thematic one: you have to pull each item in the list individually from its place in the alphabetical structure. I would like to suggest that this is the wrong way round.

An alphabetical lookup is always for a single item. Because you type the item in for a lookup in an electronic dictionary, it does not matter how the dictionary is structured. Indeed, some electronic dictionaries (e.g. COD10) show you only one entry per screen. The entries could therefore be stored on CD-ROM in random order; it would make little difference to a search for a single item. However, if they were stored by semantic field, and it was possible to scroll through the entries, a CD-ROM dictionary could fulfil both purposes: the single lookup, which is the advantage of an alphabetical organisation; and the lexical field analysis, which is the benefit of a thematic organisation. Some provision would also need to be made for composite entries of items distributed across semantic fields. But the electronic medium does not have the space considerations of print.

12.6 Further reading

A most lucid account of the development of the thematic tradition in reference works, including lexicography, is found in Tom McArthur's *Worlds of Reference* (1986), now, lamentably, out of print. Chapters 12 to 14 of his *Living Words* (1998) also deal with thematic lexicography, including an account of the *Longman Lexicon*. Werner Hüllen's *English Dictionaries 800–1700: The Topical Tradition*

(1999) treats in some detail the major works during the development of the tradition.

Genuine editions of *Roget's Thesaurus* (e.g. Kirkpatrick 1995) contain Roget's original introduction in which he outlines the rationale for the work and its underlying conception.

13 Compiling dictionaries

Any dictionary, apart perhaps from the occasional scholarly undertaking, is a commercial venture. It requires considerable investment in staff, equipment, materials, and time. The investment is unlikely to be recouped for a number of years. Dictionary projects run to a budget and to a timetable. They have to be planned and managed; they require the involvement of people with a wide range of specialist knowledges and skills. Like marriage, compiling a dictionary is not something to be 'contemplated lightly'. This chapter looks at some of the issues involved in dictionary compilation and considers some of the decisions that confront lexicographers and editors of dictionaries.

Some dictionaries have had their stories told. Reddick (1990) uses recent scholarship to recount how Samuel Johnson went about compiling his *Dictionary of the English Language*. Elizabeth Murray's biography of her grandfather, James Murray, entitled *Caught in the Web of Words* (1977), traces the genesis of the *Oxford English Dictionary* and especially James Murray's contribution as the principal editor of the first edition. Herbert Morton has written an account of *Webster's Third* and its editor, Philip Gove (Morton 1994). And the volume entitled *Looking Up*, edited by John Sinclair (1987), gives insight into the development of the COBUILD learners' dictionary.

13.1 The plan

No dictionary can begin to be compiled without considerable forethought and planning. Commercial publishers do not normally release their plans to the public, though some of the thinking that underlies a particular dictionary or edition often finds expression in the preface or introduction. The one famous published plan is Samuel Johnson's (see 4.5) *Plan of a Dictionary of the English Language* (in Wilson 1957), written to satisfy his bookseller/publisher sponsors and, at their instigation, to seek the patronage of the Earl of Chesterfield, unsuccessfully as it turned out. Whether made public or not, the plan of a dictionary has to address a number of important questions and make decisions about issues that will affect the nature of the finished product.

One of the earliest decisions to be made relates to the target user group. Indeed that decision may already have been taken before the planning process starts. Deciding, for example, to produce a dictionary for children aged 7 to 10 (Years 3 to 6 of primary school) will need to be a starting point from which other questions and decisions will flow. Similarly, if a learners' dictionary is proposed, that needs to be in view from the outset of the planning. General-purpose dictionaries, however, even though having a general native-speaker target audience, may have a conscious bias towards a particular subset of those users. ECED, for example, has 'the needs of families and students in mind' (dust jacket). Most dictionaries presuppose a general user, without specifying any particular subgroup; CCD4 is 'for everyone whether reading, writing or studying, and . . . for all who love the English language' (p. ix), whereas *Chambers* attempts to be all-inclusive in its identification of potential users:

> *Chambers* is a dictionary of unrivalled value to users of English – to students, scholars, writers, journalists, librarians and publishers. It is replete with words of technical importance to scientists, lawyers, accountants and people in business. *Chambers* is the reference dictionary for the UK National Scrabble® Championship; it is the favourite dictionary of crossword setters and solvers; it is the treasure chest for all word-game players and word lovers.
>
> (dust jacket)

There is some benefit in specifying as wide a market as possible for one's product!

Almost as crucial as the target audience is the decision on the size of the dictionary, since this will have a significant effect on a number of further issues at the planning stage. Size itself correlates both with cost and with the price at which the dictionary can be sold. A 'concise' dictionary (see 3.2) would probably have between 60,000 and 90,000 headwords and cost between £16 and £20 (at 2001 prices); 'desk-size' dictionaries are substantially larger and sell at around £30. Size will also have an effect on the format of the printed product, both in terms of its overall dimensions and the layout of its page, though other factors will significantly affect the latter as well, such as how many columns the page has. Most dictionaries have two columns of text to the page, but some recent dictionaries, both desk-size (NODE) and concise (ECED), have three columns.

Both size and target users will influence a further decision in the planning stage, concerning the coverage of the dictionary. A learners' dictionary will seek to pay more attention to the core vocabulary of the language, rather than to more specialist and technical words. A 'pocket' dictionary will also have less room for specialist vocabulary. But, in an effort to be up-to-date, general-purpose dictionaries will want to include, certainly in their desk and concise editions, words from fields such as computing, medicine, technology, business and finance, and the environment. Similarly, dictionaries will want to include current colloquial and slang words that have earned their place in the record of the vocabulary, even vulgar or taboo words. More optional may be the inclusion of words from other varieties of English around the world, though it would be unusual to exclude words at least from American English. More optional still would be dialect words from within the British Isles, though this could be a feature of the dictionary (e.g. Scots words in *Chambers*). Just as significant an influence on scope and size would be the decision to include encyclopedic entries, i.e. names of people and places, which can be quite lengthy, e.g. in CED4, which claims more than 18,500, as against the single liners in ECED and only 9,000 of them.

After all these decisions are taken, the headword list has to be chosen to reflect the target user group, the agreed size, and the intended coverage. As we have noted before (3.4), all dictionaries make a selection from the total vocabulary. How does a dictionary achieve its desired coverage but avoid becoming unbalanced in its selection of words, by, for example, having a disproportionate number of words beginning with the letter 'b' in its headword list? There are, for instance, many more words beginning with 'c' in English than beginning with 'g', in fact between two and three times as many. One of the solutions to this problem was proposed by Edward Thorndike in the US in the 1950s, in preparation for a series of Thorndike–Barnhart dictionaries. He divided the alphabet up into 105 'blocks' of approximately equal size, to reflect the distribution of English words among the letters of the alphabet. The letter 'c', for example, has ten blocks, while 'g' has only four. In fact, the final block for a letter may not contain as many words as the others, nor may letters with only one block, or the final block covering 'x', 'y' and 'z'. A number of dictionaries have followed Thorndike's system, which is reproduced in Table 13.1, taken from Landau (1989: 242, 2001: 361), but with the number of words added for each block found in COD10 (CD-ROM) headword list.

The total number of headwords given for the COD10 CD-ROM is 64,679, which would give a mean of 616 for each of the 105 blocks. The COD10 headword list includes abbreviations, derivational affixes and combining forms, which may not have been taken into account by Thorndike. Given the incidence of some low numbers for understandable reasons, only 345 for Q-74, the single block for the letter 'q', for example, and in the final block for some letters – e.g. 324 in F-37, the numbers are fairly consistent. Unusually high numbers are probably explicable: K-51 (854) is a single letter block, U-98 (958) contains words beginning with the negative prefix *un-*, whose numbers are likely to be variable in a dictionary. Overall, Thorndike's system, as tested on COD10, seems to have some validity, although, more than half a century later, it may need adjusting to the current vocabulary and to the current practices in respect of what are included as headwords.

Indeed, the planning stage needs to decide what the macro-structure and the micro-structure (see 3.3) of the dictionary will look like. In macro-structure terms, the tendency is towards a single alphabetical list of headwords that includes compounds, defined derivatives, affixes and combining forms, as well as abbreviations, and, if the dictionary is to include them, names of people and places. In micro-structure terms, the information to be included in an entry, as well as its format and its order, needs to be decided. Will pronunciation, for

Table 13.1 Thorndike's block system of distribution of dictionary entries by initial letters

Block	Letters	No. in COD10	Block	Letters	No. in COD10
A–1	a–adk	616	L–54	lim–louh	724
A–2	adl–alh	672	L–55	loui–lz	385
A–3	ali–angk	654	M–56	m–marb	720
A–4	angl–arak	659	M–57	marc–med	561
A–5	aral–ath	632	M–58	mee–mil	820
A–6	ati–az	420	M–59	mim–monn	608
B–7	b–basd	660	M–60	mono–mz	976
B–8	base–benf	602	N–61	n–nif	735
B–9	beng–bld	772	N–62	nig–nz	747
B–10	ble–bouq	858	O–63	o–oo	706
B–11	bour–buc	698	O–64	op–ou	682
B–12	bud–bz	444	O–65	ov–oz	367
C–13	c–caq	625	P–66	p–par	729
C–14	car–cel	686	P–67	pas–peq	681
C–15	cem–chim	737	P–68	per–picj	752
C–16	chin–cled	733	P–69	pick–plea	636
C–17	clee–col	667	P–70	pleb–poss	699
C–18	com–conf	549	P–71	post–prh	632
C–19	cong–coo	431	P–72	pri–prot	564
C–20	cop–cq	677	P–73	prou–pz	574
C–21	cra–culs	656	Q–74	q–qz	345
C–22	cult–cz	340	R–75	r–recn	683
D–23	d–defd	653	R–76	reco–renn	615
D–24	defe–deteq	558	R–77	reno–rhn	556
D–25	deter–discol	678	R–78	rho–rotd	678
D–26	discom–dold	569	R–79	rote–rz	369
D–27	dole–dt	715	S–80	s–sat	640
D–28	du–dz	314	S–81	sau–sd	626
E–29	e–elk	551	S–82	sea–seo	668
E–30	ell–en	573	S–83	sep–shio	610
E–31	eo–exb	689	S–84	ship–sinf	638
E–32	exc–ez	393	S–85	sing–smd	611
F–33	f–fem	541	S–86	sme–sors	624
F–34	fen–flah	654	S–87	sort–spln	627
F–35	flai–ford	649	S–88	splo–stas	542
F–36	fore–fror	591	S–89	stat–stov	531
F–37	fros–fz	324	S–90	stow–sucg	553
G–38	g–geq	634	S–91	such–swar	553
G–39	ger–gord	707	S–92	swas–sz	319
G–40	gore–grouo	625	T–93	t–tel	729
G–41	group–gz	352	T–94	tem–thq	664
H–42	h–hav	617	T–95	thr–too	663
H–43	haw–hh	627	T–96	top–trh	668
H–44	hi–horr	740	T–97	tri–tz	852
H–45	hors–hz	663	U–98	u–unl	958
I–46	i–inam	542	U–99	unm–uz	686
I–47	inan–infn	486	V–100	v–vim	673
I–48	info–intn	594	V–101	vin–vz	349
I–49	into–iz	461	W–102	w–wess	688
J–50	j–jz	615	W–103	west–wis	676
K–51	k–kz	854	W–104	wit–wz	456
L–52	l–ld	640	XYZ–105	x–zz	478
L–53	le–lil	656			

example, be given for all headwords? what transcription system will be used? how will word stress be indicated? In terms of usage, what set of labels will be used? and will any additional usage guidance be offered? For etymology, how much information will be given? will it include some indication of when the word came into the language? As such matters are decided, they need to be recorded in a manual so that everyone who works on the dictionary, or who joins the dictionary staff at a later date, knows what policies and ground rules have been determined.

Not strictly lexicographical, but nevertheless of crucial importance, are decisions about budgeting, both of money and of time. Ladislav Zgusta (1971: 348) comments:

> I certainly do not know all lexicographic projects past and present; but of those I know not a single one was finished in the time and for the money originally planned.
>
> (cited in Landau 2001: 347)

This was indeed true of some of the more famous dictionaries – Johnson's, scheduled for three years and taking nine; the OED, with Murray contracted by the Oxford Delegacy to produce in ten years and four volumes, taking fifty years and ten (subsequently twelve) volumes. But with the advent of computer technology, Zgusta's pessimism is probably no longer justified: OED2 was published on time in 1989, and it is noticeable that the timespan between editions of dictionaries appears to be decreasing, e.g. COD7 – 1982, COD8 – 1990, COD9 – 1995, COD10 – 1999, with an updated edition of COD10 in 2001.

The costs associated with compiling a dictionary are quite different from those for other kinds of book publication, as Sidney Landau observes:

> Most books cost comparatively little to prepare (the plant cost, in publishing argot) but a great deal to produce (paper, printing, and binding costs). The opposite is true of dictionaries, where the cost of production, though hardly negligible, is small compared to the huge editorial development costs, which must be amortized over a much longer period of time than book publishers are generally familiar with. Data-management costs (systems analysis, computer programming and processing) are also much higher than they are for other books.
>
> (Landau 2001: 348)

The size of the budget and its distribution between the various processes of dictionary compilation may have a significant effect on what the dictionary will turn out to be like in the end. If time, effort and money is focused on one, perhaps novel, aspect of the dictionary, this may have a detrimental effect on the quality of other aspects: usage information may be prioritised over etymology, for example.

13.2 The data

Having decided the headword list and made all the other necessary preliminary planning decisions, the issue arises of where the data for the dictionary is going to come from. There are essentially three possible sources of data: previous dictionaries, citations, (computer) corpora. Any newly published dictionary will be either a new edition of an existing line of dictionaries or a new departure. In both cases, the dictionary stands in a long tradition of dictionary making (Chapters 4 to 6), and, whether consciously or not, previous dictionaries exert their influence. Samuel Johnson used one of Nathaniel Bailey's dictionaries, Noah Webster used Johnson's, F.G. and H.W. Fowler used the OED for the first edition of the COD. It would be foolish, even when the boundaries of lexicography are being extended, to ignore the achievements of the past, though it may be sometimes more sensible to borrow the principles rather than the content from previous dictionaries. Landau (2001: 346) goes so far as to assert: 'All commercial dictionaries are based to some extent on preexisting works.'

Publishers with long-established dictionary departments build up an extensive archive of citations, often going back many decades. They continue to have a reading programme, scouring recent publications for new words or new uses of existing words. They may have readers in-house, but will often invite interested members of the public to contribute material as well. Longman ran a 'Wordwatch' programme for a number of years during the 1980s, which contributed to the *Longman Register of New Words* (Ayto 1989, 1990). Oxford has a 'World Reading Programme', an international network of some sixty readers, who contribute some 18,000 items a month for inclusion in the 'Oxford Bank of New Words' (cf. Ayto 1999). The collection of citations has a long history, going back at least to Samuel Johnson, who extracted material from the literature of the day for inclusion in his dictionary. The OED was founded on the practice of recruiting voluntary readers to undertake the reading of specific works or authors and to submit appropriate citations. Among the instructions issued by James Murray, when he renewed the call for voluntary readers in 1879, were the following:

> Make a quotation for *every* word that strikes you as rare, obsolete, old-fashioned, new, peculiar, or used in a peculiar way.
>
> Take a special note of passages which show or imply that a word is either new and tentative, or needing explanation as obsolete or archaic, and which thus help to fix the date of its introduction or disuse.
>
> Make *as many* quotations *as convenient to you* for ordinary words, when these are used significantly, and help by the context to explain their own meaning, or show their use.
>
> (Murray 1977: 347)

Readers were to write their quotations on slips of paper the size of 'a half-sheet of note-paper', together with full bibliographical information; Murray gives the following specimen (from Murray 1977: 350):

<u>*Diplomatist*</u>, *n.*

1860. J. L. MOTLEY, United Netherlands *(ed. 1868), I. ii. 24.*

If <u>diplomatic</u> *adroitness consists mainly in the power to deceive, never were more adroit* <u>diplomatists</u> *than those of the sixteenth century.*

It is estimated that some five million quotations in this form were submitted by some 2,000 readers to the OED editors, of which 1.8 million appeared in the first edition of the dictionary (Berg 1993).

    These days, dictionary departments that have a reading programme will also derive data from computer corpora. The reading programme may be only in specialised areas, as indicated by the Editor-in-Chief of ECED:

> Where did the *Encarta Concise English Dictionary*'s editors find the information on which to base their definitions? The Bloomsbury Corpus of World English, which now has over 150 million words, provided the main evidence. We amplified this with a tailored reading programme in science, technology, business, and other key areas in order to find evidence of word use in varied fields. Lastly we used the Internet as a research source.
>
> (Introduction, p. xiii)

We noted (in Chapter 11) the COBUILD dictionary as the pioneer in the use of computer corpora for providing the data from which the dictionary is compiled. The *Bank of English*, now amounting to in excess of 400 million words, continues to supply data for Collins dictionaries, both for native speakers and for learners. Oxford and Longman consult the *British National Corpus*, and Cambridge the *Cambridge Language Survey* corpus.

    A computer corpus consists of a collection of texts in electronic form, for lexicographical purposes drawn from both written and spoken English and representative of the vast range of text-types and registers found in language (see Antoinette Renouf's chapter on 'Corpus Development' in Sinclair 1987). Computer corpora can be easily searched, so that all the occurrences of a word can be identified, rather than just those that happen to be noticed by a reader. In that sense, the data from computer corpora are more complete and more reliable than from any other source; they also provide information about relative frequency of occurrence, not only of words and homographs, but also of senses of words. The usual output of a computer search is a concordance list, such as the following for the word *conductor* (taken from the one million word *Lancaster–Oslo/Bergen Corpus* of written English):

1   . . . owski*> |^T*2HAT *0former fire-eating [[conductor]] *4Leopold Stokowski *0is a mellowed man . . .
2   . . . party, to save any tickets he receives from the [[conductor]], the number of which ends in *"7.**" ^Wh . . .
3   . . . closing curtains were combined by producer and [[conductor]] into an exquisite theatrical unity . . .

4   . . . \0Mr. Harry Tomkins) and \0Mr. George Hespe their [[conductor]]. ^I am sure everyone will agree that the . . .

5   . . . Robert Hughes, euphonium solo, and the [[conductor]] played a tubular bell solo accompanied b . . .

6   . . . and lead the others. ^As for basses and altos the [[conductor]] had to teach by singing the parts with t . . .

7   . . . was unhappy about a forthcoming concert. ^*"The [[conductor]]*-so-and-so*- he has no temperament. ^It . . .

8   . . . composers.**" ^It is true that he was the first [[conductor]] to put Elgar on the musical map, the rea . . .

9   . . . Hamilton Harty in 1933 as the permanent [[conductor]] of the Halle*?2 Concerts, the orchestra . . .

10   . . . stra declined in its ensemble. ^Another permanent [[conductor]] was needed, but the Halle*?2 Society wer . . .

11   . . . n ordinary theatre managements to choose [[conductor]], producer, designer, and so on, and then, having . . .

12   . . . all responsible should be experts*- the [[conductor]], the orchestral players, the singers, the . . .

13   . . . stage (which includes arranging that the [[conductor]] can catch the eye of the singer at neces . . .

14   . . . be guided. ^How often does an excellent [[conductor]] wish to take a passage of music at an *' . . .

15   . . . in the circumstances? ^The co-operative [[conductor]], like Beecham, will always listen and be . . .

16   . . . tage is wrong.) ^But I have known a good [[conductor]] insist on what was arguably a *'correctly**' fast . . .

17   . . . is too clean to be the score used by the [[conductor]], and it was probably the fair-copy prepa . . .

18   . . . transmitted to the voltmeter V by a nickel [[conductor]] D, nickel being resistant to corrosive a . . .

19   . . . ed to the voltmeter by an earthed nickel [[conductor]] attached to the bottom of a well E in th . . .

20   . . . coupling H which also positions the \0 + ve nickel [[conductor]] with respect to the sodium by circlips o . . .

21   . . . ectrolyte J attached to the \0 + ve nickel [[conductor]] by nickel circlips. ^Fixing and positioning of th . . .

22   . . . ce, and with far more to offer. |^The [[conductor]] rang his bell. |^*"Good-bye, Dai,**" . . .

23   . . . ^Where indeed? ^Megan Thomas spoke sharply to the [[conductor]], demanding an explanation. ^But non . . .

24   . . . demanding an explanation. ^But nonplussed, the [[conductor]] was. ^A good man, mind; knew his job. ^B . . .

25   . . . first thing about it.**" |^Stung, the [[conductor]] was. ^*"What you expect me to do?**" he . . .

26   . . . proper . . . |^Getting dark, now. ^The [[conductor]] switched on the lights. ^The beleaguered . . .

27 . . . ng the sleeping Cadwallader. ^Driver and [[conductor]] peered ahead into nothingness. ^On the b . . .

28 . . . ^*"Can't go lighting bonfires on this bus,**" the [[conductor]] said firmly. ^*"Contrary to the Company' . . .

This is provided by way of exemplification of a concordance; it is from a small corpus and does not give enough data to make it possible to draw general conclusions. But it does illustrate the three main senses of *conductor*: the musical sense (Nos 1 to 17), its use in relation to electricity (Nos 18 to 21), and the bus conductor sense (Nos 21 to 28). And it shows the kind of material that a lexicographer has to work with and interpret, in order to decide whether a form represents potentially more than one homograph, and to determine how many senses should be recognised. The advantage of a concordance is that context is provided, and can be adjusted for size, so that the grammatical and collocational behaviour of words can be ascertained and used as guides for the determination of sense divisions, as Ramesh Krishnamurthy observes in respect of the COBUILD project (Sinclair 1987: 75):

> Collocational evidence was of great usefulness in an analysis of the corpus data. The concordance lines were arranged in alphabetical order of the first character after the space following the keyword. This meant that some features of the behaviour of a lexical item in text became immediately apparent.

It is no exaggeration to say that computer corpora have revolutionised the lexicographic process (Rundell and Stock 1992), in terms both of the quality of lexical data that can be obtained and of the reliability of the conclusions that can be drawn from that data.

13.3 The method

A computer corpus, with sophisticated search programs, may produce better quality data, and an electronic database may ease the task of putting the dictionary information together, but no program has yet been written, nor is it likely to be, to automate the process of getting from data to finished dictionary. All dictionaries nowadays require the input of a range of staff with different skills and specialisms. Long gone are the days of the lonely lexicographer, like Samuel Johnson, toiling in his garret with the help of a few assistants, or even the Fowler brothers putting together the first edition of the COD at their home on the island of Guernsey, with occasional forays to the OED office in Oxford. CED4, for example, lists some twenty editorial staff, including lexicographers and computing experts, as well as seventeen 'Special Consultants' on varieties of English around the world and fifty-eight 'Specialist Contributors' on topics ranging from aeronautics to industrial relations to religion. A further thirty 'Other Contributors' are also listed, alongside their specialist topic, from horology to place names to sports. Some dictionaries have established additionally an advisory board; ECED has a forty-strong 'Academic Advisory Board on English Usage', drawn from universities in the UK, Australia, Canada and the US.

The input of all these people is required for the formulation of the dictionary entries. Not only will external consultants contribute their expertise on varieties of English and technical jargons, but it is likely that a member of editorial staff will specialise in one type of dictionary information, e.g. pronunciation, etymology, grammar, usage. Some will develop expertise in defining, or in selecting the appropriate example, or in researching and writing biographical entries. The hardest, and most important, part is often considered to be that of defining. Landau (2001: 354) considers the qualities required of a good definer to be:

> First and foremost, he or she must be able to write well and easily.
>   They must have analytical minds that seek to chop things up into parts . . .
>   Definers must have a broad, but not necessarily deep, fund of information.
>   . . . definers must have a feeling for the language, *Sprachgefühl*, a sense of aptness of expression, an appreciation of nuance, style and idiom.

However, dictionary editors may seek to impose a particular uniform style of defining on their lexicographers, as Philip Gove did for W3 with his 'single-statement defining style' (Morton 1994). Compare the rambling definition of *arson* from the first edition with the crisper single-phrase from W3:

> The malicious burning of a dwelling house or outhouse of another man, which by common law is felony. The definition of this crime is varied by statutes in different jurisdictions, and generally it has been widened to include the similar burning of other property, as of churches, factories, ships, or of one's own house. (W1)

> the wilful and malicious burning of or attempt to burn any building, structure, or property of another (as a house, a church, or a boat) or of one's own usu. with criminal or fraudulent intent (W3)

When a large number of people are contributing to a single work, one of the major concerns is to maintain a consistency of writing and presentation. Dictionary projects will, therefore, document their decisions about content and style in a set of guidelines or a manual, so that any contributor or new member of staff can be informed of the house rules for the particular publication. The manual will specify not just conventions for the macro- and micro-structure of the dictionary, but also points of detail, such as use of abbreviation and punctuation within an entry.

Besides using a computer corpus for obtaining data, dictionaries are now usually constructed using a computer database. A number of commercial products of this nature are available, but the larger publishers have their in-house systems. Such a database allows several lexicographers or specialists to be working on entries at the same time, e.g. for pronunciation, etymology and so on;

and it allows each to see the work of the others. It also allows freelance lexicographers to work at a location remote from the dictionary offices. It facilitates
the editorial and checking processes, and provides with relative ease the version
for eventual printing, as well as any electronic (CD-ROM or online) version.
Not only that, but once a dictionary database has been established, it can provide the material for dictionaries of other sizes (e.g. concise or pocket) and for
other user groups (e.g. children or school students). It also provides the basis for
easier updating and revising for the production of new editions.

The computer has changed the way dictionaries are compiled and produced,
but it has not done away with the need for skilled lexicographers to practise the
art, or craft, of constructing and writing dictionary entries. Like so many other
tasks, lexicography is computer-aided rather than computer-automated.

13.4 The result

After all the effort, skill and expertise devoted to the lexicographical task, the
result is a book, of a particular size and format, printed using a number of
selected typefaces, offered to the dictionary-buying public. How a dictionary
handles, what the dictionary page looks like, how the information is arranged,
are important factors in selling a dictionary, irrespective of the quality of its
content. The impression of accessibility is of significance. The column on a
page must invite scanning up and down. The headwords, alternative spellings,
compounds, derivatives, phrasal verbs and idioms usually stand out in a bold
typeface, as do the sense numbers. The headword itself is offset to the left. Italics
are usually used for word class and usage labels, for illustrative examples, and for
words cited from other languages in the etymologies. Cross-references are normally in small capitals. Where a word belongs to more than one word class, and
they are treated in the same entry, the beginning of the second and subsequent
word class is clearly marked, e.g. with a bold diamond in CED4, with a large
bold dot in COD10. Some information may begin on a new line within an
entry, e.g. 'derivatives' and 'origin' (i.e. etymology) in NODE and COD10.
The careful use of layout and typeface contributes to the ease with which a user
is able to locate the exact piece of information that they are seeking about a
word.

Another 'result' of the lexicographic process is a CD-ROM. One CD-ROM
is much like another to look at, so there is no issue here of how it 'handles'. But
there are serious issues about how the information is displayed on the screen,
what search options are available, and how intuitive it is for the (naive) user to
operate. CD-ROM dictionaries usually display two windows: a word list window and an entry window. The word list window contains the headwords in
alphabetical order, together with a box for typing a word that the user wishes to
look up. Typing in the word locates its place in the headword list; it may also
bring up the entry automatically in the other window, or a further operation
may be required (a mouse click or pressing the 'Enter' key). It is normally
possible to scroll through the headword list, and if this is automatically linked to

the entry window, then by this means to scroll through the dictionary entries. The entry window may contain a single entry, for the selected headword; alternatively it may contain that entry together with contiguous ones that will fit onto the screen. In the latter case, it is usually possible to scroll the entry window, as if scanning a dictionary page. The entries on screen replicate as far as possible the arrangement and typefaces of the print version, though without the double or triple columns. Scrolling through entries on the screen is, thus, not the same experience as browsing a print dictionary, but for single item lookups there is little difference.

One respect in which CD-ROM dictionaries score over their print counterparts is in their full-text search facility, though this is, perhaps, of more interest to lexicologists and other students of language than to the ordinary user. CD-ROM dictionaries vary, though, in the sophistication of their search facilities, as we have noted both for native speaker dictionaries (6.7) and for learners' dictionaries (11.5), where these facilities are probably of greater importance. We are more adept at evaluating the facilities that electronic dictionaries give us, than at knowing how individual users exploit them for their own purposes (Creswell 1996; Nesi 1999; Holderbaum 1999; Heuberger 2000; Jehle 1999).

Once a dictionary is published and it is on the market, it becomes the object of scrutiny by all kinds of critic, from newspaper journalists to academics. How the critic goes about their task, or ought to, is the topic of the final chapter of this book.

13.5 Further reading

The best place to start is with Chapter 7, 'Dictionary making', of *Dictionaries: The Art and Craft of Lexicography* (2001) by Sidney Landau, himself with experience of involvement in a number of dictionary projects. His Chapter 6, 'The corpus in lexicography', is also of relevance to the discussion in this chapter (13.2).

Bo Svensén's *Practical Lexicography: Principles and Methods of Dictionary Making* (1993) and Ladislav Zgusta's *Manual of Lexicography* (1971), though a little old now, both review some of the theoretical and practical decisions facing lexicographers in compiling a dictionary. Samuel Johnson's *Plan* and *Preface* are still worth reading for their forward-looking insights (both reproduced in Wilson 1957), and the original OED *Preface* and *General Explanations* in Volume 1 of OED1 merit study.

Some of the accounts of the making of individual dictionaries were mentioned earlier (13.1): Reddick (1990) on Johnson, Murray (1977) on the OED, Morton (1994) on W3, and Sinclair (1987) on COBUILD.

14 Criticising dictionaries

Academic lexicography, or 'metalexicography', as pursued in university departments of English or Linguistics, is concerned not primarily with the compiling of dictionaries – though academics may be involved in this, as consultants, for example – but with researching and teaching about the whole business of making dictionaries: their history, their typology, their structures, their users, and so on (Hartmann 2001). One aspect of academic lexicography looks at the products of commercial lexicography and subjects them to a rigorous critique, usually resulting in a review; though academics are not the only ones who review dictionaries. The process of critiquing and reviewing dictionaries is termed 'dictionary criticism'.

One of the crucial issues for dictionary criticism is to establish a sound and rigorous basis on which to conduct the criticism, together with a set of applicable criteria. Hartmann (2001: 49) comments:

> Anyone who has ever read (or written) a review of a particular dictionary will know that generally agreed criteria and standards for the assessment of quality and performance are still rare, if they can be said to exist at all.

This chapter discusses the business of dictionary criticism and proposes some ways in which it may be undertaken and some guidelines for assessing dictionaries.

14.1 The business of criticism

In the brief section on dictionary criticism in his chapter on lexicography in *Solving Language Problems*, Reinhard Hartmann (1996: 241) defines it as the 'time-honoured' activity of 'evaluating and assessing lexicographic products'. It is an activity that has a long history. Every new edition of a major dictionary spawns reviews in all kinds of publication, from daily and weekly newspapers to academic journals. But dictionary criticism is an activity, as Hartmann notes, 'which has been beset by personal prejudice rather than noted for the application of objective criteria' (1996: 241). This concern is echoed in Noel Osselton's article – the only one with 'Dictionary Criticism' in its title – in the *International Encyclopedia of Lexicography* (Hausmann *et al.* 1989). He notes 'a surprising lack of interest in general principles, with incidental sniping taking the place of any real exploration' (Osselton 1989: 229).

Dictionary reviews vary enormously in their approach and in their scope, even those appearing in the same publication. Despite the fact that it is an important means by which information about dictionaries is disseminated, little attention has been paid to the methods and criteria underlying the business of dictionary criticism. A 'Note on Dictionary Criticism' (by K.D.) from the Dictionary Research Centre at the University of Exeter (date unknown) notes that: 'Of general dictionaries there are a lot of reviews which lack validity and reliability . . . what is needed is a wider discussion of the standards of assessment of dictionaries.' The note goes on to argue for a more objective evaluation of dictionaries and greater clarity on what the criteria of assessment might be. It concludes: 'No definite theory of dictionary criticism has been established, and it should be made more sophisticated as one field of lexicographical research. Much remains to be done.'

Two main kinds of contribution have been made so far to the debate on criteria for dictionary criticism. One has put forward proposals for guidelines or criteria of reviewing. Roger Steiner's 'Guidelines for Reviewers of Bilingual Dictionaries' (Steiner 1984) would be a case in point, or Henri Béjoint's seven criteria for English monolingual learners' dictionaries in his comparison of *OALD*, *COD* and *LDOCE* (Béjoint 1978), or Robert Chapman's four proposals for a method of dictionary reviewing (Chapman 1977), or Herbert Ernst Wiegand's rather tongue-in-cheek 'Ten Commandments for Dictionary Reviewers' (Wiegand 1994).

The other kind of contribution, which is more recent, takes a set of dictionary reviews and subjects them to analysis, with the aim of discovering the enduring concerns of dictionary reviewers. Jerzy Tomaszczyk (1988) took 120 reviews of general-purpose bilingual dictionaries and distilled the concerns of the reviewers under the headings of: equivalents, directionality, reversibility, alphabetisation, retrievability, redundancy, coverage, currency and reliability. Martha Ripfel (1989) examined and compared the journalistic and academic reviews of five German monolingual dictionaries, to identify the differing evaluation and focus of the two types of review and the range of comments made by each type. Günther Jehle (1990) looked at 'popular' and 'academic' reviews of English and French monolingual learners' dictionaries, with a focus on the nature of a dictionary review as a text-type. He concludes his study thus (p. 300): 'The practice of reviewing monolingual English and French learners' dictionaries in many cases unfortunately gives the impression that the reviewer has given no prior thought to establishing the parameters within which his judgements and critical assessments might have validity' (my translation). We will attempt to suggest some methodological principles and guidelines for dictionary criticism.

14.2 Method

Reviewing a dictionary is not like reviewing most other kinds of book publication. In the case of a normal book, the reviewer would expect to read the text in its entirety, perhaps some sections of text more than once. The reviewer of a dictionary would not expect to read every word of the text: first of all, dictionaries are not meant to be read like that, and usually dictionaries contain too much text to make it a feasible undertaking – NODE, for example, claims 4 million words of text, while CED4 estimates that it contains 3.6 million words.

Also at issue is who might be an appropriate person to review a dictionary. In general, reviewers – of books, plays, films, music – are chosen because they are considered knowledgeable or expert in the subject matter or the techniques of whatever it is they are reviewing. We should expect the reviewers of dictionaries to be knowledgeable in lexicography. This is not always so, especially in newspaper and magazine reviews: being a user of a dictionary appears to be sufficient qualification sometimes, even though the same publication would not think of asking just any reader to review a novel or a book of poetry.

A reviewer, then, must be knowledgeable about lexicography, a point made by Roger Steiner in his contribution to Dolezal *et al.* (1994), and they also need a sound methodology for critically reviewing a dictionary. As with any reviewing, the first step must be to develop familiarity with the work that is being assessed. With dictionaries, this means, first of all, reading the often neglected front-matter: the preface, the guide to using the dictionary, the list of staff and consultants, and so on. This will usually give a preliminary view of the scope of the dictionary, its intended users, and the types of lexical (and other) information that are claimed to be included. Familiarisation will also include browsing the main body of the dictionary and reading a variety of types of entry, as a means of gaining an impression of the flavour of the particular dictionary under review. Finally, some dictionaries have back-matter (appendices), which may contain gratuitous additional information (e.g. counties of the UK and states of the USA) or provide useful lexical information (e.g. affixes and combining forms).

For a detailed assessment of the content of a dictionary, Robert Chapman (1977) suggests that random sampling of entries should be used, such as 'the tenth main entry on every twentieth page', in order to yield a manageable set of entries (e.g. 50); and he proposes that each of these entries should be scrutinised carefully for 'accuracy, completeness, clearness, simplicity, and modernity' (criteria from McMillan 1949). Random sampling of entries ensures that a reviewer does not look for a predetermined list of favourite items. However, a reviewer needs to make sure that the resulting sample is representative, so that it contains at least one member of each word class, that polysemy is well represented, and that there is a spread across general and specialist lexemes. A random sample may need to be supplemented by the reviewer's checklist. Likewise, where a dictionary has special additional features (e.g. synonym essays (LDEL2) or usage notes (NODE, ECED, etc)), these too need to be taken into account.

One of Chapman's other suggestions is that the reviewing of dictionaries should be undertaken by a team of reviewers. His conception of this seems to be that each reviewer would be a specialist in some area of vocabulary and would contribute an assessment of the treatment of the 'definitions in their own fields' (Chapman 1977: 158). Where team reviewing has been undertaken more recently (e.g. the well organised and comprehensive Japanese reviews of COD8 (Higashi *et al.* 1992) and of LDEL2 (Masuda *et al.* 1994)), each member of the team has taken a different aspect of linguistic description (pronunciation, definition, usage, etymology, etc.) rather than vocabulary specialism, which is probably a more sensible division of labour. Team reviews allow a more thorough treatment of each aspect of a dictionary's lexical description, both by enabling more extensive sampling to be undertaken and by tapping into a reviewer's specialist interest.

14.3 Criteria: internal and external

Criteria for evaluating a dictionary can be derived from two possible sources: 'internal' criteria and 'external' criteria. Internal criteria derive from what a dictionary says about itself, or what the editors claim for the dictionary. External criteria derive from metalexicography (the academic study of dictionaries), taking into account the linguistic requirements for a lexical description, as well as considerations of dictionary design and production.

All dictionaries, in their preface or their blurb, make claims about their features that distinguish the current edition from previous ones, or demonstrate the superiority of this dictionary over its rivals. A reviewer can take these claims as a basis for reviewing, to investigate whether the claims are borne out in the dictionary's practice: these are the internal criteria. For example, NODE contains an extensive 'Introduction', whose principal aim is to 'explain some of the thinking behind these new approaches' (p. ix). The Introduction makes the following statement:

> each word has at least one core meaning, to which a number of subsenses may be attached . . . Core meanings represent typical, central uses of the word in question in modern standard English . . . The core meaning is the one that represents the most literal sense that the word has in ordinary modern usage.
>
> (p. ix)

These are testable statements. And they are tested by Sidney Landau in his review of NODE (Landau 1999); he comes to the conclusion that 'NODE's defining strategy is ambitious, and it does not always succeed . . . Nevertheless, in most cases, the defining strategy does work.' (p. 252)

Many shorter reviews take a dictionary's view of itself at least as a starting point for the evaluation, if not as the basis for the whole approach. Newspaper and magazine reviews routinely depend on what the editors or publisher say about their product, often with little attempt to test the sometimes exaggerated claims. In that sense, there is a danger that a critique that relies solely on internal criteria may be biased too much in favour of the dictionary, unless a radically critical stance is taken to the claims that are made.

In using external criteria, a reviewer begins from a different standpoint. The criteria are determined prior to the review; they arise from the accumulated insights of the academic community (e.g. Hudson 1988; Ilson 1991). This does not mean that they need be overly 'academic', since the community must take account of the fact that dictionaries are as much reference works aimed at particular groups of users as they are linguistic descriptions of the lexical resources of the language. Rundell (1998: 316) suggests two criteria for the evaluation of improvements in the development of learners' dictionaries:

> the description of a language that a dictionary provides corresponds more closely to reliable empirical evidence regarding the way in which that language is actually used; the presentation of this description corresponds more closely to what we know about the reference needs and reference skills of the target user.

There is a need, therefore, for two sets of external criteria for the evaluation of dictionaries: one set relates to the reference function of dictionaries and the user's perspective, and is largely about presentation and accessibility; the other relates to the recording function of dictionaries, and is largely about content. Presentation and content overlap and interact with each other (e.g. the core sense and subsense division in NODE), so this is to some extent a false dichotomy. However, it will provide a useful framework for establishing criteria for dictionary reviewing.

14.4 Presentation

How a dictionary presents its material has an important influence on the accessibility of the information for its target users. In the preface to the first edition of the COD (1911), the Fowler brothers commented that they had used 'the severest economy of expression – amounting to the adoption of telegraphese – that readers can be expected to put up with' (p. iv). How they determined readers' tolerance levels is not stated, but they are surely rather different from those of today's dictionary users. Aspects of presentation that should be considered by a dictionary reviewer include at least the following.

Page layout

The size of the page varies with the size of the dictionary (desk, concise, pocket – see 3.2). It is usual to have two columns, though three may be found in some dictionaries (e.g. NODE, ECED). A significant feature is the amount of white space, determined by the size of the margins, the spacing between entries, the inclusion of other material to break up the text (e.g. usage notes, diagrams, illustrations). All these can have an effect on the appearance of the dictionary page. Attractive page layout improves accessibility.

Layout of the entries

Traditionally dictionaries have tended to pack all the information for a headword within a single paragraph, to save space; more recent editions have begun to unpack the paragraph and to use a new line to begin a new set of information. For example, NODE begins a new line for: a different word class, derivatives, phrases, etymology. In some learners' dictionaries (LDOCE3, CIDE), the layout has been used to enhance the user's access to specific meanings of polysemous words.

Length of entries

This is determined largely by the practice of 'nesting', where derivatives, compounds, idioms and so on are included within a single entry under a root word. *Chambers* uses nesting extensively, as does the COD up to the seventh edition (1982). The use of separate headwords for compounds and derivatives, where these are individually defined, creates shorter and more numerous entries, and more white space, so enhancing page layout. Likewise the inclusion of abbreviations, affixes and combining forms as headwords (rather than in appendices) creates more and shorter entries and aids accessibility.

Abbreviation

The use of abbreviations, like nesting, saves space, an important consideration in dictionary making. The Fowlers noted this as a feature of COD1; their assumption was that the users of the COD would understand and cope with a high degree of abbreviation. That is no longer the case, and many recent dictionaries (e.g. CED, NODE) now include the full forms of items such as word class labels and names of languages in etymologies. Fewer abbreviations mean greater accessibility.

   Academic reviewers tend to concentrate on the content of dictionaries, but presentation and accessibility should not be ignored, because they make a significant contribution to enabling users to be successful in extracting information from the dictionary.

14.5 Content

Hudson's (1988: 310–12) 'checklist of types of lexical fact' would provide a starting point for criteria of content, or alternatively Ilson's (1991) more inductively arrived at set of headings would serve. Such a set of criteria would encompass at least the following.

Range of vocabulary

Modern dictionaries are keen to claim that they have included the latest words from areas where neologisms are common (e.g. business, information technology, the environment, medicine), as well as coverage of other national varieties of English (e.g. American, Australian). A reviewer would need to determine whether, for its size and scope, the dictionary had adequate coverage of up-to-date, technical, international and, if appropriate, regional lexis. Where a dictionary includes such items, geographical and biographical entries would also come under this heading.

Word formation

On the one hand, this relates to whether affixes and combining forms are treated as headwords or gathered in an appendix, or not given any attention at all (cf. Prčic 1999). On the other hand, it relates to the treatment of derived and compound words, what the criteria are for separate headword status as against nested run-on. Also relevant here is the treatment of noun/adjective pairs that are not cognate, e.g. *church – ecclesiastical, law – legal, mind – mental, lung – pulmonary*. The judgement to be made is whether the account of word formation enables a user to ascertain the formal (morphological) relations between words.

Homographs

The usual basis for more than one headword for a single spelling is different etymologies. In some dictionaries (e.g. LDEL) each word class that a lexeme belongs to occasions a new headword. In COBUILD1 there is only one headword per spelling, whereas more recent monolingual learners' dictionaries (LDOCE3, CIDE) have multiple entries based on meaning. The criteria for determining what is a headword have important consequences for lexical description as well as for accessibility.

Sense division

For words that have multiple meanings (senses), dictionaries do not always make clear how the senses have been established (cf. Allen (1999) on 'lumpers and splitters'), or the order in which they have been arranged. A tendency is emerging (e.g. NODE, COD10) to pull back from the over-differentiation of senses that has occurred in the past (CED, *Chambers*). The issue here relates both to the adequacy of the lexical description and to how straightforward it is for the user to find the desired sense.

Defining

This is usually seen as the crucial task of the lexicographer, and there are some well established defining styles, notably the analytical (Kipfer 1984: 66–8). However, these have been extended in recent years, especially in learners' dictionaries (e.g. with whole sentence definitions). Some dictionaries include a certain amount of encyclopedic information in their definitions, especially for words referring to flora and fauna. Not only does a reviewer need to assess the adequacy of the definitions, but also whether they are stylistically appropriate for the intended users.

Beyond denotation

Under this heading is included other aspects of a word's lexical behaviour over and above its denotation, such as its lexical relations (synonymy, antonymy, hyponymy – as indicated systematically in COBUILD1), its typical collocations, and any shared connotations. Sometimes this information is incorporated into definitions, but it is rarely handled systematically, though the 'synonym essays' in LDEL2 and ECED constitute a rare exception. Yet this information also contributes to an understanding of a word's meaning.

Pronunciation

There are two issues here: the transcription system, which is almost universally IPA now in British dictionaries, and the accent to be represented. While many dictionaries now give alternative American pronunciations, no account is taken of the fact, for example, that the majority of British speakers say /bʊt/ rather than /bʌt/ and /græs/ rather than /grɑːs/. Some native speaker dictionaries (e.g. NODE) are now giving pronunciations only for words that are problematical, but what may be designated a problematical pronunciation is a matter of judgement (Allen 2000).

Grammar

Dictionaries have traditionally given word class (part-of-speech) labels, and for verbs distinguished 'transitive' and 'intransitive' uses; NODE acknowledges that these may be opaque terms for modern users and substitutes 'with obj' and 'no obj'. Rarely have native speaker dictionaries given much more information about grammar beyond this; CED, and now NODE, are exceptions. By contrast learners' dictionaries have aimed for full coverage, which raises the question about how grammatical information is represented for effective access. A reviewer needs to evaluate how much information about the grammatical operation of words is necessary for a dictionary to fulfil its recording function, as against the need not to provide too much unnecessary information for the intended users.

Usage

Dictionaries routinely label words or senses of words with 'restrictive' labels, to indicate that the word or sense may be used only in a specific context. Such labels may relate to: time (obsolete, archaic), dialect (North American, Australian English, Scottish), formality (informal, colloquial), evaluation (derogatory, pejorative, euphemistic), status (slang, taboo), field or topic (Astronomy, Music, Telecommunications). The extent to which dictionaries are consistent in using their range of usage labels and how they apply them are matters for the critic to evaluate. Some dictionaries include 'usage notes', especially to give guidance on controversial areas, e.g. the preposition to be used after *different*, the distinction between *disinterested* and *uninterested*. A critic may note how 'conservative' or 'progressive' a stance is taken by a dictionary on such issues.

Examples

All dictionaries give example sentences or phrases to illustrate word meaning, grammar or usage. They are particularly numerous and prominent in learners' dictionaries, where they are seen as playing a crucial role. A number of questions need to be asked by the critic, relating to: the extent of the use of examples, what role they are seen to play in exemplification, where the examples come from (corpus or invented), and how consistently the dictionary's policy on examples is implemented.

Etymology

Since the etymological dictionaries of the eighteenth century, it has been customary to include information about etymology in native speaker dictionaries, though not in learners' dictionaries (Chapter 10). It might be argued that such information has no place in a dictionary of the contemporary language and should be confined to 'historical' dictionaries (such as OED and SOED), though Hudson (1988) includes etymology in his checklist of lexical facts. The amount of etymological detail that general dictionaries include is variable; in some cases it is just the language of immediate origin, or the etymology may be traced back as far as possible, and perhaps with cognates in related languages. It is a matter of critical evaluation whether the information in the dictionary under review is appropriate to its size, purpose and intended users.

Special features

A dictionary will often seek to distinguish itself from its rivals by including a special feature, e.g. the synonym essays and other boxed comments in LDEL2, usage and other notes in NODE, word formation boxes in COD10, misspellings in ECED, frequency information in COBUILD and LDOCE3. Sometimes these are a genuine enhancement of the information that the dictionary gives; sometimes they are more of a marketing gimmick. Other special features may be incorporated in the front-matter or the appendices, e.g. the essay on English as a world language in CED, or the punctuation guide in COD8/9. The question is whether they add to the lexical description and the coverage and usefulness of the dictionary.

14.6 Perspective

Besides following an appropriate method and making judgements against an explicit set of criteria, it is also possible for a reviewer to conduct dictionary criticism from a number of different perspectives. The discussion so far has more or less presupposed that dictionary criticism is undertaken from the perspective of the academic linguist or metalexicographer, applying lexicological and lexicographical theory and insight to the task. Certainly, in the reviews that have appeared in the *International Journal of Lexicography*, this has been, understandably, the predominant perspective adopted. But it has not always been appropriate. For example, there was a review of OALD4 by Dwight Bolinger (1990), which took the dictionary to task for not representing accurately some very subtle syntactic peculiarities of verbs, which, had they been so treated, would have probably baffled most users of the dictionary. Bolinger had, uncharacteristically, not appreciated the need for what Rundell has called 'a more utilitarian lexicography' (Rundell 1998: 337), where there is a tradeoff between the needs of the user and the meticulous accuracy of the lexical description.

An alternative perspective to that of the metalexicographer would be that, for example, of the target user. The dictionary would be judged, by the method and on the criteria stated, from the point of view of the needs, expectations, prior knowledge and reference skills of the intended group of users. For an example, see Jackson (1995) which makes a comparison of LDOCE2 and the German learners' dictionary, *Langenscheidts Großwörterbuch Deutsch als Fremdsprache*.

A third possible perspective would be that of the language teacher – particularly in respect of learners' dictionaries – who would judge the dictionary from the point of view of its suitability for the language teacher's task and for the students that they are teaching, whether in a first or a second language context. Higashi *et al.* (1992) review COD8 from this perspective in the Japanese context, perhaps inappropriately, since COD8 was not intended as a pedagogical dictionary, although the COD seems to have been used widely for this purpose in Japan.

The reviewer's perspective can act as a focus for the attention to be paid in the critique to different aspects of the dictionary's presentation and content, especially since it is difficult to treat every aspect in a single review.

14.7 Purpose

In conclusion, we may reflect on the purposes for which dictionary criticism is carried out. Some reviews, especially in newspapers and magazines, have as their main purpose to inform the public of the existence of a new edition of, usually, a well-known dictionary; the content of the review then often reflects the publisher's press release or the dictionary's blurb. Other dictionary reviews, like any book review, are directed at an interested public (teachers, students, crossword addicts) and have as their purpose to inform this audience of the content of the dictionary and its fitness for their needs.

Reviews of dictionaries that appear in academic journals, such as the *International Journal of Lexicography*, while informing the journal readers about the existence and contents of the dictionary, are also intended in many instances to make a contribution to academic lexicography. Such reviews are often more thorough, pursue a more rigorous methodology, and draw on the accumulated wisdom and expertise of the academic community of dictionary scholars. There is one further purpose that academic reviews may have. Since their critique is drawn from an expert knowledge of dictionaries, dictionary making and dictionary use, they often propose ways in which dictionaries may be improved. So, they are offering advice to working lexicographers and dictionary publishers, and contribute towards the development of both practical and academic lexicography.

If dictionary reviews are to fulfil this function, or indeed if they are to make a serious contribution to the academic study of lexicography, then it is important that dictionary criticism is conducted on a sound basis, with a clear methodology and a set of explicit criteria.

One of the purposes of this book, and of this chapter in particular, is to give you, the reader, the background to enable you to look at dictionaries, both historical and contemporary, with a more informed insight. On the basis of your study, you might attempt the review of a dictionary.

14.8 Further reading

There is no full-length treatment of dictionary criticism. The place to start is with Reinhard Hartmann's *Teaching and Researching Lexicography* (2001), where he deals with the topic in Chapter 4, Sections 4.3 and 4.4, which also contain references to other relevant articles and books.

From there it would be useful to read some of the reviews that have appeared, for example, in the *International Journal of Lexicography*. The reviews, mentioned earlier, of COD8 by Higashi *et al.* (1992) and of LDEL2 by Masuda *et al.* (1994), are particularly recommended; but most numbers of the journal contain dictionary reviews of varying extent and comprehensiveness. The other journal in which dictionaries are regularly reviewed is *English Today*.

References

Allen, R. (1999) 'Lumping and splitting', *English Today*, 16(4), 61–3.

Allen, R. (2000) 'Size matters', review of *Collins English Dictionary, The New Oxford Dictionary of English* and *Encarta World English Dictionary*, *English Today*, 16(2), 57–61.

Atkins, B.T.S. (ed.) (1998) *Using Dictionaries: Studies of Dictionary Use by Language Learners and Translators*, Lexicographica Series Maior, no. 88, Max Niemeyer Verlag, Tübingen.

Ayto, J. (1989) *The Longman Register of New Words*, Longman.

Ayto, J. (1990) *The Longman Register of New Words, Volume Two*, Longman.

Ayto, J. (1999) *Twentieth Century Words*, Oxford University Press.

Bailey, R.W. (ed.) (1987) *Dictionaries of English: Prospects for the Record of Our Language*, Cambridge University Press.

Béjoint, H. (1978) 'Trois dictionnaires anglais récents: lequel choisir?', *Les Langues modernes*, 5, 465–74.

Béjoint, H. (1981) 'The foreign student's use of monolingual English dictionaries: a study of language needs and reference skills', *Applied Linguistics*, 2(3), 207–22.

Béjoint, H. (1994) *Tradition and Innovation in Modern English Dictionaries*, Clarendon Press, Oxford.

Béjoint, H. (2000) *Modern Lexicography: An Introduction*, republication of Béjoint (1994), Oxford University Press.

Benson, M., Benson, E. and Ilson, R. (1986) *Lexicographic Description of English*, John Benjamins.

Berg, D.L. (1993) *A Guide to the Oxford English Dictionary*, Oxford University Press.

Bogaards, P. and van der Kloot, W.A. (2001) 'The use of grammatical information in learners' dictionaries', *International Journal of Lexicography*, 14(2), 97–121.

Bolinger, D. (1990) 'Review of the *Oxford Advanced Learner's Dictionary*, Fourth Edition', *International Journal of Lexicography*, 3(2), 133–45.

Burton, T.H. and Burton, J. (eds) (1988) *Lexicographical and Linguistic Studies: Essays in Honour of G.W. Turner*, D.S. Brewer, Cambridge/St Edmundsbury Press, Suffolk.

Chapman, R.L. (1977) 'Dictionary reviews and reviewing: 1900–1975' in J.C. Raymond and I.W. Russell (eds) *James B. McMillan: Essays in Linguistics by His Friends and Colleagues*, University of Alabama Press, 143–61.

Clear, J. (1996) '"Grammar and nonsense": or syntax and word senses' in J. Svartvik (ed.), 213–41.

Cowie, A.P. (1999) *English Dictionaries for Foreign Learners: a History*, Clarendon Press, Oxford.

Creswell, T.J. (1996) 'American English dictionaries on CD-ROM', *Journal of English Linguistics* 24(4), 358–68.

Cruse, D.A. (1996) *Lexical Semantics*, Cambridge University Press.

Crystal, D. (1995) *The Cambridge Encyclopedia of the English Language*, Cambridge University Press.

Dolezal, F.F.M. *et al.* (eds) (1994) *Lexicographica 9/1993: Wörterbuchkritik: Dictionary Criticism*, Max Niemeyer Verlag, Tübingen.

Duden (2000) *Die deutsche Rechtschreibung, Duden Band 1*, twenty-second edition, Dudenverlag.

Ellegård, A. (1978) 'On dictionaries for language learners', *Moderna Språk*, LXXII, 225–44.

Fernando, C. and Flavell, R. (1981) *On Idiom: Critical Views and Perspectives*, Exeter Linguistic Studies 5, University of Exeter Press.

Friend, J.H. (1967) *The Development of American Lexicography 1798–1864*, Mouton.

Godman, A. and Payne, E.M.F. (1979) *Longman Dictionary of Scientific Usage*, Longman.

Green, J. (1996) *Chasing the Sun: Dictionary Makers and the Dictionaries They Made*, Jonathan Cape.

Hartmann, R.R.K. (1989) 'Sociology of the dictionary user: hypotheses and empirical studies' in F.J. Hausmann *et al.* (eds), 102–11.

Hartmann, R.R.K. (1996) 'Lexicography' in R.R.K. Hartmann (ed.) *Solving Language Problems*, University of Exeter Press, 230–44.

Hartmann, R.R.K. (2001) *Teaching and Researching Lexicography*, Pearson Education.

Hartmann, R.R.K. and James, G. (1998) *Dictionary of Lexicography*, Routledge.

Hatherall, G. (1984) 'Studying dictionary use: some findings and proposals' in R.R.K. Hartmann (ed.) *LEXeter '83 Proceedings*, Lexicographica Series Maior, no. 1, Max Niemeyer Verlag, Tübingen, 183–9.

Hausmann, F.J., Reichmann, O., Wiegand, H.E. and Zgusta, L. (eds) (1989–91) *Wörterbücher, Dictionaries, Dictionnaires: ein internationales Handbuch zur Lexikographie* vols 1–3, Walter de Gruyter.

Hebert, H. (1974) 'Lingua frankly', review of OALD3, *The Guardian*, 25 March 1974.

Herbst, T. and Popp, K. (eds) (1999) *The Perfect Learners' Dictionary(?)*, Lexicographica Series Maior, no. 95, Max Niemeyer Verlag, Tübingen.

Heuberger, R. (2000) *Monolingual Dictionaries for Foreign Learners of English: A Constructive Evaluation of the State-of-the-Art Reference Works in Book Form and on CD-ROM*, Austrian Studies in English 87, Braumüller, Vienna.

Higashi, N. *et al.* (1992) 'Review of the *Concise Oxford Dictionary of Current English*, Eighth Edition', *International Journal of Lexicography*, 5(2), 129–60.

Historical Thesaurus of English website <http://ww2.arts.gla.ac.uk/SESLL/EngLang/thesaur/thes.htm>.

Holderbaum, A. (1999) *Kriterien der Evaluation elektronischer Wörterbücher*, Annual Report on English and American Studies 17, Wissenschaftlicher Verlag, Trier.

Hornby, A.S. (1954) *A Guide to Patterns and Usage in English*, Oxford University Press.

Hornby, A.S., Gatenby, E.V. and Wakefield, H. (1942) *Idiomatic and Syntactic English Dictionary*, Kaitakusha, Tokyo.

Hudson, R. (1988) 'The linguistic foundations for lexical research and dictionary design', *International Journal of Lexicography*, 1(4), 287–312.

Hüllen, W. (1989) 'In the beginning was the gloss', in G. James (ed.) 100–16.

Hüllen, W. (1999) *English Dictionaries 800–1700: The Topical Tradition*, Clarendon Press, Oxford.

Ilson, R. (1983) 'Etymological information: can it help our students?', *ELT Journal*, 37(1), 76–82.

Ilson, R.F. (1991) 'Lexicography', in K. Malmkjaer (ed.) *The Linguistics Encyclopedia*, Routledge, 291–8.

Ilson, R. (2001) 'Review of Atkins (1998)', *International Journal of Lexicography*, 14(1), 80–3.

Jackson, H. (1988) *Words and their Meaning*, Longman.

Jackson, H. (1995) 'Learners' dictionaries in contrast: Langenscheidt and Longman', *Fremdsprachen Lehren und Lernen*, 24, 58–74.

Jackson, H. (1998) 'How many words in YOUR dictionary?', *English Today*, 14(3), 27–8.

Jackson, H. (2002) *Grammar and Vocabulary*, Routledge English Language Introductions, Routledge.

Jackson, H. and Zé Amvela, E. (2000) *Words, Meaning and Vocabulary: An Introduction to Modern English Lexicology*, Cassell.

James, G. (ed.) (1989) *Lexicographers and Their Works*, University of Exeter Press.

Jehle, G. (1990) *Das englische und französische Lernwörterbuch in der Rezension. Theorie und Praxis der Wörterbuchkritik*, Lexicographica Series Maior, no. 30, Max Niemeyer Verlag, Tübingen.

Jehle, G. (1999) 'Learner's dictionaries on CD-ROM – mere gadgetry?' in W. Falkner and H.-J. Schmid (eds) *Words, Lexemes, Concepts: Approaches to the Lexicon. Studies in Honour of Leonhard Lipka*, Gunter Narr Verlag, Tübingen, 353–63.

Jones, D. (1997) *English Pronouncing Dictionary*, fifteenth edition, (eds) Peter Roach and James Hartmann, Cambridge University Press.

Katamba, F. (1994) *English Words*, Routledge.

Kipfer, B.A. (1984) *Workbook on Lexicography*, Exeter Linguistic Studies 8, University of Exeter Press.

Kipfer, B.A. (1986) 'Investigating an onomasiological approach to dictionary material', *Dictionaries, Journal of the DSNA*, 8, 55–64.

Kirkpatrick, B. (1995) *The Original Roget's Thesaurus*, Longman.

Knowles, E. and Elliott, J. (eds) (1997) *The Oxford Dictionary of New Words*, Oxford University Press.

Kurath, H. and Kuhn, S.M. (1954) *Middle English Dictionary*, University of Michigan Press.

Landau, S.I. (1989) *Dictionaries: The Art and Craft of Lexicography*, Cambridge University Press.

Landau, S.I. (1999) 'Review of *The New Oxford Dictionary of English*', *International Journal of Lexicography*, 12(3), 250–7.

Landau, S.I. (2001) *Dictionaries: The Art and Craft of Lexicography*, second edition, Cambridge University Press.

Lehrer, A. (1974) *Semantic Fields and Lexical Structure*, North Holland Publishing Co.

Lyons, J. (1977) *Semantics*, vols 1 and 2, Cambridge University Press.

McArthur, T. (1986) *Worlds of Reference*, Cambridge University Press.

McArthur, T. (ed.) (1992) *The Oxford Companion to the English Language*, Oxford University Press.

McArthur, T. (1998) *Living Words: Language, Lexicography and the Knowledge Revolution*, University of Exeter Press.

McLeod, I. (ed.) (1990) *The Scots Thesaurus*, Aberdeen University Press.

McMillan, J.B. (1949) 'Five College Dictionaries', *College English*, 10(4), 214–21.

Masuda, H. *et al.* (1994) 'Review of the *Longman Dictionary of the English Language* 1991 edition', *International Journal of Lexicography*, 7(1), 31–46.

Morton, H.C. (1994) *The Story of Webster's Third: Philip Gove's Controversial Dictionary and Its Critics*, Cambridge University Press.

Mugglestone, L. (2000a) ' "Pioneers in the untrodden forest": *The New English Dictionary*' in L. Mugglestone (ed.), 1–21.

Mugglestone, L. (ed.) (2000b) *Lexicography and the OED: Pioneers in the Untrodden Forest*, Oxford University Press.

Murray, K.M.E. (1977) *Caught in the Web of Words: James Murray and the Oxford English Dictionary*, Yale University Press.

Nesi, H. (1999) 'A user's guide to electronic dictionaries for language learners', *International Journal of Lexicography*, 12(1), 55–66.

Norri, J. (1996) 'Regional labels in some British and American dictionaries', *International Journal of Lexicography*, 9(1), 1–29.

Norri, J. (2000) 'Labelling of derogatory words in some British and American dictionaries', *International Journal of Lexicography*, 13(2), 71–106.

Nuccorini, S. (1992) 'Monitoring dictionary use' in H. Tommola *et al.* (eds) *Euralex '92 Proceedings*, University of Tampere, Finland, 89–102.

Osselton, N. (1989) 'The history of academic dictionary criticism with reference to major dictionaries', article 27 in F.J. Hausmann *et al.*, 225–30.

Palmer, H.E. (1938) *A Grammar of English Words*, Longmans Green.

Pearce, D.W. (1992) *Macmillan Dictionary of Modern Economics*, fourth edition, ELBS/Macmillan.

Paikeday, T.M. (1993) 'Who needs IPA?', *English Today*, 9(1), 38–42.

Prčic, T. (1999) 'The treatment of affixes in the "big four" EFL dictionaries', *International Journal of Lexicography* 12(4), 263–79.

Pruvost, J. (2000) 'Des dictionnaires papier aux dictionnaires électroniques', *International Journal of Lexicography* 13(3), 187–93.

Reddick, A. (1990) *The Making of Johnson's Dictionary 1746–1773*, Cambridge University Press.

Ripfel, M. (1989) *Wörterbuchkritik. eine empirische Analyse von Wörterbuchrezensionen*, Lexicographica Series Maior, no. 29, Max Niemeyer Verlag, Tübingen.

Le Robert Collège (1997) M.-H. Drivaud (ed.) Dictionnaires Le Robert, Paris.

Roberts, J., Kay, C. and Grundy, L. (1995) *A Thesaurus of Old English*, King's College London.

Rundell, M. (1998) 'Recent trends in English pedagogical lexicography', *International Journal of Lexicography*, 11(4), 315–42.

Rundell, M. and Stock, P. (1992) 'The corpus revolution', *English Today*, 8(2), 9–14; 8(3), 21–31; 8(4), 45–51.

Scholfield, P. (1999) 'Dictionary use in reception', *International Journal of Lexicography*, 12(1), 13–34.

Simpson, J.A. (1989) 'Nathaniel Bailey and the search for a lexicographical style' in G. James (ed.), 181–91.

Sinclair, J.M. (ed.) (1987) *Looking Up: An Account of the COBUILD Project in Lexical Computing*, Collins ELT.

Skeat, W.W. (1961) *A Concise Etymological Dictionary of the English Language*, Clarendon Press, Oxford.

Sledd, J. and Ebbitt, W.R. (eds) (1962) *Dictionaries and THAT Dictionary*, Scott, Foresman and Company.

Starnes, DeW.T. and Noyes, G.E. (1991) *The English Dictionary from Cawdrey to Johnson 1604–1755*, new edition, G. Stein (ed.), John Benjamins.

Stein, G. (1985) *The English Dictionary before Cawdrey*, Lexicographica Series Maior, no. 9, Max Niemeyer Verlag, Tübingen.

Steiner, R.J. (1984) 'Guidelines for reviewers of bilingual dictionaries', *Dictionaries*, Journal of the Dictionary Society of North America, 11(4), 315–42.

Svartvik, J. (ed.) (1996) *Words: Proceedings of an International Symposium, Lund, 25–26 August 1995*, Kungl. Vitterhets Historie och Antikvitets Akademien, *Konferenser 36*, Stockholm.

Svensén, B. (1993) *Practical Lexicography: Principles and Methods of Dictionary-Making*, translation of Swedish original published in 1987, Oxford University Press.

Tomaszczyk, J. (1988) 'The bilingual dictionary under review' in M. Snell-Hornby (ed.) *ZüriLEX '86 Proceedings*, Francke Verlag, 289–97.

Weekley, E. (1967) *An Etymological Dictionary of Modern English*, Dover, New York.

Wells, J.C. (2000) *Longman Pronunciation Dictionary*, second edition, revised, Longman.

West, M.P. (1953) *A General Service List of English Words*, Longmans Green.

West, M.P. (1964) *A Dictionary of Spelling: British and American*, Longman.

West, M.P. and Endicott, J.G. (1935) *The New Method English Dictionary*, Longmans Green.

Wiegand, H.E. (1994) 'Wörterbuchkritik. Zur Einführung' in F.F.M. Dolezal *et al.* (eds), 1–7.

Wilson, M. (ed.) (1957) *Johnson: Prose and Poetry*, Hart-Davis.

Winchester, S. (1999) *The Surgeon of Crowthorne*, Penguin.

Zgusta, L. (1971) *Manual of Lexicography*, Academia, Prague/Mouton, The Hague.

Index

accessibility 75–6, 78–82, 171, 177
acronym 13–14
affix 8, 12, 87
Anglo-Saxon 10, 118, 119, 127
antonymy 17, 97–8, 132, 146–7
authority 40, 66

Bailey, Nathaniel 37–9, 45, 166
binomial 5, 86, 99
borrowing 11, 13, 20

Cawdrey, Robert 33, 75
CD-ROM dictionaries 58, 69–72,
    141–4, 159, 171–2
citations 29, 40, 44, 48, 59, 65, 88, 166;
    see also quotations
collegiate dictionary 67
collocation 18, 27, 84, 91, 99, 132, 138,
    169
combining form 9, 12, 121
completeness 36–9, 52, 59, 65, 75, 76,
    82, 162–3, 178–9
compound 5, 8, 9, 12, 25, 53, 86, 121
computer corpus vii, 29, 131, 132, 140,
    167
concordance 29, 88, 131, 167–9
connotation 16, 96
conversion 13
coverage *see* completeness

defining vocabulary 130, 133
definition 15, 26, 43, 55, 62–3, 65,
    93–6, 131–2, 133–5, 170, 179
denotation 16, 96
derivative 8, 12–13, 25, 53, 56,
    145
dialect 110–11
dictionary 21ff, 52, 67–8, 74–6
dictionary criticism 30, 173ff

electronic dictionaries 57–8, 59, 69–72,
    77, 83, 159
encyclopedia 21–2
etymology 27, 36, 43, 55, 87, 117ff, 181
examples 26, 84, 130, 132, 136–7, 181

fixing 39–40, 44–5
formality 111–12
French 11, 20, 33, 39, 118, 120, 121
frequency 140, 144
front matter 25, 76, 175

glossary 31–2, 147
grammar 19, 22, 91, 95, 107, 108–9,
    130, 132, 135, 180
Greek 11, 33, 118

hard words 33–6, 75, 127
headword 25, 27–8, 86–8, 163, 178
homograph 2, 87–8, 179
homonym 2, 26, 87
homophone 3
hyponymy 17, 98

idiom 6, 99–100
inflection 3, 8, 19, 26, 43, 87, 105–7

Johnson, Samuel 39, 42–6, 62, 75, 161,
    165, 166

Latin 11, 20, 31, 32, 39, 118, 119, 120–2
learners' dictionaries 24, 69, 83–5, 129ff,
    153–8, 177
lexeme 2, 3–5, 18, 25
lexical field 143, 146, 153
loanword 11, 14–15, 54, 106, 120–3

macrostructure 25, 78, 163
meaning 15, 19, 55, 76, 86ff

meronymy 18, 98
metalexicography 30, 173, 176, 182
microstructure 26, 79–82, 163
morpheme 8, 19
Murray, James 48–51, 102, 161, 165, 166

nesting 68, 78, 178

obsolete 113–14
Old English 10, 117, 118, 119–20, 147, 151
Old Norse 10, 118, 119, 120
orthographic word 2
Oxford English Dictionary 23, 44, 47ff, 73, 82, 117, 124–6

part of speech *see* word class
Philological Society 47, 48
phonological word 2
phrasal lexeme 5
phrasal verb 6
polysemy 15, 88
prefix 8, 13, 145
pronunciation 18, 26, 43, 54, 102–5

quotations 46, 49; *see also* citations

reference 15–16
Roget's Thesaurus 149–50
root 8, 12
run-on 25, 27

selection 42–3, 75
sense 15, 26, 55, 68, 88–93, 133, 179
sense relation 16–18, 96–9, 139, 180
slang 112
spelling 18, 26, 43, 54, 61–2, 76, 82–3, 101–2
synonymy 17, 69, 94–5, 97, 132, 146–7
syntax 19, 27, 43, 84, 108–9, 131, 136–7

thematic order 22, 69, 143–4, 145ff
thesaurus 150–5

usage 19, 26, 109–15, 139, 180
users 76–8, 132–9, 161–2, 182

vocabulary 10–11, 25, 48, 52–3, 127, 146

Webster, Noah 61–4, 166
word 1–2,
word class 6–7, 19, 26, 54, 88, 107–8
word-form 4